Imago Dei

Also by JAMES W. HEISIG:
El cuento detrás del cuento: un ensayo sobre psique y mito (original in Spanish)
Without Staff or Sandals (edited, with introduction)

Studies in Jungian Thought
James Hillman, General Editor

Titles in this series:

Evil
edited by the Curatorium of the C.G. Jung Institute, Zurich, translated by Ralph Manheim and Hildegard Nagel

Conscience
edited by the Curatorium of the C. G. Jung Institute, translated by R. F. C. Hull and Ruth Horine

Timeless Documents of the Soul
by Helmuth Jacobsohn, Marie-Louise von Franz, and Sigmund Hurwitz

Ancient Incubation and Modern Psychotherapy
by C. A. Meier

Satan in the Old Testament
by Rivkah Scharf Kluger

The Myth of Analysis: Three Essays in Archetypal Psychology
by James Hillman

Number and Time
by Marie-Louise von Franz

Imago Dei: A Study of C. G. Jung's Psychology of Religion
by James W. Heisig

Imago Dei

A Study of C. G. Jung's Psychology of Religion

James W. Heisig

Lewisburg
Bucknell University Press
London: Associated University Presses

Associated University Presses, Inc.
Cranbury, New Jersey 08512

Associated University Presses
Magdalen House
136-148 Tooley Street
London SE1 2TT, England

Library of Congress Cataloging in Publication Data

Heisig, James W., 1944-
Imago Dei.

(Studies in Jungian thought)
Bibliography: p.
Includes index.
1. Psychology, Religious--History. 2. Jung, Carl Gustav, 1875-1961. I. Title. II. Series.
BL53.H378 200'.1'9 77-74405
ISBN 0-8387-2076-5

PRINTED IN THE UNITED STATES OF AMERICA

Contents

Acknowledgments

The list of those to whom I owe thanks for their help with this book is longer than I had thought possible. I wish to express special thanks to the Master and Fellows of Saint Edmund's House of Cambridge University for electing me to a research fellowship in 1971, and to the trustees of the Burney Fund of Cambridge for their aid in financing my researches in Switzerland and Austria during the summers of 1971 and 1972. A special debt of gratitude is also due Donald Mackinnon and Donald Cupitt for their criticisms and suggestions for the first draft of this work, and to James Hillman for his help with succeeding drafts. Among the many others whom I have consulted regularly and who have given unselfishly of their time, I cannot fail to mention Frau Aneila Jaffé; her patience, her warmth, and her knowledge have been more of an inspiration to me than words can tell. Finally, I would like to acknowledge the friendly and generous assistance I received from the staff of the C. G. Jung Institut in Zurich; from the Nationalbibliotek, the Universitätsbibliotek, and the Gesellschaft der Ärzte in Vienna; from the Landesbibliotek in Bern; and from the Staatsarchiv in Basel.

I would also like to thank the following for permission to reprint copyrighted material:

Franz Jung, son of C. G. Jung, for kindly permitting quotation from books and seminars of his father.

Pantheon Books, a Division of Random House, Inc., for permission to quote from *Memories, Dreams, Reflections,* by C. G. Jung, recorded and edited by Aniela Jaffé, translated by Richard and Clara Winston.

Princeton University Press, for extracts from *The Collected Works of C. G. Jung,* ed. Herbert Read, Michael Fordham, Gerhard Adler, William McGuire; trans. R. F. C. Hull. Bollingen Series XX. Quotations from volumes 4, 6, 8, 9i, 9ii, 10, 11. Also for extracts from *C. G. Jung: Letters.* Volume 1: 1906-1950. Volume 2: 1951-1961. Selected and edited by Gerhard Adler in collaboration with Aniela Jaffé, translated by R. F. C. Hull. Bollingen Series XCV. Quotations reprinted by permission of Princeton University Press.

Routledge & Kegan Paul Ltd. (in the United Kingdom and British Commonwealth excluding Canada), for extracts from *The Collected Works* of C. G. Jung, ed. Herbert Read, Michael Fordham, Gerhard Adler, William McGuire; trans. R. F. C. Hull. Bollingen Series XX. Quotations from volumes 4, 6, 8, 9i, 9ii, 10, 11. Also for excerpt from *Memories, Dreams, Reflections,* by C. G. Jung, recorded and edited by Aniela Jaffé, translated by Richard and Clara Winston; and for quotations from *C. G. Jung: Letters.* Volume 1: 1906-1950. Volume 2: 1951-1961. Selected and edited by Gerhard Adler in collaboration with Aniela Jaffé, translated by R. F. C. Hull. Bollingen Series XCV, Princeton University Press.

Introduction

Sir Francis Bacon once remarked that some thinkers are like ants who scurry about gathering and storing up as much useful material as they can, while others are like spiders who spin splendid and intricate webs to attract and ensnare the unsuspecting. Carl Gustav Jung, the brilliant and controversial Swiss psychologist, has been called both. To some he seems an altogether abstract and metaphysical thinker who has discarded the canons of science in order to dwell in his own private world of fantasy. Others tend to view him as a quaint and eccentric collector rummaging about through alchemical texts, fairy-tales, and Oriental scriptures for scraps to fatten up a fragile theoretical structure. For most critics he is a blend of the two: a gypsy of the intellect who never managed decisively to commit himself to one single discipline. Nothing in the history of Jung's influence on twentieth-century thought is more surprising than the force and fury of his detractors. Nothing, perhaps, but the list of his admirers.

Given the widespread controversy surrounding analytical (Jungian) psychology[1] as a whole, it is hardly surprising to find greater and still more heated differences of opinion regarding Jung's psychology of religion. It may be an exaggeration to claim with Hans Schär, Jung's best-known disciple from among the Protestant clergy, that "everything Jung has published has to do with religion to a greater or lesser degree";[2] or with the Dominican Victor White that "if it is difficult to divest Freud of the professor's gown, it is quite impossible to divest Jung of his surplice."[3] Nevertheless, so central and decisive is the religious aspect of Jung's thought that it has become the typical turning point for sympathy with or alienation from Jung's life work.

Oddly enough, for all the discussion that Jung's psychology of religion has excited, the atmosphere of scholarly interest surrounding it has grown tiresome. Devotees and skeptics alike seem generally to have fallen into the habit of thinking in clichés, instead of taking the trouble to study Jung's writings with the care they deserve. It is tempting to offer reasons for this neglect, and thereby to infer one's own exemption, but I am unsure on both counts. I can only state my intention in these pages: to offer one critical reading of Jung's psychology of religion in the hope that it does some justice to his achievement and will lead others to reread his work with greater profit.

The most immediate and persistent obstacle to such an undertaking is the sheer complexity of Jung's complete writings on eligion, which do not easily yield to summary and schematization, let alone critical commentary. In view of this fact, I choose to restrict myself to tracing the life story of the one notion that seems most central to Jung's psychology of religion, that of the *imago Dei* or God-image, and to make use of what turns up in that account for the purposes of a generalized critique. Admittedly, even this restriction does not prove altogether practical, for no sooner does one begin abstemiously to follow a single thread than one is led astray in the fascinating labyrinth of interlacing patterns that give Jung's work its distinctive flavor. In any case, it determines the basic division of the book into two parts.

The first part aims at a comprehensive account of what Jung had to say about the *imago Dei*, set in the context of the psychology of religion in which he said it. Although the approach is chronological the task is a demanding one, since *no* aspect of Jung's thought shows a clear process of evolution.[4] Indeed, the use of a temporal model to describe the unfolding of Jung's ideas may be a restraining bias that conceals as much as it discloses. Unfortunately, there is no complete research on the development of any aspect of Jung's thought to which one might confidently turn for guidance and support. It is hard to know whether the time has passed for some disciple of rare stature to accomplish for Jung what Ernest Jones has done for Freud. But it is just such a sweeping panorama based on careful investigation into all the relevant sources that is sorely needed.[5] In its absence, one can only turn to the better general introductions to Jung's thought.[6]

The second part of this study will be given to a critical evaluation, which poses additional difficulties of its own. Sifting through the mass of secondary literature has frequently proved many times more laborious than attempting to discern Jung's own mind on particular issues.[7] For the most part, comments on the commentaries will be left to the notes. The primary concern will be to clarify and to reexamine the philosophical assumptions, the factual data, and the explanatory models that provide the context for Jung's notion of the *imago Dei*. What I hope to show is that besides devising a full psychological *method* (the models of the psyche that he used in his theory and the application of those models in a therapeutic practice), Jung also gave considerable attention to constructing a *methodology* (a language for describing what he was about in his method and for defending it as a way of understanding); that these two tasks were not always kept distinct in Jung's discourse; and that Jung might have found a more suitable means of talking about what he actually did in his method than the hybrid scientific methodology that he elected to use.

Throughout this study I shall be operating under certain relevant limitations that need to be stated at the outset. Perhaps the severest disadvantage of all is that I did not know Jung personally. I count this a loss because of the frequent testimony from both his best disciples and his best critics to the important difference such an acquaintance has made on their estimate of his written work.[8] Further, I have neither undergone myself nor followed closely an extensive Jungian analysis. Again, according to the most trustworthy sources, this cannot but have some distorting effect on my interpretations.[9] Finally, I do not pretend that a few short years of research can yield a suitably balanced appreciation of Jung's work, the context in which it grew up, the opposition that it encountered, and the lifetime of experience that it expressed. Although such limitations are common to academic work, their recognition braces one for the hostility inevitably aroused by reducing to abstraction what is for others still fresh to memory or feeling. My only remedy has been considerable contact with several of Jung's closest acquaintances, who have helped to alter my judgment on some matters and to confirm my suspicions on others.

Within these limits I have attempted in what follows to encompass the entire corpus of Jung's published and unpublished writings, much of which has not yet found any place at all in serious scholarship. For most purposes it is sufficient to have a working knowledge of his autobiography and *Collected Works,*[10] but a thoroughgoing historical study requires a more solid base. In the first place, the numerous articles, reviews, reports, prefaces to books, and interviews that have not yet appeared in the *Collected Works* or that have been excluded from them, have had to be tracked down and studied. Second, it was necessary to compare revised editions of his writings with their original versions and to make note of significant changes. Third, there are the transcripts of Jung's lectures and seminars, in almost every case taken down verbatim in shorthand and later privately mimeographed. The complete collection of seminar notes alone contains well over fifty volumes of material. Except for two volumes published some years ago[11] and eleven others that have been privately printed with some minor alterations,[12] the seminar notes remain in relative obscurity in their raw, unedited form.[13] Yet they contain an impressive wealth of information that, with proper caution, deserves a place in the story of Jung's development. Fourth, there is Jung's professional correspondence, some 1,700 pages of typescript material that contains some of the clearest hints for following the growth of Jung's ideas, as well as a good deal of opinion that never found its way into his lectures and published writings.[14]

In order to give the complete Jungian corpus its due, it has seemed preferable to omit any discussion of Jung's place in the wider intellectual history of the West or even within the psychoanalytic movement as such. The choice is one of emphasis, not of exclusion. I am convinced that there is a definite advantage to examining Jung without constant reference to the archaeology of his ideas or to how they might compare with Freud's or Adler's. These are tasks that surely need doing in their own right. Meanwhile, it is best not to add another popularized account to the many already in print.[15]

Jung's writings bear the stamp of strange and powerful genius. As the story of his struggles with God will show, he was a man determined to let his inner experiences have their say, even when that meant turning a deaf ear to current standards of rational and logical discourse. To return to Bacon's analogy from the *Redargutio philosophiarum,* Jung was less like the ant that collects or the spider that spins, and more like the bee, which takes what it has gathered from garden and field into itself, digests it, and transforms it. "*Itaque hujusmodi mellis coelestia dona sperate.*"

Imago Dei

PART I

History: The Development of an Idea

1

The Early Years (1902-1920)

That Jung's notion of the *imago Dei* should show some development over the threescore years of his professional life is hardly to be wondered at. As far as we may presume that the written sources at our disposal accurately reflect his personal views at any given time, it would seem a straightforward task to trace the evolution of his thought. But in matters of religion Jung does not so easily yield to academic investigation. We have often little more to go on than passing references that only suggest a more coherent, elaborated theory lurking in the background. Even in more sustained and systematic passages, Jung frequently gives the impression of presenting the conclusion of a complex process of scientific argument, that he does not bother to articulate. Matters are further complicated by his continual efforts to revise his earlier writings.[1] Hence any attempt to examine the Jungian corpus developmentally, even a sympathetic one, has to reckon with the danger that it may result at times in an arbitrary and artificial reconstruction of his ideas. But that is a risk we must take if we would discover the way in which talk about God came to play an increasingly important role in Jung's psychology.[2]

1. 1902-1911

Jung's first extended comments on the psychology of religion did not appear in print until 1909, when he was thirty-four years of age. At the time he was a lecturer in psychiatry at the University of Zurich and senior physician at the Psychiatric Clinic where he had set up a laboratory for experimental psychopathology. In that same year he was to accompany Freud to America, where they were both to be awarded the degree of Doctor of Laws *honoris causa* by Clark University.[3]

His earliest publications had shown no particular interest in "religious phenomena" other than to record their appearance in certain cases of psychopathological disturbance.[4] For instance, in his inaugural dissertation for the medical degree Jung had described a number of occult phenomena associated with a fifteen-year-old medium, whom he diagnosed as a case of dementia praecox (now commonly referred to as "schizophrenia"). During the séances she would spontaneously recite biblical maxims, pious precepts, and religious-sounding poetry as if she were repeating a divine revelation. All of this Jung classified as belonging to one of her two "subconscious personalities"—the "sero-religious"—which represented for him nothing more than the repressed image of a pietistic pastor who had recently confirmed the girl.[5] Beyond the vaguest suggestion of a connection between hallucinatory states in general and the visions of saints, saviors, and prophets,[6] Jung does not venture in this context.

During the years immediately following, similar brief allusions to religion show up in Jung's writings. He recounts a case of "manic-mood disorder" in which the patient had illusions of himself as a new Christ and "the founder of God's kingdom on earth."[7] Similarly he refers to a woman who had tried to pass herself off as a saint and miracle worker;[8] to an epileptic who ("characteristically," according to Jung) had the tendency to slip into biblical idiom in word-association tests;[9] and to a woman plagued with dreams of her guilt before God for having decided to have her teeth extracted.[10] Only slightly more space is given to describing another woman patient who, in the midst of marital problems, twice dreamed of her father as a tall figure with a long white beard, "as if she experienced the presence of God himself." In commenting on the dreams, Jung merely points to the dominance of the father's personality over that of his daughter, without even indirectly hinting at a general principle for the etiology of religious imagery.[11]

Such generalizations do occur elsewhere at this time, however, but only in passing. At one point Jung suggests that the history of religion is rich in examples of how the unconscious can deceive us.[12] Likewise, alluding to the case of a woman patient who fancied herself the Mother of God, he remarks that "such a 'sublimation' of exceedingly earthy matrimonial desires has been a favorite plaything of women's dreams since the dawn of Christianity."[13] Again, writing on the birth of psychology as a science, Jung refers to vestiges of medieval belief in diabolical possession that survive in our own day. He concludes with the critical remark:

> With the opening of the modern era and the dawn of the first scientific ideas, the original barbaric personification of unknown powers gradually disappeared; a change arose in the conception of mental disease in favor of a more philosophic moral attitude. The ancient view that every misfortune was the vengeance of offended gods returned in a new guise to suit the times. Just as physical diseases can, in many cases, be traced back to some frivolous self-injury, so mental diseases were believed to be due to some moral injury or sin. Behind this conception, too, lurks the angry deity.[14]

At the time there was no reason to pay any particular attention to the case material and strictly incidental observations mentioned here.[15] But in 1909, in an article entitled "The Significance of the Father in the Destiny of the Individual," Jung took a first decisive step. Not only did he accept the arguments of Freud's 1907 essay, "Obsessive Acts and Religious Practices," but he went on to apply them to the God-figure of Judaism and Christianity.[16]

In approximately five hundred words Jung condenses a series of hints on how religions might be viewed as "fantasy systems" designed to resolve sexual problems. Having agreed with Freud on the decisive importance of child-parent relationships, and on their fundamentally sexual nature, he ventures a step further to claim that the same model can be seen at work behind the history of national religions. He takes as an example the religion of the Old Testament, which transformed the Hebrew paterfamilias into the figure of Yahweh to be feared and obeyed by all. The purpose of this projection was the continued adaptation of the sexual drive to the repressions of the social process—its sublimation—after the inevitable breakdown of infantile dependency. Because of the Hebrews' untamed, barbarous instincts, however, this sublimation did not succeed, and had to be supplemented with the severe compulsive practices ("ceremonials") of Mosaic law. Only the prophets were able to achieve full sublimation, to "identify" with Yahweh, and as a result became themselves the fathers of the people. Christ fulfilled the prophetic task by replacing the compulsive, legalistic relationship to an awesome God with one of personal love. When that proved ineffectual for his followers, compulsion returned: the imperfect sublimation of the Mass led to the ceremonial of the Church, from which only those saints and reformers capable of complete sublimation were able to break free. It is in this sense that modern theology, by stressing the need for "inner" or "personal" experience, is attempting to free believers from compulsion. But what remains constant throughout is the transformation of the father-child relationship into a man-God relationship. To account for the blend of virtues and faults constellated in the father, Jung notes that they transfer to the sublimation by effecting a split between God (sublime love, complete sexual repression) and Devil (unbridled sexual lust).[17]

In spite of the apparent anti-institutional tone of these remarks, Jung's ensuing correspondence with Freud shows that he considered it shortsighted to oppose Christianity outright when it might with more profit be enlisted in the service of psychoanalysis:

> I think we must give it [psychoanalysis] time to infiltrate into people from many centres, to revivify among intellectuals a sense for symbol and myth, ever so gently to transform Christ back into the soothsaying god of the vine, which he was, and in this way absorb those ecstatic instinctual forces of Christianity for the *one* purpose of making the cult and the sacred myth what they once were—a drunken feast of joy where man could be an animal, ethical and holy. That indeed was the great beauty and purpose of classical religion, which from God knows what temporary biological needs has turned into a Misery Institute.[18]

For the next two years Jung's published work shows no attempt to carry ahead this first venture into the psychology of religion. All we find are cursory references to the repressed emotions behind St. Catherine of Sienna's vision of the celestial marriage,[19] to the independence of scientific psychology from morals and religious belief,[20] and to the hope that psychoanalysis might heal and strengthen the human spirit where the Church had only crushed it.[21]

On the whole this period of collaboration with Freud was not particularly productive for Jung.[22] In fact, certain ideas were taking root that were soon to alienate him once and for all from the psychoanalytic movement. For one thing, he was growing increasingly critical of the sexual theory as Freud expounded it.[23] (He even tried once subtly to slip a revised version of it into a descriptive account of Freud's thought.[24]) For another, he had taken to a serious study of mythology and was becoming intrigued by its possibilities for psychology.[25] In a letter to Freud toward the end of 1909 he wrote:

> It has become quite clear to me that we shall not solve the ultimate secrets of neurosis and psychosis without mythology and the history of civilization, for *embryology* goes hand in hand with *comparative anatomy*, and without the latter the former is but a freak of nature whose depths remain uncomprehended.[26]

Interestingly enough, his first two actual attempts to adopt the use of mythological motifs in dream interpretation concern religious themes: a parenthetical remark on the Trinity as an instance of the expression of significance by the "multiplication of personality,"[27] and a more extended appeal to certain passages of St. Luke's gospel in order to interpret a dream whose sole content was—Luke 137.[28] But something on a much larger scale and of far more momentous consequence for the psychology of religion was being prepared by the young Dr. Jung.

2. *Psychology of the Unconscious* (1911-1912)

On 13 December 1910 Jung wrote to Freud: "Too much shouldn't be revealed yet. But be prepared for some strange things, the like of which you never yet heard from me." A few months later, after the publication of the first half of his researches, he wrote again to Freud: "My evenings are taken up very largely with astrology. I make horoscopic calculations in order to find a clue to the core of psychological truth. Some remarkable things have turned up which will certainly appear incredible to you.[29] He was not far wrong. Within a year his work was completed and appeared in book form under the title *Wandlungen und Symbole der Libido* (translated later in English as *Psychology of the Unconscious*). Its effect on the psychoanalytic movement is well-known: Jung encountered immediate and almost universal criticism at the hands of Freud's followers, and by the following year had permanently severed relations with Freud.[30]

Psychology of the Unconscious is not an easy book to read, largely because of its general imprecision of argument and almost obsessional flow of novel and unconnected ideas. As Jung himself was to comment some forty years later: "It was written at top speed, amid the rush and press of my medical practice, without regard to time or method. I had to fling my material hastily together, just as I found it. There was no opportunity to let my thoughts mature."[31] Nevertheless, the book is of singular importance to the story of Jung's development,[32] and a seedbed of suggestions for his growing interest in the psychology of religion in general and in the *imago Dei* in particular.

A passage from the Italian philosopher Guglielmo Ferrero serves as an opening motto. In it we see not only Jung's basic philosophic attitude to psychological theory, but also a foretaste of his approach to the role of religious theory in human history:

> Therefore theory, which gives to facts their value and significance, is often very useful, even if it is partially false, for it throws light on phenomena which no one observed, it forces an examination, from many angles, of facts which no one had hitherto studied, and it gives the impulse for more extended and more productive researches.[33]

The text of the book grows out of an interpretation of the fantasies of an American woman, pseudonymously called "Miss Miller."[34] In Jung's own words, the running commentary serves as a kind of "Ariadne thread to guide us through the labyrinth of symbolistic parallels."[35] While he resisted the idea that he was only engaged in a vicarious analysis of his own unconscious,[36] Jung later acknowledged

that writing the book gave him the opportunity he needed to outgrow the Freudian doctrine, with its "constricting atmosphere" and "narrow outlook."[37] Still, the influence of Freud is dominant, especially in Jung's treatment of religious questions. Far from denying the approach of his 1909 article, Jung takes it up again in studying religion as a "fantasy system" that "feeds upon the incestuous libido of the infantile period."[38] To appreciate his argument we must begin with what he has to say about the epistemological status of religious projections in general.

Jung distinguishes two kinds of thinking—directed thinking and fantasy thinking—which yield two kinds of corresponding truth—literal truth and psychological truth. *Literal truth* is achieved by *consciously directed reflection* on the physical objects of common experience; it is a critical imitation of "reality." *Psychological truth,* however, belongs to the products of all *unconscious fantasy thinking* by the mere fact that they are objects of inner experience; it is spontaneous and "turns away from reality."[39] Working within these broad guidelines, Jung focuses his attention on psychological truth, which is the realm proper to dreams, visions, fantasies, and religious beliefs. In other words, it is his intention to unravel the concealed psychological dynamics behind religious phenomena, rather than simply to dismiss them for their apparent "unreality."[40]

Jung closes the gap between forms of thinking and forms of truth by denying its relevance.[41] In his terminology, any notion of *metaphysical truth* that claims for its deliverances a privileged standpoint above the processes of thought and the nature of reality is superfluous for the purposes of psychological inquiry, which is satisfied with reducing metaphysical statements to the status of projected fantasies. He is not content merely to reaffirm Kant's distinction between the noumenon and the phenomenon, but goes on to assert that the claims of metaphysics "to be able to know the unknowable" can in fact be assimilated without remainder into the realm of psychological truth.[42]

The examination of religious phenomena breaks down into two questions: (1) the *why* of religious projections, which Jung answers by viewing them as psychic responses to unfulfilled wishes, wherein "we imagine that which we lack"[43]; and (2) the *whence* of religious projections, which he explains in terms of a common pool of "archaic inclinations" shared by all men everywhere.[44] In more traditional terminology, the first question has to do with "final causes," the second with "material causes." (Presumably the interaction between ego and unconscious would supply the "formal cause.")[45] The main emphasis of the book falls on Jung's study of "final causes" and his search for a method to understand and to cure the malady of which religious projections are the symptoms. In terms of his later development, however, the less frequent references to "material causes" are more important, for in them we see a first step toward his theory of the collective unconscious and the archetypes.[46] In any case, Jung's attempt to retain Freud's theory of wish-fulfillment[47] while at the same time introducing a "phylogenetic" approach to the unconscious, leads him to a fundamental inconsistency. For on the one hand he maintains that projected symbols have definite meanings, which are clear to the trained psychotherapist but often obscure to the patient, whose repressed desires they conceal. Yet on the other hand he speaks of the dark and inscrutable nature of the unconscious, which is reflected in the ambiguity of the mythical symbols and fantasy-images that arise therefrom.[48] As we shall see, Jung later resolved this conflict by distinguishing between "signs" and "symbols" and, more fundamentally, by all but totally abandoning the wish-fulfillment theory.

In its details the notion of religion presented in *Psychology of the Unconscious* is as decidedly experimental and unsure as its methodological premises. Yet is it argued with a brilliance and erudition that are extraordinarily difficult to capture in résumé. One would be tempted to dismiss this entire aspect of the book as a mere amplification of earlier ideas, were it not that the verbal similarities often conceal new developments and shifts of emphasis. A glance at Jung's enlargement of the notion of the libido will make this clear and at the same time provide us with the key to understanding his new attitude to religion.

For Freud libido meant the sexual drive that lay behind all human activity. Jung had long been unhappy with this formulation and so now substituted one of his own. Retaining the word *libido*, he used it instead to refer to an undifferentiated psychic energy, only one of whose expressions was sexuality. In this way Jung was able to carry on with the mechanical model of the psyche suggested by Freud and yet to relativize the theory of the sexual origin of the neuroses and discover what he considered to be the deeper levels of the mind, which had been closed to Freud. In place of his previously cautious reference to religion as a sublimation of "infantile sexuality," Jung could now take up Freud's own language and speak of it as a sublimation of the "incest-wish."[49] What he meant was not the gross sexual inclination toward one's parents that lay at the root of all sexual desire, but the yearning for the comforts of unconsciousness. In place of the literal interpretation that Freud's libido theory seemed to require, Jung offers a psychological one, made possible by freeing the libido from an exclusively sexual interpretation.[50] Even where the incest-wish does take a literal meaning in terms of an inordinate attachment to one's family or tribe, or in terms of actual physical desire, Jung wants to view it as a symptom of a deeper repression of psychic energy that ought to be flowing toward consciousness. Therefore, he argues, anything in human history that has fostered the incest prohibition has had the effect of creating the self-conscious individual.[51]

Now the function of religious beliefs and symbols in such a scheme is ambivalent. On the positive side, they redirect the incest-wish by "spiritualizing" it as a relationship to transcendent realities. Thus the dangerous repression of libido involved in the incest-prohibition is replaced by a sublimated expression. On the negative side, religion offers a *projected* compensation for repressed libido instead of a *real* one. That is to say, it typifies the naiveté of primitive man who tended to anthropomorphize and theriomorphize reality, thereby creating for himself a largely subjective universe. In spite of the fact that no one has ever seen a god, these projections continue to hold sway as long as they are charged with libidinal energy.[52]

The next step is obvious: psychoanalysis is invoked as a modern alternative to religion. Its advantage is that it makes the individual aware of his unconscious desires and enables him to control them rationally without having to resort to an illusory world of supernatural entities.[53] On the contrary, when Christianity sets up Jesus Christ as its supposed savior it conceals from the pious believer the psychological origins of his inner conflicts (his "sins") and thus narrows the reach of consciousness.[54] Jung's stance is clear:

> The stern necessity of adaptation works ceaselessly to obliterate the last traces of these primitive landmarks of the period of the origin of the human mind, and to replace them along lines which are to denote more and more clearly the nature of real objects.[55]

The only illustration of this process at work given in the book is the case of Miss Miller herself, whose religious fantasies are made to appear as the obvious products of her unconscious needs. The implication is that, had she been able to understand the meaning of her frustrated sexual longing, she would have been able to redirect her psychic energy in a conscious manner, instead of allowing it to produce a private world of symbols that were enjoyed for their own sake, keeping her all the while at a safe distance from her real problem.

In short, Jung's chief objection to religion is that it gets involved with ethics and discourages the deepening of self-awareness. Accordingly, his expressed aim is to replace patterns of belief with patterns of understanding. "This would be the course of moral autonomy, of perfect freedom, when man could without compulsion wish that which he may do, and this from knowledge, without delusion through belief in religious symbols."[56] In the end, religion only cheats man. It infantilizes him by fulfilling secretly his incest-wishes through illusory beliefs, and dehumanizes him by the compulsory and suicidal sublimation of instinct through asceticism.[57]

It is against this background that Jung takes up once again the question of God. Not surprisingly, he reserves his strongest criticisms for this most central of all religious beliefs. What the ancients meant by "God," Jung would have us see as "a part of the mind unknown to us."[58] In fact, we are given to understand that the God-concept represents "a certain sum of energy (libido)" that has been projected from its unconscious origins onto a metaphysical reality. Its function is to ensure that as individual consciousness develops it need not sacrifice the security of childhood dependence. In older religions it was the relation to the mother that accounted for the divine attributes; later the relation to the father took over:

> The idea of the masculine creative deity is a derivative, analytically and historically psychologic, of the "father-imago"[59] and aims, above all, to replace the discarded infantile father transference in such a way that for the individual the passing from the narrow circle of the family into the wider circle of human society may be simpler or made easier.[60]

By viewing God as a symbolic representation of a certain sum of psychic energy, Jung is able to conclude that in honoring God one is really honoring one's own libido.[61] His intention is not to divinize the libidinal substratum, but rather to psychologize that which men project as divine:

> Mankind wishes to love in God only their own ideas, that is to say, the ideas which they project into God. By that they wish to love their unconscious, that is, that remnant of ancient humanity and the centuries-old past of all people.[62]

This shift from the *function* of the God-concept in the individual psyche to its *genesis* in a mysterious level of common unconsciousness leads Jung to speculate further that the reason religions tend toward monotheism is that they share a single source—the libido.[63] Moreover, inasmuch as the libido is full of conflicting and opposing desires,[64] our images of God can be expected to reflect this ambiguity. For instance, Jung points to the Book of Job, which "shows us God at work both as creator and destroyer."[65] Similarly Christ, whom Jung calls "the highest expression of libido," is intimately related to Antichrist.[66] Again, Redeemers are often depicted androgynously, because "the longing of the libido raised to God (repressed into the unconscious) is a primitive, incestuous one which concerns the mother."[67]

The inescapable impression left by these comments is of an implicit atheism, insofar as the concept of God is made to originate in the unconscious in the interests of psychic equilibrium. In fact Jung even speaks of God as a pathologically engendered projection that resembles the sort of fantasy-phenomena normally attendant upon paranoia.[68] God's existence beyond the mind is eliminated from the category of literal truth because it is not empirically verifiable. To argue that it is a metaphysical truth is, according to Jung, as foolish as the medieval disputes about the number of angels crowded on pinheads or the possibility of Christ's having come as a pea.[69]

This negative tone is balanced by a more positive, if somewhat condescending note. Jung suggests that, stripped of antiquated elements, religious myths may still be useful for the unenlightened multitudes. Only a select few, the enlightened elite who are unable to bear the hypocrisy of it all, will discard religion as a crippling neurosis.[70] Hence, although Jung writes with an admiration for the role of religion in society that is not at all typical of the critical atheist,[71] he never abandons the air of informed superiority toward those who benefit from religion without ever knowing that they have mistaken illusion for truth. He is more than willing to concede that religious projections can still serve the masses as a kind of protection against the "monsters of the universe," similar to the peace and security afforded in childhood by one's parents.[72] What he objects to are the moral overtones accompanying religious beliefs. These, he claims, have now outlived their usefulness and have become a repressive force in society.[73] More particularly, he remarks that

> the Christian religion seems to have fulfilled its great biological purpose, in so far as we are able to judge. It has led human thought to independence, and has lost its significance, therefore, to a yet undetermined extent. . . . It seems to me that we might still make use in some way of its form of thought, and especially of its great wisdom of life, which for two thousand years has been proven to be particularly efficacious. The stumbling block is the *unhappy combination of religion and morality.* That must be overcome.[74]

At this stage in his development, then, Jung is unsettled in his attitude to belief in God. At best he characterizes it as a *felix culpa*; at worst, as an incestuous regression from freedom. If anything Jung has written on religion might justly be called "psychologistic," it is *Psychology of the Unconscious.* In it Jung rides roughshod over the subtleties of theology and religious mythology, frequently falls into unresolved contradictions, confuses description with hyperbole, and fails to examine the psychological premises on which he depends.[75] In the ensuing years deeper reflection and more careful research will correct much of that. Meanwhile, his public commitment to the psychology of religion has been firmly established; and—perhaps what is more important—he has discovered a method whose horizons he will pursue to the end of his life.

3. 1912-1920

For several years Jung's published work shows no significant advance in his psychology of religion, and indeed it is only with the grace of hindsight that we are able to piece together any clues relevant to his future development. In fact, generally speaking, the period between *Psychology of the Unconscious* and *Psychological Types* contains less written work of obvious moment than we might expect. The after-shock of his break with Freud brought an unusually polemical tone to his publications, overshadowing their once predominantly creative quality. But like the empty spaces in Chinese painting, the time when nothing happens is often of the deepest significance. In Jung's case, we know from his autobiography[76] that these outwardly fallow years masked a spell of intense inner turmoil, bordering at one point on schizophrenia. Jung was experimenting, on himself, with the truth of his theories of the unconscious.

A series of lectures on psychoanalysis given at Fordham University in September of 1912 are representative of the period. In them Jung attempts to give a more systematic account of his differences from Freud as they had first appeared in his analysis of Miss Miller.[77] While he continues to argue for a nonsexual theory of libido, he goes on to make explicit the model of physical energy (with its laws of conservation and transformation) that lay behind his earlier formulation.[78] He retains the wish-fulfillment theory, but stresses now that it does not yield an explanation of neurosis in terms of past causes but of present causes.[79] He reemphasizes the need to study the parallelism between unconscious fantasies and mythicoreligious motifs, and to search for a causal connection between the two.[80] Finally, he takes up briefly the question of sacramental confession in order to reiterate his conviction of the psychically hygienic value of religion, which can be cast off only by "the more highly developed men of our time."[81]

In a word, Jung's major concern at this time is with the unconscious. It is during these years that he first uses the terms *collective unconscious*[82] and *archetype,*[83] and that he begins to speak of the need for a "final" viewpoint to complement Freud's "causal" standpoint toward psychic processes and phenomena.[84] His statements on religion reflect this concern, though he does not yet appreciate the full consequences of his new position.

There is no doubt that Jung continues as before to uphold the general psychoanalytic critique of religion, especially of Christianity which, he repeats, is a fundamentally ascetic response to uncontrolled instinctuality.[85] He ventures the further opinion that we are drawing near (1916) to "the final great settlement of the Christian epoch,"[86] which is destined to be absorbed into the processes of history. Until those forces become collective, however, only a few will have the courage and the insight to ground their values elsewhere.[87] Behind such ideas as these stands the unmistakable, though as yet unacknowledged, influence of Nietzsche.

Other passages, on the contrary, prompt the suspicion that Jung has begun to modify his opposition to religion. For example, in one place he writes of the "inexorable rightness" of a religious orientation:

> Just as primitive man was able, with the help of religious and philosophical symbols, to free himself from his original condition, so too the neurotic can free himself from his illness. . . . A religious or philosophical attitude. . . is a cultural achievement; it is a function that is exceedingly valuable from a biological point of view, for it gives rise to incentives that drive human beings to do creative work for the benefit of a future age, and if necessary, to sacrifice themselves for the welfare of the species.[88]

Likewise he admits that religion may serve to put us in touch with areas of the unconscious mind that might otherwise prove inaccessible, so that it is narrow-minded to try to replace it *tout court* with "science."[89] Of course, Jung is not prepared to admit that the descriptive claims of religious beliefs are in any sense objectively true,[90] but he is not averse to granting religion a more serious and less easily replaceable pragmatic value.

We can look for the causes of this growing benevolence toward religion in the subtle changes that Jung's theory of symbolism was undergoing at the time. If the analysis of dreams and fantasy material can be enlightened by a study of mythology, if this comparison leads to the positing of an "impersonal" layer of unconscious mind, and if this hypothesis in turn can be used to explain the origin of all mythicoreligious symbols,[91] then, Jung reasons, the interpretation of the unconscious cannot be exhausted by a semantics of repressed personal desires. Here he is brought to admit for the first time the "one-sided and inadequate" nature of the wish-fulfillment theory:[92]

> The core of the individual is a mystery of life, which is snuffed out when it is "grasped." That is why symbols want to be mysterious; they are not so merely because what is at the bottom of them cannot be clearly apprehended. The symbol wants to guard against Freudian interpretations, which are indeed such pseudo-truths that they never lack for effect. . . . We must help people towards those hidden and unlockable symbols, where the germ lies hidden like the tender seed in the hard shell.[93]

This insight, in turn, generated a growing insistence on the psychological value of religious symbolism in general,[94] and the notion of God in particular.

To judge from the handful of references to God that appear in Jung's writings between 1912 and 1920, the see-saw in his theory remains. On the one hand he claims that "the concept of God is simply a necessary psychological function of an irrational nature that has altogether no connection with the question of God's existence"; the gods exist only as projections,[95] which "the naive mentality" alone will dare to hypostatize.[96] Yet, on the other hand, he refers to the whole question as one that simply lies beyond the powers of scientific cognition, which by themselves are "deficient as far as a complete comprehension of the world is concerned."[97]

What is less obvious is that the foundations of the original ambiguity have shifted. For now Jung ceases to identify the God-concept *exclusively* with the drama of repressed wishes[98] and begins to suggest it as a symbol for the impersonal unconscious as such. The occasion for this development was his study of those cases in which the conscious ego, in its attempt to assimilate the images thrown up to it from the collective psyche, is overwhelmed and identifies with them. This state of "godlikeness" (the word is Adler's) seems to require a further revision of Freud's theories.[99] Jung concluded that whereas primitive religions are based on the *projection* of the unconscious, with its "primordial images which are the ancient common property of humanity," the condition of "ludicrous self-deification" must rather be viewed as an individual's *introjection* of those contents from the unconscious—that "ocean of divinity"—onto the subjective plane.[100] Jung still speaks of the unconscious as a union of opposites, both God and Devil at the same time.[101] But he has come to see that the God-image is not only a symbol *from* the collective psyche, but also a symbol *for* that deep and mysterious layer of the mind.[102]

Jung's letters and puslished writings during these years give us almost no indication of his unusually active fantasy life which, as he later revealed in a seminar talk, threw him for a period into a kind of psychosis.[103] The single exception is his *Septem sermones ad mortuos,* an unusual piece of imaginative and perhaps "automatic" writing that he composed in the course of three intense days in 1916. The strange and eerie circumstances surrounding the writing of the *Sermones* are well enough known from Jung's autobiography.[104] He signed the manuscript under the *nom de plume* "Basilides of Alexandria" and distributed it among a small circle of friends. To one of them he wrote:

> Allow me to give you personally the enclosed little present—a fragment with far-reaching associations. I deserve no credit for it, nor does it want or pretend to be anything, it just is—simply that. Hence I could not presume to put my name to it, but chose instead the name of one of those great minds of the early Christian era which Christianity obliterated. It fell quite unexpectedly into my lap like a ripe fruit at a time of great stress and has kindled a light of hope and comfort for me in my bad hours. . . .
>
> I would ask you to find the little book a discreet resting place on your writing desk. I don't want a profane hand to touch my memory of those limpid nights.[105]

Taken by itself this small booklet of some 4,500 words reads like a thinly disguised imitation of mystical gnostic literature. Indeed, Jung condemned it in his old age as "one of the sins of my youth."[106] Seen in the broader context of his theoretical development, however, it is of seminal importance.[107] Because I have argued this point at considerable length elsewhere,[108] I shall refer here only briefly to such conclusions of my earlier exegesis as bear upon the notion of God in the *Sermones*.

First of all, by distinguishing between *Pleroma* and *Creatura*, Jung suggests two different ways of viewing the collective unconscious: as an unknowable, transcendent reality *in se*, and as the more restricted libidinal energy *in nobis*. It is this latter that he calls "God." What this identification of God and Creatura means in effect is that silence is maintained regarding the possible identity of God and the unconscious as they exist in themselves, while the purely abstract God-concept that stands behind the images of "gods" and "demons" is seen as the functional equivalent of the abstract notion of psychic energy. As a result, Basilides-Jung makes men and gods correlatives, by which he means that God-images are in fact projections of the unconscious mind. Now all these images can be reduced to four principal "gods": *Helios* (=Father), *Eros* (=Son), *Life* (=Spirit), and *Devil*. This fourfold model of the unconscious presents a contrast between two pure symbolic opposites—god and devil—and two pairs of opposites within man—love and life. With time this idea will give rise to Jung's so-called quaternity.[109]

The final stage in the doctrine of the *Sermones* consists in the resolution of all these projections by passing from the "outer world" into the "inner world," where one gives up gods and demons in order to worship the one God of Man: the *Star*. In the Star we have an image of the union of the opposites of ego-consciousness and the collective unconscious, which depend mutually on one another. Creatura (= divinity) and creature (= humanity) combine to produce the Man-God, a clear precursor of what Jung was later to call the "Self."[110]

Although it is difficult to ascertain how much was generally known of Jung's private life and researches apart from his published writings, it is clear that during these years he was being dismissed as a "mystic" by many who chose to remain loyal to Freud. As early as 1912 Jung had had to defend himself against the accusation.[111] In 1913 Abraham claimed that for want of understanding Freud, Jung was trying to turn psychoanalysis into an *ancilla theologiae*.[112] In 1916 Ernest Jones wrote that Jung's psychology "loses itself in a perfect maze of mysticism, occultism and theosophy. . . [and] abandons the methods and canons of science."[113] Two years later an anonymous reviewer referred to Jung's work as a "wholly modern mysticism."[114] Such complaints were to plague Jung for the rest of his life.

Apart from the uninhibited musings of the *Septem sermones*, Jung's writings during the years 1912 to 1920 are somewhat cautious and restrained. It is not until 1921 that he begins once more to stride like a giant, ignoring the limitations of his earlier thought and yet determined to remain faithful to what the isolation, the loneliness, and the intense spiritual torment of these "fallow years" had taught him about the human soul.

4. *Psychological Types* (1920)

H. G. Baynes, the first English translator of *Psychological Types*, opened his preface to the book by calling it "Jung's crowning work."[115] Only time would show how short-sighted he had been. For despite the marked success that the book enjoyed (witness its extraordinary sales and the effective introduction of the terms *extravert* and *introvert* into common parlance), both Jung and the majority of his followers were later to consider it a footnote to his mature writings. As a résumé of the first twenty years of his professional researches, however, *Types* holds a place of special importance. In this sense it is less scattered and more organized than *Psychology of the Unconscious* had been, though Jung is still in the habit of suggesting solutions that complicate rather than resolve his original problems.[116] Nowhere is this more evident than in his comments on religion and God.

Jung's fundamental methodological principle for the study of religion remains the same: psychology,[117] as a science "in its infancy," must be careful to operate wholly within the limits of the empirical method, avoiding all entanglement with metaphysics.[118] So too Jung's basic approach to the interpretation of religious phenomena is unchanged: they are to be seen as unconscious projections whose origin and function are the proper objects of psychological analysis. In the previous section I brought together a number of clues to argue that Jung's attitudes toward unconscious symbolism in general had been undergoing a slow but radical change. The justification for this piece of reconstruction, as well as its implied relevance to the psychology of religion, is amply supplied by *Types*.[119]

Jung's entire argument is grounded in his practical experience, personal and clinical, that "the contents of the unconscious lay the same claim to reality on account of their obstinate persistence as do the real things of the external world."[120] From his experience he had also observed that images and motifs of a mythological nature, which have no origin in personal acquisition, can spring up spontaneously in dreams and fantasies. These contents (the so-called collective unconscious) demonstrate in turn a certain "purposive nature of the psyche" that cannot be explained by purely causal-reductive methods.[121] Convinced of the scientifically empirical nature of these facts, Jung evolved a theoretical structure to integrate them into psychology.

First of all, he argued that the collective unconscious is the product of a history much longer than that of ego-consciousness—one where man was ruled not by will power, which is largely a product of civilization, but by inborn modes of action and psychic apprehension. The former have long been known as "instincts"; for the latter Jung suggests the name "archetypes" or "primordial images."[122] Genetically viewed, an archetype, like the instincts, is a kind of mnemonic deposit that has arisen through the condensation of countless processes of a similar kind.[123] This claim (that the human mind is not born a *tabula rasa* but comes preequipped with a commonly inherited substratum of primordial images) gives rise to another: Viewed functionally, the psyche must not be seen as a machine that can be programmed to adjust to the environment. Rather, man must acknowledge that in the very structure of his mind "is written the history of mankind. This historical element in man represents a vital need to which a wise psychic economy must respond. Somehow the past must come alive and participate in the present."[124] In recognition of this need Jung developed a theory of psychotherapy, which he called "the constructive method."

Jung uses the word *constructive* (or *synthetic*) to characterize his method as a hermeneutic of those unconscious products which express in symbolic language "finality," orientation to a goal or purpose.[125] In order to recognize these symbols and to decipher their meaning, one can draw upon parallels from mythology and the history of religions,[126] inasmuch as "every myth is a projection of unconscious processes."[127] Here Jung introduces the notions of "individuation" (the process of the differentiation of the human personality by the extension of consciousness to the understanding of unconscious contents) and "the transcendent function" (the power of the psyche to form symbols that mediate between the opposites of ego-consciousness and the unconscious).[128]

Having arrived at this more positive theory of the symbol, as a "life-promoting" and "redeeming" function of the psyche rather than as a merely pathological projection of repressed personal wishes,[129] Jung could hardly fail to alter his attitude toward religion as well. *In fact he now hazards the view that the psyche demonstrates a "religious function."*[130] This entails several things for Jung.

First, any orientation whatsoever, as soon as it becomes absolute and unconditional, deserves the name "religious" from the psychological point of view.[131] In terms of the individual subject, Jung sets "god" and "highest value" in apposition;[132] and in terms of collective culture, he views a "collective attitude" as the equivalent of a "religion."[133]

Second, such an orientation is a psychic necessity: "We also know from the psychology of primitives that the religious function is an essential component of the psyche and is found always and everywhere, however undifferentiated it may be."[134] This Jung takes to be the meaning of Tertullian's dictum: *anima naturaliter christiana.*[135]

The third trait of the religious function of the psyche is the basis of the first two. Jung claims that all vital forms of religion owe their absolute quality and their healing power to the fact that they release archaic instincts by means of fantasy: "The symbolic concepts of all religions are recreations of unconscious processes in a typical, universally binding form."[136] For this reason the religious function cannot be ignored or replaced without grave risk to psychic health.[137]

Fourth, the actual *function* of the religious function is that of symbol-formation, according to which a compensatory relationship is established between ego-consciousness and the collective unconscious: "When a problem is grasped as a religious one, it means, psychologically, that it is seen as something very important, of particular value, something that concerns the whole man, and hence also the unconscious (the realm of the gods, the other world, etc.)."[138] Hence we see a clear refusal to equate all religious phenomena with pathological disturbances. (It is in this sense that he dismisses attempts to diagnose paranoia in Christ as "nothing but ludicrous rationalistic twaddle."[139])

Finally, the religious function is distinguished from religious *dogmas,* which it is claimed serve to protect believers from confronting the unconscious directly:

> Christianity, like every closed system of religion, has an undoubted tendency to suppress the unconscious in the individual as much as possible, thus paralyzing his fantasy activity. Instead, religion offers stereotyped symbolic concepts that are meant to take the place of his unconscious once and for all.[140]

Jung's criticisms against religion, then, are aimed specifically at dogmatic religion, and more especially at Christianity insofar as "under the influence of Christianity. . . a collective culture came about in which the individual is liable to be swallowed up because individual values are depreciated on principle."[141]

It is only against this background that we can appreciate how Jung now orders his attitudes toward the notion of God. To begin with, he does not in the least renege on his commitment to resolve into their psychological components all projections naively adopted to support religious beliefs. He states, not without a touch of irony, that Western man is still so barbarous and uneducated that he needs a taskmaster God to supply him with moral laws and duties from above.[142] The science of psychology must struggle to combat these tendencies toward projection: "God must be withdrawn from objects and brought into the soul."[143] In this way, what is lost by refusing God the status of objective existence (from the psychological point of view), is compensated by viewing God as a symbol of "the supreme vital value," whose roots lay deep in the unconscious mind.[144] Further, Jung contends that we can explain the attractiveness of the reasoning in Anselm's ontological argument by pointing to that psychological disposition which tends to elevate the idea to a higher level of reality than the perceptions of the senses.[145] As an argument, however, Jung finds it logically nonsensical and in no way validated by his own findings.

In *Types* Jung continues to speak of God as a differentiated libido-complex, but his more developed notion of the symbol and its transcendent function leads him to two important distinctions. First, he distinguishes between the God-concept that differs from person to person and the "collective idea" of God that is pervasive throughout human history.[146] Second, he claims that in both cases it is *man's idea of God,* and not *God as he is in himself,* that is the object of psychological inquiry. This latter point was always implicit in Jung's concern that psychology should be viewed as a science rather than as a metaphysic. Now it is made explicit through his introduction of "God-image" as a technical term.[147] Unlike the parental imago, which has an objective point of reference, the God-image corresponds to nothing definite in the external world. Whether collective or individual, the God-image is to be seen as a symbol, which means that it can never be reduced entirely to subjective origins, even when certain affinities with the subject's personal history are demonstrable:

> Symbolization in the shape of the God-image is an immense step beyond the concretism, the sensuousness, of memory, since, through acceptance of the "symbol" as a real symbol, the regression to the parents is instantly transformed into a progression,

> whereas it would remain a regression if the symbol were to be interpreted merely as a *sign* for the actual parents and thus robbed of its independent character.[148]

Jung's most concentrated attempt in *Types* to grapple with the problem of God, and indeed his longest single passage on the psychology of religion to date, appears in a section entitled "The Relativity of the God-concept in Meister Eckhart." Here Jung discovers in the writings of the founder of German mysticism a point of view that suits his own psychological approach to religion: "a reciprocal and essential relation between man and God, whereby man can be understood as a function of God, and God, as a psychological function of man."[149] In fact, he is reading Eckhart very much according to his own model of the psyche, according to which

> the God-image is the symbolic expression of a particular psychic state, or function, which is characterised by its absolute ascendency over the will of the subject. . . . An accumulation of energy in the unconscious. . . activates images lying dormant in the collective unconscious, among them the God-image, that engram or imprint which from the beginning of time has been the collective expression of the most overwhelmingly powerful influences exerted on the conscious mind by unconscious concentrations of libido.[150]

At the same time, Jung does not completely identify his stance with that of Eckhart. He clarifies the distinction thus: psychological science sees God merely as a "function of the unconscious"; metaphysical orthodoxy sees God as "absolute, existing in himself." Eckhart—and here mystical tradition demonstrates its similarity to the primitive mentality—combines the two points of view in seeing God and the soul as mutually dependent realities.[151] Thus Eckhart's notion of the continual rebirth of God in the soul as the differentiation of "God" from "Godhead" is seen by Jung as the psychological equivalent of the conscious differentiation of archetypal contents from the collective unconscious; and this can occur only if the ego has first seen that the God-image is not a representation of external reality but only of the psyche.[152]

One final point merits mention. Since the God-image is seen as a *symbol* mediating between the ego and the unconscious, it cannot be understood merely as an image representing the collective unconscious, but must embrace symbolically the entire subject, or the "Self," as Jung calls it occasionally here.[153] After his usual manner of interpreting the Scriptures psychologically, Jung remarks concerning Isaiah 7:14: "Significantly, Emmanuel (the redeeming symbol) means 'God with us,' i.e. union with the latent *dynamis* of the unconscious."[154] Logically, this would lead him to see Christ (the "Redeemer") as a symbol for the union of the ego and the unconscious, i.e., of the Self. Yet Jung fails to make the connection at this time.[155] The positing of Self and God as psychologically synonymous remains implicit at best.[156]

A good deal has been sacrificed in attempting to deal in broad strokes with the religious themes of *Psychological Types,* for it is a book of uncommon erudition and imagination, permeated everywhere by the keen and discerning eye of the doctor of the soul. Nevertheless, its importance in the history of Jung's notion of the *imago Dei* can be stated in simple terms: the significance that the God-concept had lost when seen as a projection of unfulfilled wishes has begun to be restored through his growing concern in archetypal symbolics.

2

The Middle Years (1921-1949)

1. 1921-1937

When Jung finished *Psychological Types* he was forty-five years old and in the prime of life. In studying his writings of the following years, one cannot but be impressed by the extraordinary vigor and versatility of a mind coming to maturity. During the period 1921 to 1937 Jung's actual psychological *theory* did not undergo any serious change; both his method of analysis and his topographical model of the psyche continue essentially as before. It is rather in the *application* of his point of view to related areas of interest that we observe new developments. While maintaining a firm foothold in his clinical practice,[1] Jung felt impelled to broaden his researches in the fields of philosophy, art, literature, theology, oriental studies, gnosticism, astrology, and alchemy:

> Psychology, which once eked out a modest existence in a small and highly academic backroom, has, in fulfillment of Nietzsche's prophecy, developed in the last few decades into an object of public interest which has burst the framework assigned to it by the universities. . . . Through it mythology and the psychology of primitives have acquired a new focus of interest, it will revolu tionize the science of comparative religion, and not a few the ologians want to apply it even to the cure of souls.[2]

The link between theory and praxis was supplied by his hypothesis of the archetypes of the collective unconscious, of whose truth Jung became increasingly convinced the more he made use of it.

Perhaps the greatest testimony to Jung's intellectual vitality at this time were the public and private seminars that he began to conduct in 1925 and that continued up until 1941. Whatever the condition of the individual reports made from those sessions—and they range from highly suspect students' notes to more reliable, nearly verbatim transcripts—they pay clear tribute to Jung's genius and dedication. One is astonished by the wide reach of material he commanded when speaking off-the-cuff, as also by his efficient handling of the most abstruse questions arising in discussion. And everywhere, through the more than fifty volumes of notes, Jung's personality shines through: his tenderness, his anger, his irrepressible sense of humor.[3]

No less important to Jung's intellectual growth were the annual Eranos meetings at Ascona, Switzerland. Initiated by Frau Olga Fröbe Kaptyn in 1933, these workshops gave Jung an opportunity to air his theories and to exchange views with a select group of distinguished scholars from a number of different disciplines. From its very inception until 1951 Jung was a frequent contributor to the sessions and the uncontested focal point of its activities.[4]

Although the years 1921-1937 did not see a systematic presentation of Jung's psychology of religion[5]— nor even an extended treatment of the sort found in *Psychology of the Unconscious* and *Psychological Types*—his interest in religious problems was growing steadily stronger. In hindsight we might say that the ground was being laid for the more sustained and specialized work of later years

Jung's overall attitude to religion remains as ambivalent as ever. He both criticizes its inhibiting qualities and praises its potential benefits for psychic health. Further, we still search in vain for a clear definition of what he means by *religion.* At times he uses the term in its ordinary, commonsense vagueness; at other times he wants to redefine the notion to include the worship of whatever is absolute (i.e., one's "God").[6] In this latter sense Freud's sexual theory is referred to as a sort of "religious conviction" and his notion of the superego as a covert adoption of religious ideas.[7] By the same token, mass movements are often alluded to as "religious," even where their specific ideologies are explicitly "antireligious."[8] The reason why these "isms" can be grouped together as religions, Jung claims, is their strong emotional tie to what is archetypal.[9] Yet he is careful to exclude psychology, and in particular his own approach, from this metaphorical use of the word *religion.* It remained for him a "science."[10]

Truth to tell, Jung is less concerned with defining religion than he is with talking about the psychological origins and effects of religion—in its widest connotations. Thus he frequently refers to religions as "therapeutic systems" or as "psychological methods of treating the diseases of the human soul."[11] Speaking more specifically of Christianity, Jung notes that one of its positive aspects is that it helps to develop consciousness by bringing man into contact with his unconscious mind.[12] Negatively, on the other hand, Christianity has its repressive traits as well, especially its tendency to degrade man's inner worth and to foster an unconscious collectivism wherein the individual is swallowed up.[13]

It is in the light of such ideas that Jung begins to take an interest in the differences between Protestantism and Catholicism, apropos of their relative merits for psychic health.[14] Further reflection also leads him to assume a more critical attitude toward what he had previously spoken of as the approaching end of the Christian era.[15] No longer does he view the signs of the demise of Christianity as disinterestedly as before.[16] Rather, he sees a real danger both in modern man's refusal to recognize the deep roots that Christianity has sunk into the Western mind and in his subsequent tendency to seek a surrogate in theosophy, anthroposophy, Christian science, and Eastern religions:

> The gods of Greece and Rome perished from the same disease as did our Christian symbols: people discovered then, as today, that they had no thoughts whatever on the subject. On the other hand, the gods of the strangers still had unexhausted mana. . .
>
> . . . Shall we be able to put on, like a new suit of clothes, ready-made symbols grown on foreign soil, saturated with foreign blood, spoken in a foreign tongue, nourished by a foreign culture, interwoven with foreign history, and so resemble a beggar who wraps himself in kingly raiment, a king who disguises himself as a beggar? . .
>
> . . . We are, surely, the rightful heirs of Christian symbolism, but somehow we have squandered this heritage. We have let the house our fathers built fall into decay, and now we try to break into Oriental palaces that our fathers never knew. Anyone who has lost the historical symbols and cannot be satisfied with

> substitutes is certainly in a very difficult position today: before him there yawns the void, and he turns away from it in horror. What is worse, the vacuum gets filled with absurd political and social ideas, which one and all are distinguished by their spiritual bleakness.[17]

Further developments of this general critique of religion appear in Jung's comments on the God-image. Most significantly, we find here a firm and final break with the militant agnosticism of his early years, and a growing awareness of a complexity that had once escaped his notice. In one passage, revising an earlier article, he makes this shift of viewpoint clear and emphatic:

> If we leave the idea of "divinity" quite out of account and speak only of "autonomous contents," we maintain a position that is intellectually and empirically correct, but we silence a note which, psychologically, should not be missing. By using the concept of a divine being, we give apt expression to the peculiar way in which we experience the workings of these autonomous contents. . . . Therefore, by affixing the attribute "divine" to the workings of the autonomous contents, we are admitting their relatively superior force. And it is this superior force which has at all times constrained men to ponder the inconceivable, and even to impose the greatest sufferings upon themselves in order to give these workings their due. It is a force as real as hunger and the fear of death.[18]

Here again, it is the *experience* men have of God that was ill-important, not the metaphysical and dogmatic propositions of theology, which pretend to say something about God as he is *in se*:

> Science has never discovered any "God," epistemological criticism proves the impossibility of knowing God, but the psyche comes forward with the assertion of the experience of God. . . . Only people with a poorly developed sense of fact, or who are obstinately superstitious, could deny this truth. . . . The experience of God has general validity inasmuch as almost everyone knows approximately what is meant by the term "experience of God."[19]

Jung's writings are not much help, however, in telling us what *he* means by "the experience of God." At most he informs us that it is a quality of "profound and universal significance" that attaches itself to certain psychic events.[20] More than that he refuses to say, reminding us yet again of the limits of psychological science:

> The fact that I am content with what can be experienced psychically, and reject the metaphysical, does not amount, as any intelligent person can see, to a gesture of skepticism or agnosticism aimed at faith and trust in higher powers, but means approximately the same as what Kant meant when he called the thing-in-itself a "merely negative borderline concept." Every statement about the transcendental is to be avoided because it is only a laughable presumption on the part of a human mind unconscious of its limitations. Therefore, when God or the Tao is named an impulse of the soul, or a psychic state, something has been said about the knowable only, but nothing about the unknowable, about which nothing can be determined.[21]

Consistent with his earlier position, Jung goes a step further in stressing that, psychologically speaking, all dogmas can be traced back to psychic experiences, which are only very imperfectly represented in the religious propositions of faith.[22] For this reason, dogma is seen to serve the believer as a sort of protective shield against firsthand, personal "experience of God." This function has its advantages and its drawbacks. Jung was only too well aware of the risks involved in confrontation with the unconscious, and his own life and practice had taught him that it was not something to which everyone should be exposed.[23] "I recognize that Nature is aristocratic," he wrote, "and what is even more, esoteric."[24] For certain men, a naive form of religious faith is necessary for psychic health. "A person who no longer believes that a God who knows suffering will have mercy on him, will help and comfort him and give his life a meaning, is weak and a prey to his own weakness and becomes neurotic."[25]

At the same time, Jung sees it as a sign of greater maturity when one has the psychic strength to break through the protective barriers of collective belief and open oneself to the immediate "experience of God":

> Theology does not help those who are looking for the key, because theology demands faith, and faith cannot be made; it is in the truest sense a gift of grace. We moderns are faced with the neces-

> sity of rediscovering the life of the spirit; we must experience it anew for ourselves.[26]
> For a long time and for the great majority of mankind the symbol of a collective religion will suffice. It is perhaps only temporarily and for relatively few individuals that the existing collective religions have become inadequate. Wherever the cultural process is moving forward, whether in single individuals or in groups, we find a shaking off of collective beliefs.[27]

For modern man, Jung is saying, revelation is to be sought in inner experience, outside the bounds of churchly authority. Belief is to be replaced by knowledge.[28]

Yet here Jung strikes a familiar note of warning: modern man must beware of slipping into a naive form of atheism in which he ignores the deeper meaning of the religious function and ends up in self-deification. "We are eating the gods, and there is danger of exploding, of being too full. . . . The whole of Olympus is now integrated into our poor psyches. . . . Human consciousness becomes almost divine."[29] Even the most pathological forms of religiosity often conceal behind the neurosis a deep longing for God—a *Gottesminne* that modern man would do wrong to overlook.[30] Thus Jung does not hesitate to reaffirm that it is the doctor's duty to recognize spiritual forces at work in the disturbances of those entrusted to his care, and to encourage them to wrestle with that reality, whatever name they choose to give to it.[31] In a letter to the Swiss author and philosopher W. R. Corti, Jung makes the point dramatically:

> That you "live for God" is perhaps the healthiest thing about you. . . . God wants to be born in the flame of man's consciousness, leaping ever higher. And what if this has no roots in the earth? . . . One must be able to suffer God. That is the supreme task for the carrier of ideas. He must be the advocate of the earth. God will take care of himself. My inner principle is: Deus *et* homo. God needs man in order to become conscious, just as he needs limitation in time and space. Let us therefore be for him limitation in time and space, an earthly tabernacle.[32]

If Jung does not attempt to reconcile his apparently contradictory remarks on the God-image, neither is he unaware of them. In fact, it is here that the theoretical usefulness of the notion of the archetypes, symbolic dominants of the collective unconscious, becomes clear. In the first place, as archetype, the God-image, like all projections, occurs spontaneously, independently of an individual's conscious religious convictions.[33] To be sure, Jung has not entirely given up the idea that the psychogenesis of some gods may be explained by unfulfilled wishes,[34] parental imagos,[35] or the desire for protection from life's trials.[36] But he had also become aware of the inadequacy of attempts to explain all God-images *only* as symptoms of personal neuroses, ignoring the work of the collective unconscious.[37] The truly important thing, he insists, is that we recognize "God" as a living presence in the psyche,[38] indeed, as "the supreme and ultimately decisive factor,"[39] which is not reducible to the category of a personal acquisition.

Second, as an archetypal symbol, the God-image is a source of inexhaustible intelligibility, a bearer of possible meaning that can never simply be "explained away."[40] It is open to any number of possible explanations, both as to its interpretation and as to its origins:

> The fact is that archetypal images are so packed with meaning in themselves that people never think of asking what they really do mean. That the gods die from time to time is due to man's sudden discovery that they do not mean anything, that they are made by human hands, useless idols of wood and stone. In reality, however, he has merely discovered that up till then he has never thought about his images at all. . . .
>
> All ages before us have believed in gods in some form or other. Only an unparalleled impoverishment of symbolism could enable us to rediscover the gods as psychic factors, that is, as archetypes of the unconscious. No doubt this discovery is hardly credible at present. . . . Since the stars have fallen from heaven and our highest symbols have paled, a secret life holds sway in the unconscious. That is why we have a psychology today, and why we speak of the unconscious. All this would be quite superfluous in an age of culture that possessed symbols.[41]

Thus, whether one opts to explain the nonpersonal forces at work in man in religious or in psychological terms, the main concern for Jung is that some contact with that reality be maintained. For Jung himself, of course, despite his commitment not to disenchant the religious-minded of their metaphysical projections, psychological science offers the most appealing explanation:

> It is always a sign of progress when a man realizes that the Supreme Being is relative to himself, as he is relative to God. . . . The gods are really parts of our psyche. . . . As soon as a man increases his consciousness, the gods decrease in size and power.[42]
>
> But since the gods are without doubt personifications of psychic forces, to assert their metaphysical existence is as much an intellectual presumption as the opinion that they could ever be invented.[43]
>
> Unperturbed by the philosophical pros and cons of the age, a scientific psychology must regard those transcendental intuitions that sprang from the human mind in all ages as *projections,* that is, as psychic contents that were extrapolated in metaphysical space and hypostatised.[44]

All of these statements, typical of the period under consideration, must be seen only as an expression of Jung's psychological point of view regarding the *genesis* of the God-image. In no way do they cancel or contradict, so far as Jung was concerned, the possible *functional value* of even the most far-fetched philosophical or theological standpoints.

Third, as an archetype the God-image is a mediating force between consciousness and the unconscious, and thereby a vital element in the process of individuation.[45] The goal of this process is the birth of the Self,[46] whose principal symbol, Jung now asserts, is the "mandala,"[47] a "mystical circle expressing the totality of the individual."[48] Now, at least in mandalas found in the West, the image of the highest value or "God" is to be seen in the center.[49] The conclusion seems obvious: the image of the deity and the image of the Self are psychologically equivalent. In actual fact, however, Jung hesitates to draw such a conclusion in his published writings at this time.[50] Even in his seminar lectures, where the connection is made more clearly,[51] on at least two occasions he reacts unfavorably to the idea.[52] In general he prefers the simpler and more cautious description of the God-image as a "projection of unconscious contents."

On the other hand, we find a number of references to the symbol of Christ as an image of the Self,[53] especially in the seminar notes.[54] Hence he argues that true *imitatio Christi* does not consist in "casting one's burdens on Jesus"—what he calls a "suckling psychology"[55]—but means undertaking the same experiment with life that Jesus had, the way of individuation.[56] Christ's uniqueness is merely symbolic: he represents the goal to which all men are called, each in his own way, namely, Self-realization.[57]

Fourth and finally, the God-image shows its archetypal roots in its symbolic appearance as a union of the opposites—male and female, good and evil. Jung's study of the mandala in its typical quaternity structure, and of alchemy, with its stress on the reconciliation of the opposites, provided him with a stimulus to develop this insight further. The Christian dogma of the Trinity, he thereby came to see, was a projection that the more advanced consciousness of modern man finds unacceptable.[58] In some of his writings and seminars he suggests that the "missing fourth" is the principle of evil, whose symbol is the devil.[59] If we are to account for the "shadow side" of God, his terrifying aspect that often appears in the visions of the mystics[60] and also in the Old Testament portrait of Yahweh, the God of wrath, then we cannot view God simply as a *summum bonum,* as only good.[61]

Moreover, since the Trinity is wholly masculine,[62] it is in need of completion by the feminine principle, which in fact is also seen to occur in mystical visions and in certain apocryphal literature.[63] Jung observes accordingly that Christian tradition often locates the feminine principle in the figure of the Holy Ghost. This is particularly obvious in the Gnostic tradition, which identified the Holy Ghost as *Sophia.*[64] Elsewhere he identifies woman and devil, thereby combining the two qualities in a single image of the "fourth" person of the Trinity.[65]

In conclusion, we may recall that it was during this period that Jung began his researches into alchemy. He had read Herbert Silberer's *Problems of Mysticism and its Symbolism* when it first appeared in 1914, but was unimpressed by his interpretation of alchemy at the time. From 1918 to 1926 his interest lay principally in Gnostic literature, which he finally abandoned as too alien to his purposes. Then in 1928 he received a copy of a book on Chinese alchemy, *The Secret of the Golden Flower,* from his good friend Richard Wilhelm, the famous Sinologist. It was a study of this book that kindled Jung's enthusiasm at the prospects of discovering in the bizarre and esoteric doctrine of the mystical science of alchemy an unexpected support for his notion of the individuation process.[66] He soon learned that such themes as the ritual of the Mass, the Christ-event, and the relativity of God and man were treated by the Western alchemists in a manner wholly sympathetic to his own psychological point of view.[67] At last, he believed, he had found what he was searching for: a common meeting ground for psychology and religion. Indeed, alchemy was to remain his principal academic interest for the rest of his life, and in time he was to build up a library of alchemical texts from the sixteenth and seventeenth centuries—the "golden age" of alchemy—that ranks with the finest in the world.

2. *Psychology and Religion* (1937)

In 1937, at the invitation of the Dwight Harrington Terry Foundation, Jung traveled to Yale University in America to deliver three lectures on the series' perennial theme, "Religion in the Light of Science and Philosophy." In the following year the text of those talks appeared, in their original English form, under the title *Psychology and Religion*.[68] Among all of Jung's writings on religion this little book holds a place of special importance as a sort of manifesto of his psychology of religion. Retrospectively, it represents his first attempts to gather his thoughts together in a relatively organized fashion. Prospectively, it marks a turning point in his development, for it is the first of the several mature and sustained efforts to grapple with religious themes that, for better or for worse, have come popularly to be associated with Jung's approach to the psychology of religion. Once that is said, we need not be too disappointed if *Psychology and Religion* offers us little new in the way of point of view or style of argumentation. Let it suffice that here Jung demonstrates how he has made up his mind on some questions and turned his attention to others that are to occupy him in the years ahead.

For the organization of his ideas Jung reverts to the familiar pattern of a commentary on three dreams extracted from an earlier article.[69] Approximately one third of the lectures is given over to the background material necessary for his work of interpretation; in addition a fair amount of alchemical material is cited;[70] what remains deals with a number of specifically religious questions that Jung relates to the dreams but does not relate to each other. The most promising theoretical model, his first attempt at an actual definition of religion, is not used here so fully as it might have been. Accuracy of exposition, therefore, impels me once again to set out Jung's views *seriatim,* leaving a number of questions still open.

After a brief explanation of his "phenomenological" and nonmetaphysical approach to religion, Jung offers the following definition:

> Religion, as the Latin word denotes,[71] is a careful and scrupulous observation of what Rudolf Otto aptly termed the *numinosum,* that is, a dynamic agency or effect not caused by an arbitrary act of will. On the contrary, it seizes and controls the human subject, who is always rather its victim than its creator. . . .
>
> Religion appears to me to be a peculiar attitude of mind which could be formulated in accordance with the original use of the word *religio,* which means a careful consideration and observation of certain dynamic factors that are conceived as "powers"; spirits, daemons, gods, laws, ideas, ideals, or whatever name man has given to such factors in his world as he had found powerful, dangerous, or helpful enough to be taken into careful consideration, or grand, beautiful and meaningful enough to be devoutly worshiped and loved.[72]

Being grasped by such unconscious factors, Jung insists, is an absolute experience and a fact of prime import for psychology. "Religious experience is absolute; it cannot be disputed. You can only say that you have never had such an experience, whereupon your opponent wll reply: 'Sorry, I have.' And there your discussion will come to an end."[73] Again, he observes that "one could even define religious experience as that kind of experience which is accorded the highest value, no matter what its contents may be."[74]

At the same time, Jung warns us not to confuse *religion* with *creed.* "Creeds are codified and dogmatized forms of original religious experience. The contents of the experience have become sanctified and are usually congealed in a rigid, often elaborate, structure of ideas." Nor is religion to be identified, he tells us, with mere pious sentimentality, which frequently serves as a way of escaping from awkward emotional demands, indeed from the true religious experience of the unconscious mind.[75]

It is in this context that Jung repeats his warning that although many find themselves by conviction outside the walls of organized, creedal religion, they thereby incur the grave risk of falling prey to a simple-minded atheism that can effect a harmful inflation of the ego, or to the "mental epidemics" of mass movements wherein the individual is totally absorbed. For no man can live entirely without projections and illusions.[76] In fact, for most men, Jung would argue, the shelter of faith is much more conducive to mental health than scientific knowledge, precisely because its origins are in the unconscious and beyond the control of ego-inflating reason:

> In itself any scientific theory, no matter how subtle, has, I think, less value from the standpoint of psychological truth than religious dogma, for the simple reason that a theory is necessarily highly abstract and exclusively rational, whereas dogma expresses an irrational whole by means of imagery. . . The theory has to disregard the emotional values of the experience. The dogma, on the other hand, is extremely eloquent in just this respect. One scientific theory is soon superseded by another. Dogma lasts for untold centuries.[77]

Thus Jung professes his tolerance toward those whom he judges to have achieved a healthy relationship with their unconscious through recourse to the protective arms of the Church:

> So long as such a defense works I shall not break it down, since I know that there must be cogent reasons why the patient has to think in such a narrow circle. But if his dreams should begin to destroy the protective theory, I have to support the wider personality. . . I reinforce a means of defense against a grave risk, without asking the academic question whether the defense is an ultimate truth. I am glad when it works and so long as it works.[78]

By standing aloof from the "metaphysics" of religious beliefs, Jung tries to direct our attention to what is for him the primary *fact*: that God—"that psychological function which wields the greatest power in your system"[79]—is an autonomous force in the psyche. While this in no way supports or proves the transcendent existence of God, it does demonstrate what Jung refers to for the first time as "the existence of an archetypal God-image."[80]

None of what has been said so far is without clear and frequent precedent in the story of Jung's development as I have traced it in the previous sections. Nor do any of the above thoughts undergo significant alteration in the years to come. There is, however, another aspect of *Psychology and Religion* that is less definitive and more in the style of imaginative gropings. I am referring to Jung's interest in the God image as a symbol of psychic totality.

It is clear in these talks that Jung is advancing steadily in his attempt to relate the God-image to the psychological notion of the Self, along very much the same lines as he had been moving since 1928, when his interest in mandala symbolism and alchemy first suggested the idea.[81] His study of Oriental religions led him to conclude that historically the mandala (with its usual quaternity structure) "served as a symbol to clarify the nature of the deity philosophically."[82] Yet, when he turns to mandala symbolism as found among modern men—for example, as found in the dreams, fantasies, and drawings of his patients—Jung finds the deity absent:

> I have seen many hundreds of mandalas, done by patients who were quite uninfluenced, and I have found the same fact in an overwhelming majority of cases: there was never a deity occupying the center. The center, as a rule, is emphasized. But what we find there is a symbol with a very different meaning. It is a star, a sun, a flower, a cross with equal arms, a precious stone, a bowl with water or wine, a serpent coiled up, or a human being, but never a god.[83]

What then does the mandala, this spontaneously reproduced circle with an internal division into four parts, mean to modern man? Jung describes his interpretative method and its results *in nuce:*

> I have always been particularly interested to see how people, if left to their own devices and not informed about the history of the symbol, would interpret it to themselves. I was careful, therefore, not to disturb them with my own opinions, and as a rule I discovered that they took it to symbolize themselves or rather something in themselves.
> . . . The use of the comparative method shows without a doubt that the quaternity is a more or less direct representation of the God who is manifest in his creation. We might, therefore, conclude that the symbol spontaneously produced in the dreams of modern people means something similar—*the God within.*
> A modern mandala is an involuntary confession of a peculiar mental condition. There is no deity in the mandala, nor is there

> any submission or reconciliation to a deity. The place of the deity seems to be taken by the wholeness of man.[84]

Now, the "wholeness of man" is nothing other than what Jung calls the "Self." Hence his final judgment: the image of the Self is "not a substitute but a symbol for the deity. . . . If we want to know what happens when the idea of God is no longer projected as an autonomous entity, that is the answer of the unconscious psyche."[85]

The spontaneous God-imagery produced by the modern psyche, Jung further notes, contrasts sharply with the traditional Christian dogma of the Trinity, inasmuch as the "Quaternity" preserves the principles of evil and femininity.[86] While he cites a good deal of historical and alchemical material in support of this view, he does so with a certain reserve, adding with a touch of cynicism that the Church does well to avoid contact with such notions as long as she wants to safeguard her dogma against the onslaughts of the immediate experiences of nature.[87]

The fuller elaboration of the quaternity theme, as also of the relationship between Self and God, is left for future labors. What is of interest in *Psychology and Religion* is that Jung has taken a decisive step, setting his face toward a new horizon where the human and the divine unite in the process of individuation.

3. 1938-1942

On a radiant summer morning in August 1940 a small group of scholars gathered together in Ascona to hear the Basel mathematician Andreas Speiser speak on the theme "The Platonic Doctrine of the Unknown God and the Christian Trinity." It was the eighth annual meeting of the Eranos workshop and, in contrast to former years, only one lecture had been arranged. After lunch one of the guests fetched a Bible from the library and retired to a shady corner of the garden near the shores of Lago Maggiore, where he sat reading and taking notes. On the following day he astonished the assembly by responding to his colleague's paper with a brilliant lecture on "The Psychology of the Trinity-Idea." Slowly and ponderously the 65-year-old man spoke, as thoughts he had been nurturing for many years finally began to emerge into their full maturity. For many, what he had to say was a disarming surprise; for not a few others, a great shock. But for those who knew him best, it was a moment they had long awaited—the moment when Professor Jung would undertake his first full-scale treatise on the notion of the *imago Dei.*[88]

To describe the growth of Jung's thought during the period 1938 to 1942, one can hardly do better than take this lecture on the Trinity as a touchstone. First, some general remarks. There is no doubt that, as far as Jung's psychology of religion is concerned, the preoccupations of these years are a direct result of the position he had taken in his 1937 Terry lectures.[89] His writings, his lectures, and his correspondence all corroborate this fact. Jung continues to view religion in general, and the *imagines Dei* in particular, as psychic facts that—to leave aside all questions of metaphysics and ontology—are open to scientific investigation and that modern man cannot ignore except at his own peril.[90] Religion plays an important and indispensable role in the psychic welfare of most men.[91] Even the "modern man" who can no longer believe, and who understands that "the development of consciousness requires the withdrawl of all the projections we can get our hands on,"[92] must not cut himself off from his unconscious by an inflated rationalism. Here psychological science can fill a gap left by the *Götterdämmerung* far better than the artificial and foredoomed attempts to embrace alien religions from the East.[93] In this sense, Jung observes in one place, we might even call psychology a "religion *in statu nascendi.*"[94]

In a short preface to the published version of his lecture on the Trinity, Jung attributes the adverse criticism his ideas had provoked to a certain "timid defensiveness" of Christian symbolism, which allows the psychologist to study non-Christian religions with full liberty but draws the line at his invasion of Christian dogmatics. Arguing that the *theological* validity of a dogma is in no way denied when one reflects on its *psychological* meaning, Jung begs of those blessed with the charisma of "belief" that they be tolerant toward those others who are only capable of "thought."[95]

Jung begins by distinguishing between *trinity* and *triad.* In the religions of antiquity and of the East, the images of a triadic God are countless, and probably share a common archetypal base with the Christian Trinity. But the special quality of the latter is its *triunitas,* which differentiates it from the *tri-theism* of the triadic gods. Further, Jung introduces a distinction between the *form* and the *content* of the Trinity, that is, between its *logical* (consciously and rationally conceived) and its *psychological* (unconsciously produced, archetypal) characteristics. The logical formula for the triad given in Plato's *Timaeus*—the tension of opposition between the One and the Other which is resolved in the Third—may be an acceptable intellectual model for the form of the Trinity. For its content we must look elsewhere.[96]

Psychologically viewed, the Trinity is composed of Father, Son, and Holy Spirit. Now while "Father" leads logically to "Son," this formal model breaks down with the appearance of the Holy Spirit, who is the "breath" or "life" that proceeds from both and is lived by both. Here, Jung tells us, we come up against a psychological notion stemming from a primitive and undifferentiated mode of thought according to which qualities were not able to be abstracted but were merely juxtaposed to one another: a man and his life, or his sickness (seen as a demon), or his health and prestige (mana), et cetera.[97]

At this point Jung attempts to combine the logical and the psychological by comparing the changing images of God to the stages in the development of human consciousness, of which he distinguishes three.[98] The first, the *World of the Father,* "typifies an age which is characterized by a pristine oneness with the whole of Nature." The problem of evil is nonexistent and the Oneness of God is unchallenged by an Other. But when doubt dawns and the reality of evil becomes a problem, the stage is set for the *World of the Son.* The One has to be supplemented by the Other, for by "an irreversible increase in man's consciousness" the Father becomes the God-man and reveals himself and his Fatherhood through the Son. Hence, the age when the Greeks began criticizing the world, Jung asserts, was the preparation for the birth of Christianity. One aspect of the God of Christian revelation was the Holy Ghost, who appears on the earthly scene with the departure of Christ. By corresponding to the life common to Christ and the Father, the Holy Ghost puts an end to the "doubt" and reconciles the opposition between the One and the Other, carrying the work of redemption to mankind at large. In the *World of the Holy Ghost,*[99] therefore, we have the final stage in the evolution of the God-image and a still higher level of consciousness, symbolized by the Trinity, which is a higher form of God-concept.[100]

What Jung has done, in effect, is to interpret the Trinitarian doctrine not as a description of a process that occurs in the Godhead, entirely outside of man, but as an expression of the process of images within the human mind. In one sense, then, the process may be viewed logically as a Platonic *eidolon* related to an eternal *eidos,* whose origins—"God"—are unknowable (except to God's equals, Jung notes, for whom theologians occasionally mistake themselves, fogetting the role that human reflection has played in the development of doctrine). On the other hand, there is an obvious surplus of meaning that the logical model cannot provide, but that falls within the scope of psychological science.[101] It is here that Jung leaves his polemics against Speiser's Platonic interpretation of the Trinity and turns to a problem more familiar to him: the archetypal nature of the God-image.

After categorically asserting that the quaternity is a universal archetype representing completeness,[102] Jung at once concludes that the Christian Trinity is "perfect" but "incomplete" because it has omitted the reality of evil and imperfection, preferring to characterize God as a *summum bonum.* Accordingly, evil is both explained away as a mere *privatio boni* with no absolute existence and personified as the Devil (who in Jung's view, far better represents the *reality* of evil than the euphemistic thinking that makes it appear only as an absence of good).[103] In contrast to the Church Fathers, who resisted the idea of representing God as a quaternity, Jung undertakes to argue that, as the personification of evil, the Devil must assume his rightful place in the Godhead. In the Old Testament the Devil was one of the "sons of God," he observes; while the theory of the *summum bonum* makes him simply the "ape of God" who stands outside of the Trinity, the *umbra trinitatis.* So to minimize his importance is to ignore the scriptural evidence for his role in the drama of redemption:

> If the power of the Evil One had been as feeble as certain persons would wish it to appear, either the world would not have needed God himself to come down to it or it would have laid within the power of man to set the world to rights, which has certainly not happened so far.[104]

Of course, Jung is not claiming anything about the actual ontological status of the Devil, any more than he intends to pass judgment on the ontological nature of the Trinity. He simply wants to reaffirm that evil is an effective and menacing reality standing in opposition to good, a psychological reality that expresses itself symbolically both in religious tradition and in personal experience.[105]

Although foreshadowed in the Old Testament, the Devil makes his full debut in the New Testament as the adversary of Christ, as an autonomous power beyond God's control. Jung is far from clear in his attempt to account for this dual procession of Christ and the Devil:

> This statement is possible only by virtue of something else that is not Jesus, not Son or Logos. The act of love embodied in the Son is counterbalanced by the denial of the Devil. . . .
>
> If we think in non-trinitarian terms, the logic of the following scheme seems inescapable:[106]

For Jung, this opposition between Christ and Antichrist is archetypal and therefore has countless parallels in mythology. He gives as an example its "synchronicity" with the dawning of the Age of Pisces (whose symbol is two fishes joined by commissure and moving in opposite directions), which points to "the increasing realization of duality postulated by the Son."[107]

Psychologically speaking, such images represent the conflict between good and evil, a conflict that persists until such time as they are understood as relative values. In a Christian age, Jung admits, such an idea is out of the question, and evil must be seen as an absolute opposite to the *summum bonum* of the Trinity. Only with the further development of consciousness is the opposition resolved in a fourth principle, which restores the unity and in which the Father is seen to share a common life with his "light" and "dark" emanations. The resultant symbol is the quaternity:[108]

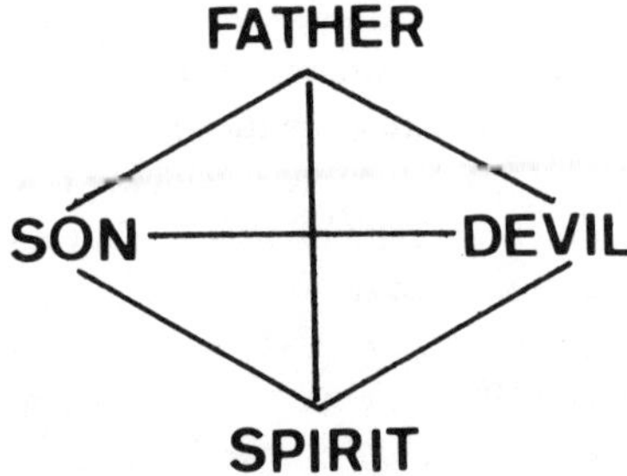

This archetype of completeness, driven underground by the opposition between spirit and nature—which is symbolized in the Christian Trinity—surfaced occasionally in alchemical philosophy and elsewhere, but always *extra ecclesiam.* And its meaning was ever the same: the union of heaven and earth, of God and man—symbolized in the cross at the center of the quaternity:

> On the one hand we have the polaristic identity of Christ and the adversary, and on the other the unity of the Father unfolded in the multiplicity of the Holy Ghost. The resultant cross is the symbol of the suffering Godhead that redeems mankind. This suffering could not have occurred, nor could it have had any effect at all, had it not been for the existence of a power opposed to God, namely "this world" and its Lord. The quaternity scheme recognizes the existence of this power as an undeniable fact by fettering trinitarian thinking to the reality of this world.[109]

In the *World of the Holy Ghost* man bears within himself the tension of the opposites—Christ and Antichrist—and it is his task to seek a completeness and inner unity that does not cut itself off from the cross: "this world and its reality." What will be the result? "It may well be the revelation of the Holy Ghost out of man himself. Just as man was once revealed out of God, so, when the circle closes, God may be revealed out of man."[110] In any case, to ignore the problem of good and evil that is cast up by the currents of the unconscious, to deceive oneself into thinking ethical demands no longer have any meaning, is to become dangerously inflated by the powers of reason and distant from "the mystery of inner experience which is thereby denied us."[111] In this vague and hortatory tone, full of double meanings and subtle ironies, Jung takes his leave of the reader.

Set in the wider context of his other writings at this time, the broader import of Jung's argument becomes somewhat clearer. From his interest in the individuation process—which he takes as a sort of intellectual scaffolding to study the symbols of transformation in the Mass,[112] the relation of alchemical literature to the religious problems of modern man,[113] and the *Exercitia Spiritualia* of Ignatius of Loyola[114]—we can safely conclude that the "development of consciousness" of which Jung speaks in connection with the "three Worlds" is to be understood as the process of integrating conscious and unconscious mind. Further, we can suppose that Jung's stress on Christ as an archetype of the Self[115] somehow stands behind the implied parallel between the Incarnation and the growth of consciousness as it appears in his lecture on the Trinity. Yet, inasmuch as the precise relationship between God, Christ, Self, and unconscious is still unresolved at this time,[116] it is not possible to detail the parallelism any further just yet.

4. 1943-1949

The next few years were difficult ones for Jung. Early in 1944 he was smitten by a severe cardiac infarct that brought him to the brink of death and required a period of convalescence involving almost total renunciation of his clinical practice. About a year later he wrote to Kristine Mann:

> As you know, the angel of death has struck me down too and almost succeeded in wiping me off the slate. I have been practically an invalid ever since, recovering very slowly from all the arrows that have pierced me on all sides. Fortunately enough my head has not suffered and I could forget myself in my scientific work.[117]

Indeed, given the heart attack and a number of other physical ailments that afflicted Jung in his eighth decade, it is remarkable to what extent he was able to carry on his research—and with a vitality and scholarly care that contrasts sharply with the frequent references to death in his letters.

Shortly before his illness, Jung finished *Psychology and Alchemy,* a lengthy book based on two earlier studies and augmented by nearly one-half with new material. Amidst the latter is to be found an opening essay entitled "Introduction to the Religious and Psychological Problem of Alchemy," which is probably the best single exposition of the psychology of religion to come from Jung's pen. Here we see him at his disciplined best, wandering very little from his theme and summarizing his major conclusions as clearly as he was able. Although I shall subsume the ideas of that essay into a wider framework that takes account of further developments in Jung's thought, it is at least worth mentioning that there is no better outline of his views on religion in the whole of his published and unpublished work.[118]

We do not find much significant change in Jung's general attitude to religion at this time. His writings reconfirm his support of authentic Christianity and his attack against its repressive prejudices, which are, as he says, "not of the deepest and best understanding of Christianity but of the superficialities and disastrous misunderstandings that are plain for all to see."[119] Regarding the latter, Jung directs his main complaints against the tendency of Western theology so to objectify God that he is no longer permitted to reach down into the soul, but can be worshiped only as *totaliter aliter.* As a result, the imitation of Christ also loses its force as a demand to seek out and follow the ideal of one's own life.[120] For the psychologist, on the contrary, the "reality of religion" is grounded in a certain "faculty of relationship to God" that is found in the psyche and that he calls now for the first time the "God-archetype."[121] If the God-archetype is entirely projected onto an external object, it thereby loses its effectiveness for consciousness and remains in its primitive, unconscious state. And if it is entirely introjected, it tends to inflate consciousness, with the same effect of rupturing contact with the unconscious. Thus the symbols of religion demonstrate their true therapeutic value only when they assist one in coming to terms with the unconscious mind.[122]

Of course, as Jung again says in reply to his theological critics, such a view says nothing about the existence or nonexistence of a transcendent referent for the God-archetype, but only about the psychological reality of the *imago Dei:*[123]

> The religious point of view, understandably enough, puts the accent on the imprinter, whereas scientific psychology emphasizes the *typos,* the imprint—the only thing it can understand.

> The religious point of view understands the imprint as the working of an imprinter; the scientific point of view understands it as the symbol of an unknown and incomprehensible content.[124]

The psychologist begins, then, precisely at the point where organized religion has failed. It is his task to revitalize religion by recognizing that "the archetypes of the unconscious can be shown empirically to be the equivalents of religious dogmas";[125] and this in view of the fact that religious symbols seem to have lost their meaning for modern man:

> Religion is a "revealed" way of salvation. Its ideas are products of a pre-conscious knowledge which, always and everywhere, expresses itself in symbols. . . . Every extension and intensification of rational consciousness, however, leads us further away from the sources of the symbols and, by its ascendency, prevents us from understanding them. That is the situation today. . . . But if we understand these things for what they are, as symbols, then we can only marvel at the unfathomable wisdom that is in them and be grateful to the institution which has not only conserved them but developed them dogmatically.[126]

Today man finds himself in a despiritualized world, where the real is identified with the material, and thus, Jung concludes, he easily falls prey to his unrecognized but no-less-powerful archaic instincts, as German National Socialism was amply demonstrating.[127]

Because the churches have not adapted themselves to what, according to Jung, were undeniable developments of modern consciousness, they offer little refuge for the thinking man.[128] Psychology, on the other hand, seems to come to his aid by opening up the way to the encounter with the unconscious and its "spiritual," archetypal contents:

> The fact is that with the knowledge and actual experience of these inner images a way is opened for reason and feeling to gain access to those other images which the teaching of religion offers to mankind. Psychology thus does just the opposite of what it is accused of: it provides possible approaches to a better understanding of these things, it opens people's eyes to the real meaning of dogmas, and far from destroying, it throws open an empty house to new inhabitants.[129]

It is just this "knowledge and actual experience" that psychology offers to the man who can no longer establish a connection between religious symbols and his own soul through the usual channels,[130] much the same as the spagyric art had done for the alchemists:

> Whereas in the Church the increasing differentiation of ritual and dogma alienated consciousness from its natural roots in the unconscious, alchemy and astrology were ceaselessly engaged in preserving the bridge to nature, i.e. to the unconscious psyche.[131]

With these two points in mind—the presence of a primordial God-archetype in the unconscious and the need for modern man to rediscover religious symbolism through the psyche—we may now turn to Jung's comments on the Trinity, seeking the clarification that seemed to elude us in his 1940 Eranos lecture.[132]

In his discussion of triads as archetypal forms, Jung incorporates new material drawn from Babylonian and Egyptian mythology and expands his discussion of the *Timaeus* to include reference to Plato's quaternity-structures.[133] Somewhat later he adds a brief chapter on the history of the Christian dogma of the Trinity from the New Testament up to the Lateran Council of 1215.[134] The only noticeable effect of these interpolations is that they enable Jung to assert more forcefully the archetypal nature of the triadic structure, and to note that, from the psychological point of view, any mention of the "inspiration of the Holy Spirit" in the growth of dogma can be understood as referring to the unconscious factors at work molding the anthropomorphic material and giving it a numinous quality.[135] Hence, for these two reasons alone, merely to dismiss the dogma as logically nonsensical would be to forgo its profound psychological meaning.[136]

The major emphasis of the revision, however, falls on the two questions with which I concluded the résumé of the original lecture: the parallel between the development of dogma and the individuation process, and the positing of Christ as an image of the Self.

Jung now makes explicit his view that, psychologically seen, the Trinity denotes both "a process of unconscious maturation taking place within the individual" and "a process of conscious realization continuing over the centuries."[137] The connection with his earlier assumption that the psychic ontogeny of man-writ-small recapitulates the psychic phylogeny of man-writ-large could not be clearer. The details of his revised argument bear this out.

The *Age of the Father* represents the "passive, unreflecting condition of the child"; it is habitual, law-regulated, and largely unconscious. The shift to the *Age of the Son* begins with the archaic pattern of patricide, when the son puts himself in the father's place. This in itself signifies no development, for the old customs are retained. A differentiation of consciousness first occurs only when the individual begins to reflect and discriminate, to suffer the conflict of moral opposites resulting from his "freedom from the law." The image of Christ crucified between the two thieves is an eloquent symbol of this tension. This second stage thus represents a coming to awareness. The third and final stage points beyond the Son to the *Age of the Holy Ghost,* wherein the Father is recovered and integrated with the Son. In other words, consciousness comes to recognize the unconscious as a higher authority that stands behind and beyond the powers of reason. "Just as the transition from the first stage to the second demands the sacrifice of childish dependence, so, at the transition to the third stage, an exclusive independence has to be relinquished."[138] This third age, in short, means

> articulating one's ego-consciousness with a supraordinate totality, of which one cannot say that it is "I," but which is best visualized as a more comprehensive being, though one should of course keep oneself conscious all the time of the anthropomorphism of such a conception. Hard as it is to define, this unknown quantity can be experienced by the psyche and is known in Christian parlance as the "Holy Ghost," the breath that heals and makes whole.[139]

Now if the Trinity denotes the *process* of conscious development according to its threefold movement, it is not the proper image for the *goal* of that development. Indeed, for Jung, a psychological appreciation of the triadic structure leads to the further recognition of an aim whose symbol is a quaternity. That is to say, the archetype of the triad serves as a model to establish a one-to-one relationship between the theological dogma of the Trinity and the psychic evolution of man: Father = unconsciousness; Son = consciousness; Holy Ghost = the union of conscious and unconscious mind. The weakness of the parallel is that God and man are wholly separate from one another.

The incarnation wherein mankind finds its place *within* the divinity is not properly accounted for. To explain this psychologically, a different archetypal basis is needed.

As we have already seen, the archetype of the quaternity is both the symbol for psychic *totality,* the Self, and also, through its association with the mandala figure, for one's highest value, or God.[140] The Trinity, on the contrary, denotes an image of abstract *perfection,* from which rational reflection has omitted the evils and imperfections of earthly existence. As archetypes of the collective unconscious, symbols of Self or God betray their origins, appearing as a union of opposites: good and evil, male and female, spirit and nature, God and man. The Trinity, however, as a consciously elaborated dogma, is a *summum bonum,* wholly masculine and spiritual, *totaliter aliter* as far as man is concerned. The psychologist must follow his empirical evidence—he must favor the symbol of the quaternity. He looks to account for the "missing fourth" by showing man's alienation from the unconscious. This in turn permits him to discover the psychological significance of certain nondogmatic traditions as well: Satan and Christ as the dark and light sons of the Father, the feminization of the Holy Ghost, the continuing incarnation of God in mankind through the working of the Paraclete, and the mutual dependence of man and God on one another.[141]

Behind Jung's approach to the conflict between Trinity and quaternity stands his developed map of the psyche. God the Father is, in fact, the equivalent of the *unconscious*; Christ and Satan are symbols for the tension between good and evil that originates with the birth of *ego-consciousness*; and the continuing incarnation through the Holy Ghost represents the process of *individuation.* The resultant divine quaternity thereby denotes the *Self* as the goal of human life. Its only symbolic difference from the Trinity (i.e., as a psychological image) is the addition of the fourth figure, the Devil. This development is of course implicit in the interpretation of the Trinity as a model for the evolution of consciousness. Yet it was impossible as long as the Trinity was presumed to be a fitting archetypal symbol for the Self. Therefore, Jung concludes, we are impelled to criticize the dogma psychologically.

Late in 1943 Jung wrote to a Protestant pastor:

> A confession of faith in the Holy Spirit is beyond Christ (for which I politely beg your pardon) and hence, it seems to me, more helpful for the attainment of salvation (which still hasn't materialized) than the backward-looking memory of the prefiguring God-man who prepared the way for the Paraclete. And it is the Paraclete that represents the revelation of God in the individual-as-he-is, the nothing-but-man.[142]

Granted that this passage may be translated in the terms given above, we are still left with the fact that Jung had often referred to Christ as the symbol of the Self throughout earlier writings, whereas here he seems to have abandoned that idea. But the matter is much more complex, and only a careful study of his specific comments on this question and on the lapis-Christ parallel as found in the medieval alchemists[143] can give us a foundation for clarifying what is far from clear in Jung's own work.

The fact is that for Jung Christ both is and is not a symbol of the Self. If we look at the New Testament, he tells us, we see myth taking the place of history in the portrait of Christ:

> He is completely overlaid, or rather smothered, by metaphysical conceptions. . . . The whole pre-Christian and Gnostic theology of the Near East. . . . wraps itself about him and turns him before our eyes into a dogmatic figure who has no need of historicity.[144]

All questions of Christ's true inner nature aside, this means psychologically that Christ became the object of his contemporaries' (collectively unconscious) expectations, and that there was therefore a general projection of divinity onto the Christ figure. His story bears all the characteristics of the "hero's" life: improbable origin, divine father, hazardous birth, precocious development, miraculous deeds, symbolic death, post-mortem effects, et cetera. In iconography he is often depicted in the mandala as an all-embracing totality. Theologically, he is God and the mystical body of the Church. Ritually, his body is sacrificed and eaten. All of this points to the underlying archetypal idea of the Self that is present in man as an unconscious image. "It was the archetype of the Self in the soul of every man that responded to the Christian message, with the result that the concrete Rabbi Jesus was rapidly assimilated by the constellated archetype. In this way Christ realized the idea of the Self."[145]

Whereas it is true that "anything a man postulates as being a greater totality than himself can become a symbol of the Self," Jung argues that not every image is fully adequate. Since Christ is not a totality (he lacked evil and sin), he is not an image of the Self in its fullest definition. As an incarnation of God, suffering at the hands of the world, he represents, however, the suffering that the ego must endure at the expense of the unconscious on its way to individuation.[146] In this sense Jung claims that the Christ figure is "perhaps the most highly developed and differentiated symbol of the Self, apart from the figure of the Buddha."[147] Nonetheless, the dogma of Christ represents only the good; evil is left to his counterpart, the Devil. Hence, Christ does not represent the Self as the true union of opposites that it is. The unconscious counterpart to the all-good Christ-image, the Antichrist or Devil, is missing.[148]

Moreover, for the first time we now find in Jung's published writings a clear and unambiguous statement—such as appeared previously only in his seminar talks—that God and the Self are psychological equivalents, inasmuch as the symbols for the Self cannot be distinguished from the images of God.[149]

Presuming theoretical consistency in all of this, we are led to the following conclusions: (1) God the Father is the psychological image for the collective unconscious; (2) God as Trinity denotes the birth of consciousness out of the unconscious; (3) God as quaternity is the symbol for the goal of the individuation process, namely, the Self;[150] (4) the Christ figure represents the opus psychologicum, the struggle toward the goal, or the process of individuation itself; and (5) the Holy Ghost stands for the ideal form of the *imitatio Christi,* that is, the individual's decision to struggle toward the Self through the passion of earthly existence, and thereby both to complete and to transcend the incarnation that began in Christ. Jung's emphasis here and in his later work on the Christ figure as an archetype of the Self must, therefore, be understood as an attempt to breathe new life into a symbol that has become remote and meaningless for modern man:

> Complete redemption from the sufferings of this world is and must remain an illusion. Christ's earthly life likewise ended,

> not in complacent bliss, but on the cross. . . . The goal is important only as an idea; the essential thing is the *opus* which leads to the goal: *that* is the goal of a lifetime.[151]

So far I have avoided the question of the role of the feminine principle in the Trinity. In the light of the foregoing, however, Jung's position grows clearer and more understandable. The Trinity, he argues, is an entirely masculine symbol, and as such it gives expression to an archetype of transcendence, of an absolute perfection that lies beyond the range of human possibility. The absence of woman, and *a fortiori,* the omission of Mary from the Godhead, are an indication of the suprahuman sphere that is being symbolized. (This same archetype is constellated, Jung tells us, in primitive initiation rites where young men are separated from their mothers, in the exclusion of women from the sacred mysteries, and in priestly celibacy.[152])

The quaternity, on the other hand, adumbrates a different archetype which, consequent upon the Christian doctrine of the Incarnation, presses for the inclusion of the feminine principle. The proclamation of Mary as θεοτόκος at the Council of Ephesus in 431; the Collydrians' heretical worship of Mary as a goddess; the alchemists' interpolation of the even numbers (which symbolize the feminine principle) of earth, underworld, and evil between the odd numbers (the masculine principle) of the Christian Trinity; the Gnostic doctrine of the Holy Ghost as *Sophia;* the *Sapientia* of medieval natural philosophers; the feminization of the Holy Ghost by the early Christians of Egypt—all of this bears witness to such an underlying unconscious image.[153] The doctrine of the mystical union of Christ with his Church, and all other such images of the "androgyny" of Christ, were clearly insufficient.[154] The doctrine of Mary's Assumption Jung finds much more satisfying psychologically. Its proclamation as a dogma, he continues, "is a consistent and logical restoration of the archetypal situation, in which the exalted status of Mary is revealed implicitly and must therefore become a *'conclusio certa'* in the course of time."[155] For the taking of Mary's soul into heaven *with her body*—"a much more material body than Christ's"—represents materiality (the diametrical opposite of spirit and the true abode of evil, corruption, and the Devil) assuming its rightful place in the divinity.[156] The Assumption is thus seen by Jung as a prefiguration of the quaternity, although it is the Devil and not the woman who remains, as we have seen, the usual image for the "missing fourth."

The importance of Jung's essay on the Trinity and its later revision can hardly be overestimated. Not only did it force him to concentrate his efforts on the question of the *imago Dei* and to clarify his position over against the theological approach to dogma; but it also provided him with a number of problems that were to define the direction of his final years. It is to the story of those years that we turn in the following chapter.

3

The Late Years (1950-1961)

1. 1950-1953

Thirty-seven years after writing *Psychology of the Unconscious,* Jung resolved to use the enforced leisure of old age and illness to submit the book to a thorough revision. The result was the somewhat longer *Symbols of Transformation.* If one lays the two texts side by side, the cumulative changes in Jung's outlook become apparent, especially with regard to his psychology of religion. The close etiological ties between the *imago Dei* and the personal history of the patient are slackened, and much more room is given to the activity of the collective unconscious. The child-parent relationship no longer suffices as an adequate model for the psychology of religion,[1] and the wish-fulfillment theory of neurosis, so prominent in the original edition, is now almost totally absent. Accordingly, direct allusions to Freud increase both in number and in their explicit hostility, Jung having long since given up defending Freud against his critics and having turned instead to defending himself against the Freudians. In general, the skeptical and rationalistic tone of *Psychology of the Unconscious* is replaced by a more tolerant and positive treatment, wherein psychology is no longer advanced as an adequate substitute for religion. Later advances in the archetypal theory are carefully woven into the text in support of this position. Indeed, hardly a single allusion to God slips by without some alteration in the text. What remains clear, however, is Jung's continued conviction of the psychic damage wrought by false forms of religion.

Jung's other writings of the period show little affinity with the questions raised in connection with the rewriting of *Psychology of the*

Unconscious.[2] The main stress lies rather on a problem inherited from his researches into the psychology of the Trinity: the relationship between God and the Self, and its role in psychic development. This concern is evident in several comments made in passing regarding the mandala (and quaternity symbols in general) as a *tertium comparationis* for images of God and Self,[3] the question of the "missing fourth" in the Christian Trinity,[4] and the psychological meaning of Christ as an archetypal symbol of the Self.[5] More important is that it appears as the leitmotiv of two of Jung's most significant contributions to the psychology of religion: *Aion* and *Answer to Job*.

Under pressure from many of his readers who asked for a more thorough treatment of the relationship between the Self and the Christ-figure, and apparently inspired by a dream he had during a temporary illness, Jung worked on and off at such a project for several years.[6] The final results, completed in 1950[7] and published in the following year under the title *Aion,* represent Jung's most difficult and complex book. In attempting to outline the ideas in it that are relevant to this study of the *imago Dei,* I can give only a glimpse of the wider reaches of the work.

As his title indicates, Jung is concerned in *Aion* with a specific period of historical time, namely "the Christian aeon." Since we are still very much "rooted in Christian soil" and since Christ is "the still living myth of our culture," says Jung, it follows that self-understanding requires an appreciation of that process of psychic development of which we are the offspring. To this end he undertakes to study the changing patterns of symbolism adumbrating the Christ-figure—the archetypal image of the Self in our aeon.[8]

At several points in his exposition Jung breaks off to clarify further the methodology of his approach to the *imago Dei.* First of all, he repeats his deliberate evasion of all questions of faith and metaphysics, claiming that for the psychologist it is only the deliverances of inner experience that count as "facts." And so, when faced with the ultimate theological question raised by the book—Is the Self a symbol of Christ or is Christ a symbol of the Self?—the psychologist has no alternative but to choose the latter.[9]

We may pause for a moment here to recall Jung's famous debate with Martin Buber in 1952. In an open letter to *Merkur,* Buber had attacked Jung for overstepping the limits of his science and substituting a modern brand of Gnosticism for faith.[10] In reply, Jung emphatically disassociated himself and his "science" from all creedal commitments:

> I do not doubt his [Buber's] conviction that he stands in a living relation to a divine Thou, but I remain of the opinion that this relation stems from an autonomous psychic content which would be defined in one way by him and in another by the Pope. Thus I do not myself presume in the least to pass judgment as to whether or how far we have to do here with a metaphysical God who has revealed himself to the devout Jew as he was before the Incarnation, to the Church Fathers as the subsequent Trinity, to Protestants as the one Saviour and to the present Pope as accompanied by a *coredemptrix.* Or should we doubt that the advocates of other traditions, including Islam, Buddhism, Taoism, etc., have the same living relation to "God" or Nirvana or Tao that Buber has to his own peculiar notion of "God?"[11]

Although Jung thus totally repudiated the label of "Gnostic" that Buber had affixed to him, the latter's reply was once again to accuse Jung of a faith-destroying Gnosis: "It—and not atheism, which annihilates God because it must reject the hitherto existing images of God—is the real antagonist of the reality of faith."[12] Given such criticism, it is not surprising to find Jung reiterating his position frequently both in his published writings and in his private correspondence.[13]

Second, Jung takes occasion in *Aion* to reiterate his approach to religious dogma. Although dogma is, properly speaking, a symbolic expression of inner experience and thereby a means to keep one in touch with his unconscious, it ceases to fulfill this function when its images become too alien from contemporary language. That the very word *dogma* has come generally to acquire the pejorative connotation of unexamined prejudices is a symptom of this state of affairs. Confronted with this situation, some turn to Eastern religions, a solution that Jung continues to lament as a naive denial of Western man's historical roots.[14] Others choose to follow the existing religious conventions blindly, unaware of their origins and meaning; of these Jung is no less critical:

> The bridge from dogma to the inner experience of the individual has broken down. Instead, dogma is "believed"; . . . .

> Dogma no longer formulates anything, no longer expresses anything; it has become a tenet to be accepted in and for itself, with no basis in any experience that would demonstrate its truth. Indeed, faith has itself become that experience.[15]

For his part, Jung offers a third alternative, which is to approach the history of dogma as a part of the broader and deeper process of psychic growth that has occurred throughout the Christian era. At this point we may return to the main argument of *Aion*.

In his attempt to trace a portion of the archetypal history of mankind, Jung concentrates chiefly on the parallel between the Christ figure and the image of the fish. Despite the extravagant complexity of his analysis, the theoretical basis for his endeavors is relatively simple: In order for the Christ figure to become the center of a dogmatic tradition, there must be a certain unconscious preparedness for it, a sort of "psychic matrix," as Jung calls it, into which the dogma was assimilated over the centuries. The connecting link is the archetype of the God-man, "which on the one hand became historical reality in Christ, and on the other, being eternally present, reigns over the soul in the form of a supraordinate totality, the Self."[16] To establish this relation Jung studies nondogmatic symbols of the Self—in particular, the fish, which he finds intimately related, in turn, to the alchemical *lapis*—and the manner in which these symbols were seen to express subjectively the meaning of the dogmatic Christ:

> The fish symbol is a spontaneous assimilation of the Christ-figure of the gospels, and is thus a symptom which shows us in what manner and with what meaning the symbol was assimilated by the unconscious. . . . The fish symbol is thus the bridge between the historical Christ and the psychic nature of man, where the archetype of the Redeemer dwells. In this way Christ became an inner experience, the "Christ within."[17]

The last third of *Aion* deals similarly with Gnostic symbols of the Self, which Jung would claim give us access to the psychic repercussions of the Christian message in its first beginnings.[18]

In his study of astrological, alchemical, and Gnostic symbols of the Self, Jung employs his familiar interpretative tools: the mandala and the quaternity. Convinced that both the findings of empirical psychology and the study of comparative mythology verify these latter as images of psychic totality,[19] and also following his earlier analysis of Christ as an image of the Self[20] (his personal biography being neither knowable nor psychologically significant),[21] Jung proceeds to an altogether new application of these ideas.[22]

There is a remarkable temporal and thematic coincidence, Jung observes, between the history of Christianity and astrological predictions. The birth of Christ corresponds to the beginning of the Age of the Pisces with the *conjunctio maxima* of Jupiter and Saturn in Pisces in 7 B.C. The story of the Magi in St. Matthew's Gospel proves, Jung claims, that Christ was viewed astrologically from a very early date.[23] Moreover, there is a remarkable correspondence of meaning:

> Through the fish symbolism, Christ was assimilated into a world of ideas that seems far removed from the gospels—a world of pagan origin, saturated with astrological beliefs to an extent we can scarcely imagine today. . . . Being the twelfth sign of the Zodiac, Pisces denotes the end of the astrological year and also' a new beginning. This characteristic coincides with the claim of Christianity to be the beginning and end of all things, and with its eschatological expectation of the end of the world and the coming of God's kingdom. *Thus the astrological characteristics of the fish contain essential components of the Christian myth; first, the cross; second, the moral conflict and its splitting into the figures of Christ and Antichrist; third, the motif of the son of a virgin; fourth, the classical mother-son tragedy; fifth, the danger at birth; and sixth, the savior and bringer of healing.* It is therefore not beside the point to relate the designation of Christ as a fish to the new aeon then dawning.[24]

Taking the symbol of the two fishes joined by commissure as representing Christ and Antichrist, and following charts of the astrological aeon of the Pisces, Jung notes that the transition from the dominion of the first fish (Christ) to that of the second (Antichrist) took place between the eleventh and thirteenth centuries. This period, Jung tells us, was noted for its spirutual instability and chiliastic dreams. One of the most influential voices of the time was Joachim of Flora (d. 1202), who expected the opening of the seventh seal and the revelation of the "everlasting gospel" in the near future, as well as the birth of a "new age of the spirit." It was an age of both revolutionary heresies and the revitalization of monasticism through the beginning of the mendicant orders. The Holy Ghost Movement, which Joachim had initiated, was full of such contradictory manifestations and thereby, Jung asserts, represents the "antichristian psychology" that corresponds to the dawn of the age of the "antichristian fish."

What is more, the twelfth and thirteenth centuries witnessed the start of Latin alchemy, in which the *lapis philosophorum* was taken as a substitute for Christ in much the same way as the Holy Ghost Movement tried to complete the message of Christ with the "everlasting gospel." In the ensuing Renaissance, we see a period of materialism and worldliness. As the fishes are depicted at right angles to one another, so too was the vertical Gothic style gradually supplanted with a horizontal one, witnessed in the explorations of the world and of nature. The subsequent loss of spirituality, culminating in the Enlightenment, led to the present world wide situation, "which can only be called 'antichristian.' "[25] We are now drawing to the end of the Age of the Pisces and the beginning of the Age of Aquarius (ca. 2000), which will "constellate the problem of the union of opposites" that had been divided during the Christian aeon.[26]

We may leave to one side the many historical questions that the above summary of Jung's argument raises, and direct further attention to those themes pertinent to the psychology of religion. But before we do so, a word should be added concerning the correspondence Jung has observed between temporal occurrences and astrological predictions.

Although the symbiosis of Christianity and astrology led to certain mutual influences,[27] we are still unable to establish, Jung claims, any causal link between the birth of Christ and the inception of the Age of Pisces, or between the subsequent events of Christian history and the astrological charts for the time, or even between the simultaneity of the New Testament fish imagery and astrological symbolism. The connection can be seen only, therefore, as an acausal coincidence of *meaning,* a phenomenon that Jung calls "the synchronicity of the archetype."[28] He had coined the term *synchronicity* some twenty years previously,[29] and for some time there was a rumor going about that he was preparing a book on parapsychology. But it was not until an Eranos lecture in 1951, followed by a considerably longer essay in 1952, that he brought the notion again to public attention.[30]

Jung's description of synchronicity as an "acausal connecting principle" is clear enough:

> Synchronicity . . . means the simultaneous occurrence of a certain psychic state with one or more external events which appear as meaningful parallels to the momentary subjective state.[31]

Instead of identifying scientific explanation with causal explanation, the principle of synchronicity states that psychological interpretation must often be content to suspend judgment on such questions and work with the simple fact of a correlation of meaning. In this way such baffling issues as the accuracy of astrological forecasts and oracular literature like the *I Ching*, as well as the unexplored world of parapsychological phenomena, need not be excluded categorically from scientific psychology.[32] Jung's own method of explanation, as we have seen it at work in *Aion,* is to view the coincidence as resting on archetypal foundations, so that by an unknown (and perhaps ultimately unknowable) causal process, an archetype is constellated both in consciousness and in some event or series of events in the external world. Alternatively, the principle is applicable to the intrapsychic question of the *imago Dei,* and here it becomes obvious to what extent synchronicity functions as a shorthand expression for the nonmetaphysical viewpoint of psychology that Jung had been advocating for the previous forty years. Thus the meaningful coincidence of a God-image and a certain psychic state can be viewed as the constellation of an archetype of the collective unconscious, without thereby denying, or asserting, an ulterior transcendent cause of either the archetype or the specific image in question.[33]

Returning now to the religious themes of *Aion,* we observe that the parallel Jung has unearthed between the two astrological fishes in the sign of Pisces and the Christ-Antichrist opposition falls neatly into line with his earlier evaluation of Christ as an archetypal symbol of the Self. On the one hand, he repeats, the image of Christ suspended on the cross between the two thieves aptly expresses the moral tension between consciousness and unconsciousness, good and evil, that results from an increase of consciousness—itself a stage on the path to Self-realization. As such it symbolizes the duty of individuation, which falls on us all by nature, and the suffering of those who take up their fate. As God and man, Christ represents consciousness tormented by the greater totality, the Self.[34]

On the other hand, Christ is not the image of that final stage, but points forward to an apocatastasis wherein the opposites will be reunited. Christ is a symbol of perfection but not of totality, and thus can be understood only over against his complement, the Antichrist.[35] In support of this idea, Jung notes that among the Church Fathers Christ shares a number of symbols in common with the Antichrist (or Devil), including that of the fish.[36] Further, the relation of Christ and Devil as complementary opposites—for instance, in the motif of the two hostile brothers—is to be found in Gnosticism, apocryphal literature, heretical doctrines, and alchemical philosophy, a fact that stems ultimately, Jung holds, from the ambivalent image of Yahweh that Christianity inherited from the Old Testament.[37] Thus, in the same way that the struggle of the two fishes represents "the newly arisen world of consciousness," so do Christ and Antichrist represent aspects of a greater totality, the original *imago Dei,* which has split into opposites in the process of its incarnation in mankind.[38] The self-revelation of God in Christ, then, symbolizes how the problem of the opposites arises when God becomes an object for reflection. The God-image, as a spontaneous archetypal symbol for the Self, is a true *conjunctio oppositorum* in its original unconscious condition.

Since Jung sees every repression of this opposition as a backward-looking urge for pristine unconsciousness, he continues to express interest in the doctrine of the Assumption of Mary as a psychological advance, inasmuch as it complements the wholly masculine Godhead. Such interests, he asserts, are wholly consistent with the Christian aeon in its second, "antichristian" half.[39] For like reasons, the opposition between Christ and the Devil is seen as a more accurate reflection of the archetype of the *imago Dei* than those theological trends which would eliminate the Prince of Darkness and attribute all evil to man while elevating God to the status of a *summum bonum.* This tradition of thought led, in Jung's view, to the metaphysical definition of evil as a *privatio boni,*[40] which he attacks vigorously and extensively for the first time in *Aion.*

Jung finds the notion of the *privatio boni* unacceptable on two counts. First, it denies the evident reality of evil, which is a commonplace but painful part of all human life. Likewise, the reality of certain of *God's* activities is overlooked, for the "theory of the *privatio boni* does not dispose of the eternity of hell and damnation."[41]

Second, and here lies the crux of Jung's argument, the *privatio boni* view of evil is not an adequate expression of the psychological reality of moral judgment. Psychologically speaking, "good" and "evil" are evaluative categories, applied to given facts of experience. They are not themselves facts, but human responses to facts, which may differ from one person to another. "Psychology does not know what good and evil are in themselves; it knows them only as judgments about relationships."[42] Their psychological "marks" are the feeling-tones that accompany them,[43] and these are *opposites.* One cannot be regarded as a diminution or privation of the other; from the point of view of psychology, they are *equally real.* From the *metaphysical* point of view, which Christian theology takes, it may be necessary to treat good and evil as objective extremal realities, and then to say that they cannot be coordinate, equal realities. Good is prior, deriving from the Creator's fullness of being. Evil is a secondary disorder or privation of the good. To the psychologist, however, such an explanation looks like a "euphemistic petitio principii," whose only benefit is that it gives expression to the noble impulse to encourage the good and diminish the bad.[44]

In conclusion, let us return briefly to the fundamental theoretical insight that had prompted the speculation of *Aion.* For Jung, an examination of the history of God-talk reveals

> transformations of the God-image which run parallel with changes in human consciousness, though one would be at a loss to say which is the cause of the other. . . . For the present, it is not possible for psychology to establish more than that the symbols of wholeness mean the wholeness of the individual. On the other hand, it has to admit, more emphatically, that this symbolism uses images or schemata which have always, in all the religions, expressed the universal "Ground," the Deity itself.[45]

Thus, whether he considers the development of the Old Testament God of Wrath to the New Testament God of Love,[46] the heretical apocryphal aberrations of Christian doctrine,[47] the esoteric teachings of hermetical and astrological thought, or the poetry of the mystics, the psychologist finds in each instance a basic and spontaneous psychic process at work that is intimately bound up with the development of individual and collective consciousness. This process is so deeply embedded in the psyche that even though man must work for the elimination of projections and their resolution into understanding, still he cannot live without the gods: "*the destruction of the God-image is followed by the annulment of the human personality.*"[48] The ultimate ground of images of God and Self remains, therefore, unknown and uncontrollable.

A few months before the appearance of *Aion,* Jung wrote rather lightheartedly to a colleague, "Now I am ripe for an auto-da-fe."[49] Yet within weeks he had set himself once again to the study of Christian symbolism, fully aware that he would only be delivering himself into the hands of his critics. Under such conditions, it is not surprising that Jung hesitated for some time before handing over to the publishers the next great *petra scandali* he had carved out of the reflective solitude of old age: *Answer to Job.*[50]

2. *Answer to Job* (1951)

In the spring of 1951, in the grip of a serious illness, Jung—then nearly seventy-six years old—took up his pen and sought once again to exorcise the daimon that had so often possessed him in moments of apparent weakness. The outcome, written in a single draft at high speed and almost without corrections, was the brilliant and controversial little book *Answer to Job.* As Jung later recalled:

> If there is anything like the spirit seizing one by the scruff of the neck, it was the way this book came into being.[51]
>
> Throughout I felt as if I were the *causa ministerialis* of my book. It fell on me suddenly and without warning during the fever of an illness. I look on its contents as a display of divine consciousness in which, willy-nilly, I have a share. It was necessary for my inner equilibrium that I make this development conscious.[52]

Almost immediately upon its publication in 1952, and for many years thereafter, *Job* aroused violent reactions in theological circles.[53]

Among other things, it was called "frivolous,"[54] "provoking and jeering,"[55] "grotesque, blasphemous and perverse,"[56] "a half-spiritual, half-joking farce,"[57] and even "childish and paranoid."[58] For his part, Jung did not appear to take the criticisms of the theologians very seriously, reacting to them with more annoyance than sympathy.[59]

In its problem, *Job* is a direct continuation of *Aion*: it traces the growth of consciousness through a study of changing images of God, both within and without the limits of defined doctrine. Jung states his intentions succinctly:

> If Christianity claims to be a monotheism, it becomes unavoidable to assume the opposites as being contained in God. But then we are confronted with a major religious problem: the problem of Job. It is the aim of my book to point out its historical evolution since the time of Job down through the centuries to the most recent symbolic phenomena, such as the *Assumptio Mariae,* etc.[60]

At the same time, the work gives deliberate expression to Jung's subjective and emotional response to the problem of the *imago Dei.* In fact, nowhere else does his preoccupation with this problem achieve the heights of personal involvement that it does in *Job*, and as such the book is a true masterpiece of irony. Beneath the humor, the sarcasm, the occasional flippancy, and what Jung calls the pervasive "critical common sense" of the book, one senses the storm and stress of a mind passionately seeking in imagination what it had been unable to discover in the accepted interpretation of Christian symbolism.[61] For one of traditional faith, *Job* must needs require a supreme effort. But to have passed over into Jung's unique perspective can also be an uncommonly rewarding experience.[62]

In a prudent gesture of self-defense, Jung goes to some lengths in a short introduction to reassert his point of view as a psychologist,[63] distinguishing what he now calls "physical truth" from "psychological truth." Accordingly, religious statements are said to "refer without exception to things that cannot be established as physical facts, and can even be characterized as physical impossibilities." They are "psychic confessions which in the last resort are based on unconscious, i.e., on transcendental, processes."[64] Two long passages may help to clarify the point with regard to the study of religious phenomena. In a general vein, Jung writes:

> Whenever we speak of religious contents we move in a world of images that point to something ineffable. We do not know how clear or unclear these images, metaphors, and concepts are in respect of their transcendental object. . . . Our reason is sure only of one thing: that it manipulates images and ideas which are dependent on human imagination and its temporal and local conditions, and which have therefore changed innumerable times in the course of their long history. There is no doubt that there is something behind these images that transcends consciousness and operates in such a way that the statements do not vary limitlessly and chaotically, but clearly all relate to a few basic principles or archetypes.

And with more specific reference to the question of God:

> If, for instance, we say "God," we give expression to an image or verbal concept which has undergone many changes in the course of time. We are, however, unable to say with any degree of certainty—unless it be by faith—whether these changes affect only the images and concepts or the Unspeakable itself. . . . Should any of my readers feel tempted to add an apologetic "only" to the God-images as we perceive them he would immediately fall foul of experience, which demonstrates beyond any shadow of doubt the extraordinary numinosity of these images . . . . It is, in fact, impossible to demonstrate God's reality to oneself except by using images which have arisen spontaneously or are sanctified by tradition, and whose psychic nature and effects the naive-minded person has never separated from their unknowable metaphysical background.[65]

In applying his psychological notions to the Bible, therefore, Jung has no intention of vying with the exegetes. Nevertheless, it is clear to Jung that the psychologist often has more to say about religious symbolism than the theologian, since he seeks the archetypal foundation of religious experience, without either being bound by specific creedal commitment or intending to "explain away" religious phenomena. In the symbols of faith he finds, in fact, a key for understanding the "process of differentiation of human consciousness."[66]

For this reason, the event of Christ's Incarnation (which, as we shall see, forms the central theme of the book) is given the same status as the legend of Job: both are viewed as mythologems; and the question of historical, "physical," fact is ruled out as irrelevant for the psychologist. Here we notice a slightly more relaxed attitude toward the historical Jesus:

> The fact that the life of Christ is largely myth does absolutely nothing to disprove its factual truth—quite the contrary. I would even go so far as to say that the mythical character of a life is just what expresses its universal human validity. It is perfectly possible, psychologically, for the unconscious or an archetype to take complete possession of a man and to determine his fate down to the smallest detail. . . . My own conjecture is that Christ was such a personality.[67]

Having thus clarified Jung's methodological posture, we are in a better position to understand what I called above the irony of *Answer to Job*. To begin with, we must see Job as a type-figure representing modern man, and thereby serving as a mouthpiece for Jung himself as well. Job's sufferings, his doubts, and his questions are all introjected through a kind of "active imagination by proxy"[68] —a process that Jung invites the reader to follow with him. To achieve the maximum effect, this identification is not made explicit throughout the book, but is evoked rather through an appeal to humane compassion for the injustice Job suffered at the hands of Yahweh.[69] Jung states his aims eloquently in the couse of his opening remarks, from which I quote at length:

> I shall not give a cool and carefully considered exegesis that tries to be fair to every detail, but a purely subjective reaction. In this way I hope to act as a voice for many who feel the same way as I do, and to give expression to the shattering emotion which the unvarnished spectacle of divine savagery and ruthlessness produces in us. . . . And just as there is a secret tie between the wound and the weapon, so the affect corresponds to the violence of the deed that caused it.
>
> The Book of Job serves as a paradigm for a certain experience of God which has a special significance for us today. These experiences come upon man from inside as well as from outside, and it is useless to interpret them rationalistically and thus weaken

> them by apotropaic means. . . . The violence is meant to penetrate to a man's vitals, and he to succumb to its action. He must be affected by it, otherwise its full effect will not reach him. But he should know, or learn to know, what has affected him, for in this way he transforms the blindness of the violence on the one hand and of the affect on the other into knowledge.
>
> For this reason I shall express my affect fearlessly and ruthlessly in what follows, and I shall answer injustice with injustice, that I may learn to know why and to what purpose Job was wounded, and what consequences have grown out of this for Yahweh as well as for man.[70]

To achieve this understanding, Jung is not content to lay his hand across his mouth and submit to a superior power as his biblical counterpart had done. He stands up boldly and, ordering Yahweh onto the analyst's couch, sets out to defend the righteousness of Job by mustering all his skills as an alienist. It is precisely at this point that one is apt to dismiss the whole venture as a jest in bad taste. Yet to do so would be to miss the subtle, contrapuntal motif that Jung intends to strike. For his aim is to offer modern man, faced with the problem of evil, an alternative to atheism and pious summission. Hence the motto with which the book opens: "I am distressed for thee, my brother. . . ."[71] If we first examine the completed analysis of Yahweh, we shall then be better able to disengage that alternative.

Jung's professional diagnosis of Yahweh is that he suffers from an acute lack of self-reflection, which his encounter with Job made evident. The symptoms of this condition, reaching back to his earliest dealings with man and forward to the sacrificial death of Christ on the cross, suppose this claim. For however much Yahweh's omniscience embraced the external world, his notorious failures to consult it in highly emotional situations bespeak a certain psychic disequilibrium, which surfaced in his wager with Satan against Job. The result was an inconsistency and malice that conflict with the image of steadfastness and loving-kindness reputed of him.

I would like to suggest explaining Jung's complex case against Yahweh by teasing out the personality-model covertly at work in the analysis. On such a reading, each of the principal *dramatis personae* whom Jung calls upon for testimony can be seen as a projection of the character of Yahweh in one of its aspects, so that together they comprise the variety of activities that Jung attributes to the developing psyche.

The figure of Satan is clearly circumscribed by what Jung calls the "shadow," that is, the "inferior side" of the personality, or the sum total of all unconscious elements, personal and collective. Insofar as these elements are denied a role in consciousness, they tend to coalesce into a relatively autonomous "splinter personality," which stands in opposition to the conscious ego as an alter ego in the same way that Satan opposes Yahweh in the Book of Job.[72]

The *persona*—a term that Jung uses to designate the face an individual wears in front of others, his general psychic approach to the outside world which, more often that not, disguises the inner reality—is exemplified in Yahweh's outward attitude to Job: the *mask* of supreme goodness, justice, and mercy.

Now, just as the persona serves as a bridge between the ego and the outer world, so the *anima* or *animus* is the door to the collective unconscious, a mediator between the world of the ego and the world of the shadow. As an image of the soul, it personifies the feminine nature of a man's unconscious (anima) and the masculine nature of a woman's unconscious (animus), as well as representing the projection-making function of the unconscious. In *Job*, therefore, the anima of God is Sophia (the hypostatized *Sapientia Dei*) and her New Testament equivalent, Mary.

Finally, Christ is seen as the image for the "individuating ego," and the process of individuation or the coming to birth of the Self.

With these clarifications, it is easy enough to follow the interpretation Jung gives of Yahweh's personality. The encounter with Job was something of a psychic trauma for Yahweh, inasmuch as it made him aware, even if only vaguely at first, of his own shadow-side. The force of his reaction to Job's questioning makes this clear. It is a typical defensive transference of the blame onto Job, without the least hint of a rebuke against Satan:

> Yahweh sees something in Job which we would not ascribe to him but to God, that is, an equal power which causes him to bring out his whole power apparatus and parade it before his opponent. Yahweh projects on to Job a skeptic's face which is hateful to him because it is his own, and which gazes at him with

> an uncanny and critical eye. He is afraid of it, for only in face of something frightening does one let off a cannonade of references to one's power, cleverness, courage, invincibility, etc . . .
>
> His readiness to deliver Job into Satan's murderous hands proves that he doubts Job precisely because he projects his own tendency to unfaithfulness upon a scapegoat. . . . Yahweh has become unsure of his own faithfulness.[73]

But a seed of discontent has been sown; a sore has been irritated, for "Job is no more than the outward occasion for an inward process of dialectic in God. His thunderings at Job so completely miss the point that one cannot help but see how much he is occupied with himself."[74] The diagnosis is inevitable:

> The character thus revealed fits a personality who can only convince himself that he exists through his relation to an object. Such dependence on the object is absolute when the subject is totally lacking in self-reflection and therefore has no insight into himself. . . . If Yahweh, as we would expect of a sensible human being, were really conscious of himself, he would, in view of the true facts of the case, at least have put an end to the panegyrics on his justice. But he is too unconscious to be moral. Morality presupposes consciousness.[75]

Now, greater self-awareness would have shown Yahweh that he was not identical with his persona. For Jung the evidence here is overwhelming: Yahweh gets angry at men whom he might have created differently had he thought of it at the time; he neglects to consult his omniscience again and again; he makes a convenant with man only to break it later; he flagrantly violates at least three of his own commandments in his dealings with Job; he lets a "doubting thought," Satan, bamboozle him to the point where poor Job ends up by invoking God for protection against God; he demands human sacrifice in appeasement while claiming to be all-good and all-loving. In short, Yahweh is a personality swarming with unreconcilable opposites, totally unlike the *summum bonum* that later theology tried to call him.[76]

Ideally, of course, Yahweh should have acknowledged his shadow side that Job had seen, but he preferred to let it remain unconscious.[77] The impetus to self-awareness was to come from elsewhere.

For about the same time as Yahweh is torturing Job to avoid confrontation with himself, rumor spreads that Yahweh has remembered his feminine playmate, the firstborn of all creation, an unstained reflection of his image: Sophia, the Wisdom of God.[78] This anamnesis is to be seen as prompted by the need for self-reflection, "for if Job gains knowledge of God, then God must also learn to know himself. It just could not be that Yahweh's dual nature should become public property and remain hidden from himself alone."[79] Hence an anima-figure presents itself to Yahweh as a kind of psychopomp into the world of the unconscious. Sophia affects Yahweh in two ways: whereas previously he had blamed evil on man's disobedience, he now begins to look on Satan, his first Son, as the responsible one; and whereas once he had made a convenant with his chosen people, treating them as a jealous husband does his bride, forcing them into a submissive, feminine role, now he begins to recall his own eternal coexistence with Sophia and to rediscover a relationship of love—rather than fear—with mankind. In both respects, a momentous change is seen as imminent, not in the world but in God himself—God will become man.[80]

In this way the motivation for the Incarnation is traced back to Yahweh's encounter with Job. Jung asks: "Could a suspicion have grown up in God that man possesses an infinitely small yet more concentrated light than he, Yahweh, possesses? A jealousy of that kind might perhaps explain his behavior."[81] Later his answer is more resolute:

> Job's superiority cannot be shrugged off. Hence a situation arises in which real reflection is needed. That is why Sophia steps in. She reinforces the much needed self-reflection and thus makes possible Yahweh's decision to become man. It is a decision fraught with consequences; he raises himself above his earlier primitive level of consciousness by indirectly acknowledging that the man Job is morally superior to him and that therefore he has to catch up and become human himself. . . . Yahweh must become man precisely because he has done man a wrong.[82]

Birth by the Virgin Mary, who is the incarnation of Sophia, is symbolic of Yahweh's love for mankind. Yet at the same time, "Mary is elevated to the status of a goddess and consequently loses something of her humanity," just as Christ himself was not a real human being, but a God. In other words, the Incarnation was incomplete because "Yahweh's perfectionism is carried over from the Old Testament into the New."[83] Too close an identification with his persona inhibits his taking more than a couple of intitial steps along the path of individuation.

With the problem of evil shifted onto the shoulders of Satan, who is thenceforth banned from the heavenly court, Yahweh's integration of the shadow is far from complete:

> God, with his good intentions, begot a good and helpful son and thus created an image of himself as the good father—unfortunately, we must admit, again without considering that there existed in him a knowledge that spoke a very different truth. Had he only given an account of his action to himself, he would have seen what a fearful dissociation he had to go into through his incarnation. Where, for instance, did his darkness go—that darkness by means of which Satan always manages to escape his well-earned punishment? Does he think he is completely changed and that his amorality has fallen from him?[84]

But it is the "Spirit of truth," the Paraclete whom Christ promises, who is destined to bring to light what Yahweh has overlooked. The first "disturbance in man's unconscious" appears with the Revelation of St. John.[85]

In the Apocalypse we find a compensation for the God of Love whom Jesus had preached; we are reminded of the wrathful side of Yahweh, which Christ had not overcome, indeed to which he had been sacrificed.[86] For St. John this opposition remains external to God and is depicted in the hostility between Christ and Antichrist, which was eventually to result in the latter's defeat. Even so, in the figure of Christ we see irrepressible signs of the shadow appearing. "This apocalyptic 'Christ' behaves rather like a bad-tempered, power-conscious 'boss' who very much resembles the 'shadow' of a love-preaching bishop."[87] What all this points to is a development beyond Christianity, which had long been sinking roots but which only now comes to blossom, at the end of the aeon of the Pisces. The meek Lamb who is transformed into an irascible ram is an image of the feelings repressed in the Christian quest for perfection, a perfection that quite overlooked the psychic need for completeness.

This incompleteness of the Incarnation of God in Christ, as revealed by the Paraclete, thus points forward to a further stage in the process of Yahweh's growth. Its symbol appears in the Apocalypse as the birth of the son of the sun-woman, whose parallelism to the myth of Christ makes him seem like a second Messias to appear at the end of the world. The basis for this parallel is to be sought in the archetype of the Self to which both Christ and the son of the sun-woman owe their numinosity; and the woman herself is seen to have strong affinities with Sophia and Mary, to be an anima-figure. Further, as the offspring of the *hieros gamos* of Christ and his bride, this new Messias is an image of a union of God and man that transcends the possibilities of the Christian era—in Jung's term, a "Christification of many."[88]

The burden mankind faces in its relationship to Yahweh after the encounter with Job and the life of Christ is that *God wanted to become man and still wants to.* In Christ God had incarnated his good side, but his evil side still remained projected onto his creatures. Thus the pressure for a further advance:

> From the promise of the Paraclete we may conclude that God wants to become *wholly* man; in other words, to reproduce himself in his own dark creature (man not redeemed from original sin). The author of Revelation has left us a testimony to the continued operation of the Holy Ghost in the sense of a continuing incarnation.[89]

After the Incarnation of Christ, Yahweh's process of individuation is to be sought in the world of man: "God acts out of the unconscious of man."[90] In this way Jung rejects the notion of redemption that involves man's submission to a loving Father, insisting rather that redemption means that a man becomes conscious of the opposites in God as they are reflected in man himself. Hence he can claim that, in addition to the morality of Christ, we also need a "morality of evil," that is, the complete integration of the unconscious. This conscious realization of the *imago Dei* in man is the work of the Holy Spirit, the Spirit of Truth, who carries to its conclusion the work of Christ.[91]

As had been the case with Yahweh, so now mankind is also in need of the wisdom of Sophia, as a bridge between consciousness and the unconscious. It is in this light that Jung applauds the papal pronouncement of the dogma of Mary's Assumption into Heaven as an image of the ongoing incarnation. It must surely have pleased Jung greatly to have read of the dogma's solemn declaration in 1950, after his own explicit prediction of the event two years earlier. Indeed, he calls it in *Job* "the most important religious event since the Reformation," and warns that Protestants would do wrong to ignore it or misunderstand it.[92] The dogma points ahead to a union of God and man, of heaven and earth, of Yahweh and Sophia. It is a timely recollection of the marriage of the sun-woman and the Lamb, from whose union the new man is to be born. For just as both consciousness and the unconscious are necessary for the birth of the Self, so can Christ and Mary be properly considered co-redeemers of mankind.[93]

With this final movement the answer to Job rests complete, and the projections and anthropomorphisms that made up Jung's material return to their original, undisguised identification as symbols for the growth of the psyche. The basic line of thought as we have followed it here is hardly new to Jung; nor indeed can it be said to have been expounded in an especially lucid manner in *Job*. But the book stands as a testimony, a self-portrait of Jung in his inner struggles with God, and maintains its charm and its maturity despite the exegetical distortion and dubious logic of his argument. In this sense, it is as if Jung were writing autobiographically when he penned the following lines concerning St. John:

> *In confinio mortis* and in the evening of a long and eventful life a man will often see immense vistas of time stretching out before him. Such a man no longer lives in the everyday world and in the vicissitudes of personal relationships, but in the sight of many aeons and in the movement of ideas as they pass from century to century.[94]

3. 1954–1961

In the final years of his life, the preparation of papers for professional meetings, clinical work with patients, and travels abroad—all once such a major part of Jung's career—came at last to an end. He spent much more time in solitude or among a small group of relatives and friends.[95] Yet he was far from inactive intellectually; not only did he keep up an immense and impressive correspondence with his colleagues and critics, but he somehow found the strength to add still more titles to his long list of published writings. Indeed, to judge only from a bibliographical list, one could hardly discern that old age, retirement, and frequent illness had overtaken him.

Jung's major achievement at this time was the completion of a massive work on alchemy, which had been some twelve years in the making, *Mysterium Conjunctionis.*[96] In the preface to this work he referred to it as "my last book"; and in a letter to Victor White dated 19 January 1955 he wrote: "My last work, *Mysterium Conjunctionis,* is now in printing and I have no more ideas—thank God," But time and an irrepressible drive for intellectual activity were to banish this spirit of surrender. Two more books—*The Undiscovered Self*[97] and *Flying Saucers: A Modern Myth*—as well as a number of major articles were still to be written. In all of this material, and especially in his letters, religious themes play a considerable but secondary role. In fact, Jung did not develop his views on the psychology of religion much beyond the arguments of *Aion* and *Job*, and for this reason my account of these final years will consist more or less of a summary recapitulation of ideas we have met with, in one form or another, in his earlier work.

To begin with, Jung's aggression against the theologians over the methodological independence of the psychology of religion grows more intense and more heated at the end of his life. His stance is firm and unswerving, in line with what he had been saying for nearly thirty years: that as a psychologist he considered himself neither an atheist, a Gnostic, an agnostic, a mystic, a metaphysician, nor a theologian,[98] and that his theories did not claim to prove the existence of a transcendent God or to say anything at all about the nature of such a being.[99] Rather, he was an empirical scientist who studied subjectively felt experiences, without wishing to preempt the task of the philosopher or theologian.[100] In the interests of science, therefore, all religions, and their symbolism and rites, are to be seen as equally relative to the psyche. Nothing is to be said regarding the claims of any doctrinal tradition to ultimate truth. Not only *can* such a view be taken of religious phenomena, says Jung, but it *must* be, if we are not to fall into Freud's error of eliminating one of the most important aspects of human psychology.[101]

Further, Jung refers more explicitly to his personal attitude to God, a matter on which he had always shown a mixture of irritation and reticence when theologians or the faithful pressed him on it. In opposition to the traditional notion of religious "belief," Jung characterizes himself as possessed of a "knowledge" based on personal experience of forces that transcend the conscious psyche. In an interview held in 1955 he remarked:

> All that I have learned has led me step by step to an unshakable conviction of the existence of God. I only believe in what I know. And that eliminates believing. Therefore I do not take his existence on belief—I *know* that he exists.[102]

A similar comment, made during a 1959 television interview on the BBC brought Jung a storm of letters to which he replied in the *Listener:*

> I did not say in the broadcast, "There is a God," I said, "I do not need to believe in God: I *know*." Which does not mean: I do know a certain God (Zeus, Yahweh, Allah, the Trinitarian God, etc.) but rather: I do know that I am obviously confronted with a factor unknown in itself, which I call "God" in *consensu omnium ("quod semper, quod ubique, quod ab omnibus creditur")*. . . . I should consider it an intellectual immorality to indulge in the belief that my view of a god is the universal, metaphysical Being of the confessions or the "philosophies." . . . Since I *know* of my collision with a superior will in my own psychical system, *I know of God.*[103]

And again, we find in one of his letters this fuller comment, which I quote at length:

> We find numberless images of God, but we cannot produce the original. There is no doubt in my mind that there is an original behind our images, but that it is inaccessible. We even could not be aware of the original, since its translation into the terms of our psychical possibilities is necessary and indispensable to make it perceptible at all. How would, e.g., Kant's *Critique of Pure Reason* look when translated into the psychical imagery of a cockroach? And I assume that the difference between man and the creator of all things is even immeasurably greater than between a cockroach and man. Why should we be so immodest as

> to assume that we could catch a universal being in the narrow confines of our language? We know that the God-images play a great role in psychology, but we cannot prove the physical existence of God. As a responsible scientist I am not going to preach my personal and subjective convictions which I cannot prove. . . . When I keep to statements which I think I can make evident then it does not mean that I deny the existence of anything else that might exist beyond it. It is sheer malevolence to accuse me of an atheistic attitude, simply because I try to be honest and disciplined. . . . I am well satisfied with the fact that I know experiences which I cannot avoid calling numinous or divine.[104]

Much the same mixture of tolerance and skepticism is found in Jung's general remarks on religion during these years. On the one hand he continues to speak of an "instinctive" religious need in man that is denied or repressed only at the risk of harm to the development of the personality.[105] And on the other hand he recognizes that adherence to certain religious dogmas seems especially suited for the psychic health of the morally weak, of those whose minds remain at a relatively unreflective stage of growth: "The great religions are psychotherapeutic systems that give a foothold to all those who cannot stand by themselves, and they are in the overwhelming majority."[106] The reason for this ambivalence, as always, is to be found in what Jung understands by religion and how he approached its study.

Underlying Jung's talk of religion, then, is its definition in terms of an individual's submission to and dependence on the numinous in psychic experience. In contrast to this, there are creeds (on occasion also called loosely "religions") that circumscribe a set of doctrines held in common as a confession of faith.[107] For Jung, of course, direct and personal experience is the indispensable element in the individuation process and thus psychologically of higher value than the creedal attitude, even if at times it proves threatening to existing ecclesial modes of thought.[108] This happens because such experience involves contact with the unconscious mind, which is the seat of all religious experience and the origin of all religious dogma, which is in fact a definite expression of collectively shared archetypes.[109] While the symbols of Christian dogma may serve *creedal man* as a kind of apotropaic safeguard against the invasion of unconscious forces, they offer *religious man* a starting point for self-reflection. Hence it is not surprising to find Jung insisting on the fact that he is a Christian, and at the same time continuing to view the trend toward Oriental religions as a mistaken response by the West to the apparent decline of Christianity and the lamentable division among the churches of Christendom.[110]

Images of God, whether in dogmatic form or not, hold a special place among the archetypal symbols. For not only are they "projected and autonomous dominants of the psyche," but they also represent the supreme values and the source of meaning in one's life.[111] That this was so for Jung himself is beyond doubt. A letter to a young Benedictine monk makes the point exquisitely: "I find that all my thoughts circle around God like planets around the sun, and are as irresistibly attracted by him. I would feel it to be the grossest sin if I were to oppose any resistance to this force."[112]

As archetypal symbols, God-images reflect the fullness of opposites characteristic of unconscious phenomena. Jung never tired here of claiming that for the psychologist "good" and "evil" were traits appropriate to the *imago Dei,* which very often appears as a *complexio oppositorum.*[113] In the same way, the most fitting representation of the underlying archetype includes a feminine as well as the accustomed masculine aspect.[114] As a result, Jung found it preferable to work with a quaternity-structure to describe the nature of the God-image, rather than with the Christian Trinity.[115]

Arguing from the fact that the quaternity-structure is to be seen both in images of God and in those of the Self, Jung arrived at the generalization that "God," "Self," "highest value," and "wholeness" are functional psychological equivalents.[116] In particular, for Western man it is the figure of the incarnate God, Christ, that most naturally comes to represent the archetype of the Self in religious language,[117] in spite of the fact that the dogmatic image of Christ lacks the completeness required of an archetypal symbol: he is all *male* and all *good.*[118] In any event, Jung is critical of those theologians who try to humanize Christ too excessively and to demythologize the Gospels, for such efforts tend to ignore the psychic condition—namely, the presence of an archetype—which grants such a figure its appeal and inner meaning in the first place, quite apart from questions of historicity.[119]

A curious application of the psychology of the *imago Dei* occurs in Jung's analysis of "UFOs."[120] In his view, it is not the actual physical events that are of interest—they may or may not be true as reported, though Jung was personally impressed by certain accounts.[121] What matters for the psychologist is rather the archetypal condition that has been constellated and expressed in the projection of certain attitudes toward flying saucers. In the language of "synchronicity" (which principle Jung adopts for the purposes of his argument), the *causes* of the perceived phenomena remain unknown, but a certain *meaning* supplies a connecting link to the present situation of modern man.[122]

This meaning is, in brief, a heralding of a certain development of consciousness concomitant with the approaching astrological Age of Aquarius.[123] Treating UFO's as "visions," and therefore as archetypal images, Jung likens their roundness to the mandala and thence to the *imago Dei* and the Self. To the disorientation and perplexity of our times and the apparent demise of Christianity, an archetype that at one time would have found its footing in the Christ-figure now appears projected onto the skies:

> On the antique level, therefore, the UFOs could easily be conceived as "gods." . . . It is characteristic of our time that the archetype, in contrast to its previous manifestations, should now take the form of an object, a technological construction, in order to avoid the odiousness of mythological personification. Anything that looks technological goes down without difficulty with modern man.[124]

As psychic products the UFO's indicate the need for a development of consciousness whereby men who no longer believe in or hope for "metaphysical interventions" from a supernatural realm can find salvation and meaning in life. In the phrase of *Answer to Job,* they point to "the Christification of many."[125]

This theme of the ongoing incarnation as an image for the psychological process of individuation is still very much present in Jung's writings at this late stage, even if often in covert form.[126] In fact, one could say that it was his one solid bond with the living Christian tradition. For like the alchemists before him who had approached the knowledge of God through the knowledge of oneself,[127]

Jung was convinced that God was nowhere to be found if not in the depths of the human soul: "If one experiences himself and comes in the end to know more or less clearly who he is, then he has also experienced something of God and who he is."[128]

4. *Memories, Dreams, Reflections* (1961)

"An autobiography is the one thing I'm not going to write," Jung remarked in 1948. "I've seen enough autobiographies in my lifetime and the essential things were lacking in every one of them."[129] But he was not beyond coaxing, and eventually yielded to pressure from friends and disciples. One may suppose that when he finally consented in 1956 to write his memoirs he had come to understand his outer resistance as a screen for an inner desire to relive his past in the reflexive light of old age. In any case, he set to work with the aid of his private secretary, Aniela Jaffé, referring to the project always as a "biography" that she was writing and in which he himself, as he said, "was only getting my feet a little wet."[130] It is a tribute to Frau Jaffé that the final result bears the stamp of Jung's own hand so completely, both in the enchanting style of its prose and in the distinctive flavor and flow of its ideas. Although Jung requested that the book be published posthumously and be excluded from his *Collected Works,* to underrate its importance would be an injustice of the worst sort—especially in any account of Jung's religious thought.[131]

As an autobiography, *Memories, Dreams, Reflections* is something of a unique venture in that Jung chose explicitly to respect his faded recollection of outward events and to concentrate rather on his private "bouts with the unconscious."[132] To this end he made use of the categories of his mature thought to put order into the chaos of a life of inner experiences. However much this last book annoyed some of his critics, obviously one has little choice but to accept Jung's account of events to which there could be no other witnesses. What can be said, however, is that *Memories* must be approached with a certain cautious reserve. For much of what life denied Jung, imagination supplies—with regard to both the description and the interpretation of the facts.

Throughout his life, Jung tells us, he was a solitary person who believed himself possessed of a certain "daimon" to which he always sensed it his duty to be faithful.[133] He recounts the tale of his years as a struggle between two personalities within him—the "No. 1" personality, the external man, and the "No. 2" personality, the spiritual man.[134] From early youth Jung had sought to be alone in the "eternal" world of his fantasies, resisting the alienating influence of his schoolmates. (In later life, he was to encourage his patients to a similar frame of mind, rather than to expend their energies merely in adjusting to the external environment.[135])

Jung's rapport with this No. 2 personality was supported by frequent and quite remarkable phenomena that convinced him of the presence of "daimonic" forces in his soul. Everything from clairvoyance, telepathy, and prophetic dreams to poltergeists, catalytic exteriorization, and haunted houses came his way. If we follow C. D. Broad's dictum—as Jung himself surely would have—that any theories about religious experience advanced by those who have had none of their own should be regarded with suspicion, then *Memories* shows Jung's personal experience to have been so rich as to exempt him from reasonable criticism.[136]

By a strange series of mental associations—of the sort possible perhaps only to a young child—Jung came from an early age to harbor a deep fear and distrust of the "Lord Jesus," of all clergymen (and especially Jesuits), and of Catholic churches. This extraordinary and precocious dislike of official Christianity was confirmed by a number of inner experiences, all of which appear to have had the effect of inspiring a very private brand of religious sentiment in the young Jung.[137] Between the ages of three and four he had his earliest dream: the image of a giant phallus enthroned in a splendid subterranean kingdom. At the time he did not recognize the figure for what it was. All he knew was that it had some connection with the dark Lord Jesus:

> The phallus of this dream seems to be a subterranean God "not to be named," and as such it remained throughout my youth, reappearing whenever anyone spoke too emphatically about Lord Jesus. Lord Jesus never became quite real for me, never quite acceptable, never quite lovable, for again and again I would think of his underground counterpart, a frightful revelation which had been accorded me without my seeking it.[138]

At about the age of nine, he carved a small wooden manikin, which he hid away, together with a small painted stone, under one of the roofbeams in the attic of his house. In times of distress he would steal away to be with his self-styled idols. "At such times it was strangely reassuring and calming to sit on my stone. Somehow it would free me of all my doubts. . . . I was but the sum of my emotions, and the Other in me was the timeless, imperishable stone."[139] Depression and melancholy were in fact frequent companions to the boy Jung, so that he would often retire into the inner world of his fantasies for a therapeutic release that prevented him from being suffocated by the strains of his No. 1 personality.

From the age of eleven Jung began to take a keen interest in "God," whom he saw at first as somehow different from the uncanny soul-snatcher, Lord Jesus. But a moving experience of God's "dark side" was to change all that. Sometime in his twelfth year, Jung recalls, he began to have suspicions of an evil thought lying just below the threshold of consciousness. For two days he warded it off, but on the third day he yielded:

> I gathered all my courage, as though I were about to leap forthwith into hell-fire, and let the thought come. I saw before me the cathedral, the blue sky. God sits on his golden throne, high above the world—and from under the throne an enormous turd falls upon the sparkling new roof, shatters it, and breaks the walls of the cathedral assunder.[140]

This, he felt, must be an experience of grace; somehow it was God's will for him to see what he had seen. Jung treasured the revelation in the silence of his own thoughts, while outer disenchantment with official Christianity became more and more pronounced. He recalls, for instance, how fascinated he had been by the notion of the Trinity, only to suffer the disappointment of having his father pass over that long-anticipated part of the catechism with the simple comment that he didn't understand it at all. Then too, Jung was beginning to wonder how it was that God could be omnipotent and yet powerless against the Devil, who seemed free to roam about wreaking evil at will.[141] Likewise, he found First Communion a dull and empty event. And when he turned to a reading of Biedermann's *Christliche Dogmatik,* which he had found on the shelves of his father's library, his sense of the incompatibility between his private experiences and traditional doctrine seemed irreparably fixed:

> That finished it for me. This weighty tome on dogmatics was nothing but fancy drivel; worse still, it was a fraud or a specimen of uncommon stupidity whose sole aim was to obscure the truth. I was disillusioned and even indignant, and once more seized with pity for my father, who had fallen victim to this mumbo-jumbo.[142]

Although Jung's father was himself a country pastor of the Basel Reformed Church,[143] he never inspired his son with a sense of respect for the Christian faith—quite the opposite. Jung watched his father fall to pieces under the throes of personal doubts of faith, while all the time refusing to engage in discussions on religious matters with his son, recommending him instead to "believe." And so Jung grew to dislike theology "because it posed problems to my father which *he* couldn't solve and which seemed to *me* unjustified."[144] Further, while he was away at Gymnasium, Jung frequented the house of an uncle, also a pastor, and there heard theological discussions for the first time. But this experience was also disappointing, so safely did the participants seem to the boy ensconced in a "self-evident world-order." His earlier suspicions were once again confirmed: "For God's sake I now found myself cut off from the Church and from my father's and everybody else's faith. Insofar as they all represented the Christian religion, I was an outsider."[145]

In all of this one can readily see the childish exaggerations and one-sided attitudes of an adolescent struggling for independence from his unhappiness at home. At the same time, Jung recounts his story with such simplicity and clarity that the sophistication of later years seems to fall away before our eyes and reveal the primitive and unaltered form of his religious convictions. For throughout his youth Jung clung to the idea of God as something beyond proof, as a belief based on actual experience—something that he felt had separated him from the rest of men, who could only *talk* about God, but who were really "like animals, unconscious of such things."[146]

The inner battle between the No. 1 and the No. 2 personality followed Jung to his university studies and was the source of his growing interest in spiritism and psychology which, despite the almost universal opposition of family and friends, led to his choice of a profession. At this point begins the story of Jung's career, one aspect of which, together with the relevant autobiographical data, has formed the object of the foregoing chapters. It remains here only to gather up briefly the various comments on religious questions that appear in *Memories* and that are relevant to the present theme.

Consistent with the account he gives of his life is Jung's assertion here yet again of the primacy of direct religious experience over mere assent to established religious beliefs, though the latter may perform a function of inestimable value for the unreflective multitudes: "One half of humanity battens and grows strong on a doctrine fabricated by human ratiocination; the other half sickens from the lack of a myth commensurate with the situation."[147] Himself an "unbeliever," it was Jung's life's work to forge such a myth and dedicate himself wholeheartedly to it. Working within the legacy of Christian symbolism, he sought an alternative to what he considered the vague and abstract deliverances of the theologians who spin theories out of theories with no concrete base in experience. It was contact with the unconscious that could breathe new life into old images, and that enabled him to find meaning in life and escape the widespread spiritual *anomie* of contemporary man.[148]

Jung's epistemological stance as a psychologist helped him to steer clear of theological debates at the same time as he criticized their over-intellectualism. "A belief proves to me only the phenomenon of belief," he asserts, "not the content of the belief."[149] The only certitude he permitted himself was that of the subjective feeling of an actual psychical experience of powers one sensed were superior to consciousness—and it mattered little, in the end, whether one named those powers "the unconscious," "*élan vital,*" or "God:"

> For it is not that "God" is a myth, but that myth is the revelation of a divine life in man. It is not we who invent myth, rather it speaks to us as a Word of God. The Word of God comes to us, and we have no way of distinguishing whether and to what extent it is different from God. There is nothing about this Word that could not be considered known and human, except for the manner in which it confronts us spontaneously and places obligations upon us.[150]

The difficulties such a position involved him in from the side of psychological science are epitomized in his early encounters with Freud, who took it upon himself to counsel the youthful Dr. Jung, nineteen years his junior, to avoid cudgeling his brains over questions of philosophy, religion, and, above all, the occult, that "black tide of mud."[151] Looking back over those events, Jung remarks:

> Although I did not properly understand it then, I had observed in Freud the eruption of unconscious religious factors. . . . In the place of a jealous God whom he had lost, he had substituted another compelling image, that of sexuality. . . . But what difference does it make, ultimately, to the stronger agency if it is called now by one name and now by another?[152]

For his part, of course, Jung showed no hesitation in referring to the cornerstone of his psychology—the collective unconscious—as "God", convinced as he was that he was speaking of the very thing that men at all times and places have called God. "I am a man . . . . a splinter of the infinite deity," he announces in the opening pages of his memoirs.[153] And later on he refers to men as "bits of God become independent," and as "victims and promoters of a collective spirit" to which all our *imagines Dei* refer.[154] He saw the Incarnation of Christ as a symbol for an inner psychological process of development to which all men are called. Indeed, the "filiation" of the Holy Spirit represents man's being drawn into the labors of that divine drama of Incarnation which Jung, as a psychologist, calls the individuation process. Further, in the same way that the Christian myth speaks of union with God after death, Jung speculates that this growth into psychic wholeness may well continue after death.[155]

As to what God might be in himself, Jung keeps to his customary deliberate silence, except to state his preference for St. John's description—"God is Love"—since love embodies the paradoxical and uncontrollable nature of all our images of God:

> Man can try to name love, showering upon it all the names at his command, and still he will involve himself in endless self-deceptions. If he possesses a grain of wisdom, he will lay down his arms and name the unknown by the more unknown, *ignotum per ignotius*—that is, by the name of God.[156]

The opposition that Jung's lifelong interest in religion brought him at every turn served only to deepen his convictions. One can almost sense here his identification with Nietzsche, perhaps his single greatest philosophical mentor, as a member of the aristocracy of the enlightened: "I am a solitary because I know things and must hint at things which other people do not know, and usually do not even want to know."[157] And what is it that he had seen but that few others were willing to admit? The concluding lines of his autobiography speak simply, eloquently, Socratically:

> There is nothing I am quite sure about. I have no definite convictions—not about anything really. I know only that I was born and exist, and it seems to me that I have been carried along. I exist on the foundation of something I do not know. In spite of all the uncertainties, I feel a solidity underlying all existence and a continuity in my mode of being. . . . The more uncertain I have felt about myself, the more there has grown up in me a feeling of kinship with all things. In fact, it seems to me as if that alienation which so long separated me from the world has become transferred into my own inner world, and has revealed to me an unexpected unfamiliarity with myself.[158]

PART II

Critique: The Quest for a Methodology

4
On Style and Methodology

Carved in stone over the fireplace of Jung's retreat at Bollingen are the words *Quaero quod impossible.* After tracing the complicated journey of Jung's notion of the *imago Dei* through a lifetime of development, I find that to undertake a critique of a concept so central to his thought is, ironically, to make that motto one's own. Jung's writings drag the reader so hastily back and forth across the frontiers of philosophy, theology, psychology, mythology, philology, and anthropology that, willy-nilly, one tends either to stumble dizzily into a position of naive discipleship or else to break free and stalk off in skeptical, defiant indifference. In order to avoid these extremes, it is necessary to approach Jung slowly and patiently, cautious of generalization and reconciled to the aim of making but a few humble steps. To this end, I propose to direct attention first of all to the most basic questions of style and methodology, so that I may later return to comment specifically on the *imago Dei.*

Behind these efforts lies the conviction that consideration of Jung's language and methods of procedure is far from the peripheral issue it is usually taken to be, and also far from a simple, routine task. Indeed, in questions of methodology, depth psychology in general still lumbers along in its covered-wagon days. My aim here is not to construct a full-blown defense of some particular philosophical groundwork for archetypal psychology, but merely to offer some points of critical clarification—even if that means only further complicating what too many have taken for simplicity itself.

1. The Jungian Style

It is a curious fact that one of the most-discussed and yet most-neglected aspects of Jung's psychology is that of his literary style. Hardly any of Jung's commentators—whether amicably or adversely disposed to his work—has passed by the opportunity of making some remark on the peculiar characteristics of his use of language and methods of argumentation.[1] To deal with the matter exhaustively would be an immense task, one that clearly falls outside the scope of this essay. Still, I find it necessary to offer at least some brief comment on the "Jungian style" by way of preface to a treatment of his methodology.

Most of Jung's early work from the period 1902 to 1911 belongs to the then accepted genre of scientific psychology, notably his writings on the word-association test and on dementia praecox. The publication of *Psychology of the Unconscious,* however, was to disclose to the world a style much more suited to Jung's own temperament and mode of thinking. This, the typically Jungian style, gradually overcame his attachment to the existing literary conventions until it dominated his writings for over forty years,[2] perplexing and enchanting students of his works ever since.

First impressions in reading Jung tend to be disconcerting in the extreme. The reader is made to feel that he is in the presence of a thinker so overburdened with his own erudition that the usual demands for clarity and precision seem trivial in comparison. Prolonged contact enables a more balanced judgment, of course; but one's initial sentiments of frustration, or even humiliation, are not altogether without basis. There is no gainsaying Jung's phenomenal breadth of learning[3] and his brilliant, penetrating imagination. He was no dilettante, no mere armchair autodidact. What he read he weighed and pondered in the light of his one overriding concern: the mystery of the human personality. Far from falling into the facile, journalistic eclecticism that has ensnared many lesser minds, Jung submitted himself to the relentless demands of intellectual discipline. It was this, more than anything else, that accounted for the blossoming of his genius and for his wide-reaching appeal.

All of this is to be borne in mind if Jung is to be evaluated fairly—for what he was trying to do and not for what we might have liked him to be doing. Consider, for instance, his early use of mythical motifs. Within two years of commencing a serious study of mythology—during which time he was engaged in a full-time clinical practice—Jung came to wield the material boldly with the apparent finesse of an accomplished classicist, while in fact relying more often on the authority of his intuition than on a traditional examination of the notions with which he was dealing. Viewed from the perspective of a classical scholar who wishes to defend the expertise of his discipline, Jung's ventures look suspicious indeed. But from the viewpoint of Jung's own psychological concerns, such intellectual adventures were the very stuff of his method: making use of insight wherever it was to be found, freely trespassing academic domains with a higher purpose in mind. In fact, they were an integral part of the superstructure upon which he erected his psychological theory.

Hence it is my view that it is of only secondary importance to sift out the sound from the spurious in particular issues of Jung's cross-departmental researches. More fundamental is an appreciation of the general structure of his argumentation, part of which is reflected in his literary style.

According to his own theory of psychological types, Jung is best classified as an "introverted-thinking type," with "intuition" as the dominant auxiliary function.[4] If we combine his statements regarding these categories of the typology, we see, in what seems to be a piece of involuntary self-reflection, a concise statement of the main traits of the Jungian style:

> Introverted thinking shows a dangerous tendency to force the facts into the shape of its image, or to ignore them altogether in order to give fantasy free play. . . . Although it may seem to the originator of the idea that his meagre store of facts is the actual source of its truth and validity, in reality this is not so, for the idea derives its convincing power from the unconscious archetype, which, as such, is eternally valid and true. . . .
> The introverted intuitive moves from image to image, chasing after every possibility in the teeming womb of the unconscious . . . . His language is not the one currently spoken—it has become too subjective. His arguments lack the convincing power of reason. He can only profess or proclaim. He is "the voice of one crying in the wilderness."[5]

Without entering into the particulars of Jung's theories of personality, we can see in the above passages three aspects of Jung's writing. First, his style is *imaginative-synthetic*. He prefers imagery to concrete factuality, general structural pattern to specific analysis, free fantasy to directed ratiocination. His is a world where the public, observable datum achieves greatest theoretical interest when it has been first viewed as a subjective symbol and then related to a world of other symbols independent of the initial, objective context. Immediate, infrapsychic experiences exert an uncommonly strong influence on Jung's psychological interpretations. Indeed, we find him saying as early as 1925: "Dreams have influenced all the important changes in my life and theories."[6]

Second, Jung's style is held together by a *subjectivistic logic*. In place of rigorous and systematic argumentation, we find a quasi-poetic flow of thoughts in both the description and in the interpretation of data. In a private and covert fashion, ideas seem to spawn other ideas via metaphor, simile, analogy, and mere word-association.[7] One often feels oneself in the grip of ideas whose very strength lies in their intuitive ambiguity. Jung was not blind to this fact. He freely admitted that he had thrown his thoughts together in an unorganized manner,[8] and on more than one occasion begged those of his readers who noticed certain lacunae in his logic to realize that much of what he had written came not from the head but "from the heart."[9]

Third, there is a certain tone of *prophetic authority* in Jung's mature style. His words seem to call for and inspire a total conversion: "Come follow me. . . . Go thou and do likewise." This characteristic runs parallel with Jung's increased alienation from other psychological currents over the years. For in spite of his professed openness to alternative points of view and his wide-reaching interests in fields related to his own, Jung was not above a kind of Olympian disdain vis-à-vis psychologists of opposing traditions—the least likely group to be affected by his particular "vision."[10] The number of direct references in his work to other directions in psychology, both experimental and clinical, was surprisingly thin for so voracious a reader as he.[11] Even his allusions to Freud were tainted by a growing antagonism so strong that for more than forty-five years he naively maintained certain early misinterpretations. The war with the past was one that Jung never gave up entirely. His arguments to the last often reveal the pattern: "You have heard it said of old . . . but I say unto you. . . ."

As reflections of the peculiarities of Jung's temperament, these three basic traits of his style have an ambivalent effect on the reader, working at one moment to Jung's advantage, and at the next to his discredit.[12] One commentator writes:

> As a writer, Jung does not possess what one could call a well-groomed style, but his style is courageously immediate and reveals that winds from sea and forest blow through his work. This tension between a most discriminating intellect and a genuine tie to nature characterize Jung's psychology.[13]

Others, like Aldous Huxley, accuse Jung of a "turgid copiousness":

> Jungian literature is like a vast quaking bog. At every painful step the reader sinks to the hip in jargon and generalizations, with never a patch of firm intellectual ground to rest on, and only rarely, in that endless expanse of jelly, the blessed relief of a hard, concrete, particular fact.[14]

Still, it simply will not do to leap too quickly to the conclusion that Jung did not know how to write.[15] Often lyrical where one might expect more clarity of expression, Jung had a rare ability to season the driest subject matter with eloquence and convincing passion. (It was in recognition of such qualities that he was awarded the Prize for Literature of the City of Zurich in 1932.) Aphoristic *aperçu* and high sounding, quotable generalization are very much part of the Jungian style. Indeed, as Karl Stern once noted, Jung appears to have made a virtue of his weakness in precision.[16]

At this point we may return briefly to the question of Jung's use of source materials and give air to the criticism that he was too impatient, too much enamored of great and moving ideas to trouble himself over the high academic standards of the various disciplines into which he ventured for help. Some examples may help.

If there is one field in which Jung's academic work has earned him greatest respect, it is that of alchemy.[17] The fact is, however, that most historians of science, at least till recently, were too little interested in psychological interpretations of alchemy, and most students of psychology too little informed about alchemy, to force the question into the open for review. Consider *Mysterium Coniunctionis,* Jung's masterpiece of alchemical research. In it strands of guesses, facts, suspicions, and hypotheses are all woven together in a torrent of seemingly endless allusions, which only the most encyclopedic of minds could ever hope to sort out. Now this might all redound to the author's credit, were it not that Jung himself has to be faulted with a good deal of the confusion he causes his readers. If one examines the original draft of the work, one discovers, incredibly enough, that by itself it would have made a relatively short book: a nucleus of basic concepts tied together logically, in the form of a hypothetical construct. But rather than elaborate this text by studying its assumptions and its consistency with the available data, Jung preferred to adopt it *tout court* as a sort of mold into which he could empty his files on alchemical literature. The first draft is marked everywhere with red "xs" indicating insertions; then there are insertions within the insertions, and so on—sometimes getting so complicated that the final typist was not always able to get everything in the right place. The outcome was a massive volume of over 550 pages, in which the original cluster of ideas had all but perished under the weight of its embellishments.

Much the same "technique" was adopted by Jung in many of his privately conducted seminars. Let us take the discussions he led for a period of nearly five years on Nietzsche's *Thus Spoke Zarathustra.*[18] The core of Jung's commentary on the work consists of a complex of calculated but loosely connected intuitions, yielding, in turn, a provisional diagnosis of the condition that eventually drove its author into madness. In place of a systematic examination of the operational judgments of such an analysis, Jung concentrates on supporting his suspicions, after the manner of a self-fulfilling prophecy—elaborating the text through a tumult of parallels and comparisons drawn from virtually every corner of his reading and clinical experience. The end product was ten impressive volumes of extraordinary learning and ingenuity, which nonetheless failed either to alter or to criticize the framework from which he had set out and the material he had mustered in its support. His only defense against the charge of a *circulum vitiosum* was to appeal to his own authority, claiming that Nietzsche's book "should be reserved for people who have undergone very careful training in the psychology of the unconscious."[19] It is for such methods that critics have often accused him of a scholarly superficiality that is seductive and deceptive to the unprepared.[20]

Finally, I would add a word on neologisms in Jung's works. Strictly speaking, Jung did not coin new terms. Rather, he resurrected words from classical antiquity to suit the purposes of his theory (e.g., anima/animus, persona, archetype); he made use of current psychological jargon and added his own connotations (ego, self, unconscious); and he took over words from nonpsychological contexts (introvert/extravert, individuation, complex, quaternity). His justification for this is given succinctly in one place in his writings:

> In describing the living processes of the psyche, I deliberately and consciously give preference to a dramatic, mythological way of thinking and speaking, because this is not only more expressive but also more exact than an abstract scientific terminology, which is wont to toy with the notion that its theoretic formulations may one fine day be resolved into algebraic equations.[21]

In fact, his own special vocabulary was endeared to Jung, and he resented when it was ignored by those who took over his ideas.[22] It would, of course, be intolerant to refuse him the right to forge his own idiom. What is not so immediately evident is that it might be equally intolerant to demand of him the clarity and consistency of meaning that would facilitate a confrontation with the broader base of linguistic usage within psychology. With a few notable exceptions, this has not occured, and critics of analytical psychology complain of an unfortunate and symptomatic isolation of Jung's terminology, happily repeated by initiates among whom it tends to breed the smugness and self-righteousness that are the constant hazards of heretical, nonconformist, or contrapuntal literature.[23] What such criticism tends to overlook is that ambiguity serves a deliberate, double purpose in Jung's thought and language: the preservation of the richness of the psyche and the signaling of an intellectual task that remains ever half-done.[24]

In short, a simple, straightforward statement about the Jungian style is impossible. As literature his works blend brilliance, charm, and learning with bombast, erratic scholarship, and a curious, idiosyncratic logic. That so many have affixed the label of "romantic" to him hardly comes as a surprise. The title hangs loosely on him, but is not altogether inappropriate. His was a romanticism like that of Heinrich Schliemann: the one exploring the archaeology of the psyche, the other that of lost civilizations; each on a search for the great synthetic idea, careless over details, drawing more inspiration from the poets and philosophers than from his fellow scientists, and each the discoverer of a world overlooked by those preoccupied with detail and precision.

2. Jung's Methodology

The traits of the Jungian style described above do not belong simply to his "personal equation" as an author, but also reflect the various techniques and models that he adopted for gathering, describing, and explaining psychological phenomena (his "method"). Further, even during the years of his collaboration with Freud, and more especially after their separation, Jung had seen the necessity of putting psychological method on a sound philosophical basis (a "methodology"), which would both clarify its presuppositions and establish its validity as a science. In fact, he did not himself approach the problem systematically, but left only scattered fragments throughout his writings. At least two motives compel me to stop at this point to collect and organize Jung's methodological reflections before proceeding to a consideration of his method as such.

First, Jung himself was convinced that, however little he reckoned himself a professional philosopher, he had presented an adequate methodology that would protect his theories from the charge of philosophical naiveté and recommend them as scientifically sound. This conviction stands virtually unchallenged up to the present moment among those engaged in the practice and teaching of analytical psychology.

Second, it is my view that if the genius of Jung's work is to be properly located and given its due place in the history of psychology, an alternative methodological groundwork to his own is essential. Much of the debate and confusion surrounding fact and theory in analytical psychology can, I believe, be traced back to a fundamental incommensurability between Jung's psychological method and the kind of philosophical claims he made for it.[25]

Jung's methodological statements seem to fall into three main categories: a commitment to the primacy of experience, a quasi-Kantian subjectivism, and a defense of the "energic" point of view. The common denominator to each of these classes of statements is the firm belief that his methods were "scientific" and had nothing at all to do with "metaphysical" speculation. On this latter point I shall have more to say in the following section.[26]

In the first place, then, we have Jung's many statements regarding the *primacy of experience,* which we may group in three subclasses. To begin with, there are the references to what Jung calls "the phenomenological standpoint." If we note the various contexts in which he mentions *phenomenology,* we find that he uses the term in a very loose and broad sense, in much the same way as he speaks of his *empiricism.* There is no hint that he intends to identify with any of the various continental philosophical currents stemming from Brentano and Husserl.[27] Phenomenology means for Jung simply a concern with the observable world of facts that is unprejudiced by theoretical presuppositions—in contrast to what were for him the empty abstractions of speculative metaphysics.[28]

More commonly, we find Jung speaking directly of "experience" as the "empirical basis" of his psychological method. Time and again he identifies "facts" and "reality" with "experience," and leaves the matter at that. He was convinced that the psychologist need only accept the principle *Was wirkt, ist wirklich* to assure himself of a critical starting point.[29] Typical of the scores of references in his works is the following:

> Not being a philosopher, but an empiricist, I am inclined in all difficult questions to let experience decide. Where it is impossible to find any tangible basis in experience, I prefer to leave the questions unanswered. It is my aim, therefore, always to reduce abstract concepts to their empirical basis, in order to be moderately sure that I know what I am talking about.[30]

In defending his views against his critics, Jung likened himself on occasion to Galileo, who begged his detractors to take a look through his telescope and decide for themselves, It was a plea for the stubbornness and self-evidence of the "facts" that Jung had met continually in his psychotherapeutic practice and indeed in his own inner life.[31]

Finally, Jung affirms the primacy of experience by drawing attention to the provisional and hypothetical nature of all psychological theory. No statement is exempt from the possibility of correction upon the discovery of new data. "The empiricist must therefore content himself with a theoretical 'as if.' "[32] In stressing this point, Jung all too often slips into a deceptively polemical mood for which his imagination must often supply the opponent, there being no reasonable scientist or philosopher of science who would in principle disagree with him. At times we are forced to attribute the belligerence of Jung's remarks to his desire to establish the scientific foundations of his work and the right to disagree with current opinion.[33] As for the testing of hypotheses, Jung is content to appeal to the success of psychotherapeutic treatment, inasmuch as the final duty of the doctor "is always to the individual, and he is persuaded that nothing has happened if the individual has not been helped."[34] Experimentation of the sort possible in many of the physical sciences he held to be patently impossible for the clinically oriented psychologist.[35]

Let us now turn to a second class of statements, those involving what I have called Jung's *quasi-Kantian subjectivism.* The sum total of references to Kant in Jung's writings suggests that he had opted deliberately to escape the trials of epistemological analysis by enlisting the support of what he deemed a sympathetic tradition. For Jung's purposes, the complexities of Kant's arguments would have been an unnecessary distraction, but the general idiom of the philosopher's major conclusions was most appealing and Jung made free use of it. Unfortunately, certain of Jung's followers have failed to make note of this in their eagerness to defend his methodological principles.[36]

Jung recognized that in psychology, as indeed in all science, there is no absolute objectivity, that "assumptions are unavoidable."[37] This is so not only because preconceived aims and interests are always at work in the processes of understanding,[38] but also, he adds, because in psychology—where the subject becomes the object of its own investigation—there is no external point of reference. Jung's favorite analogy for this state of affairs lay in the comparison of the futile search for a *tertium comparationis* between the psyche and its contents to Archimedes' boast, "Give me a fulcrum on which it rests, and I will move the earth." In this vein he writes:

> I do not imagine for a moment that I can stand above or beyond the psyche, so that it would be possible to judge it, as it were, from some transcendental[39] Archimedean point "outside." I am fully aware that I am entrapped in the psyche and that I cannot do anything except describe the experiences that there befall me.[40]

The psychologist, then, seems compelled to a subjectivistic point of view, according to which knowledge of the mind and its relation to the external world must appear like Till Eulenspiegel's pulling himself out of the swamp by his own pigtail. Jung's overall dependence on commonsense realism, however, shows that he resisted such a conclusion. Caught in the Kantian dilemma, but with a predispositional distaste for idealism, Jung could find no other exit than to reaffirm his faith in an objective reality:

> We are absolutely incapable of saying how the world is constituted in itself—and always shall be, since we are obliged to convert physical events into psychic processes as soon as we want to say anything about knowledge. But who can guarantee that this conversion produces anything like an adequate "objective" picture of the world? . . . We must for better or worse content ourselves with the assumption that the psyche supplies those images and forms which alone make knowledge of objects possible.[41]

With the presupposition of objective realism behind him, Jung does not hesitate to carry his subjectivism still further. If all experience of the world is ultimately filtered through the psyche, he states, then one may well inquire after the conditions that the psyche imposes on the world in order for it to become an object of human perception and knowledge. Kant had already demonstrated, at least to Jung's satisfaction, that "there can be no empirical knowledge that is not already caught and limited by the *a priori* structure of cognition."[42] Kant's refusal to see the mind as a *tabula rasa* at birth, Jung argues, had paved the way for future psychology, with its understanding of unconscious processes, to posit an inherited, collective psychic structure that conditions all experience, conscious and unconscious.[43] To the Kantian categories Jung leaves the analysis of conscious knowing. For the unconscious, however, he infers another set of potential patterns of psychic behavior, the "archetypes," which are not merely analogous to the categories but actually supply their very foundations. Methodologically, therefore, the archetypes represent the ultimate transcendental conditions for the psyche's apprehension of itself and its contents.[44]

Now, although Jung draws on Kant's doctrine of the *categories* to describe the function of the archetypes in understanding the phenomena of the unconscious mind, his notion of the collective unconscious as the seat of the archetypes leads him to confound matters by speaking of them as transcendental *objects* that point to an imperceptible, noumenal reality whose existence can be grasped only by intuition.[45] The inconsistency was never resolved. I shall have more to say of this in a later context.

Finally, we come to the third class of methodological statements, which describe Jung's *energic point of view.* As a check against the opposing tendencies to naive realism and transcendental idealism that we have seen in his empiricism and his subjectivism, Jung was forced to recognize that in some sense fact and theory are correlative concepts, incomprehensible without one another:

> I trust that it does not conflict with the principles of scientific empiricism if one occasionally makes certain reflections which go beyond a mere accumulation and classification of experience. As a matter of fact, I believe that experience is not even possible without reflection, because "experience" is a process of assimilation without which there could be no understanding.[46]

There are two complementary models of "reflection" that Jung employs in his study of psychic "experience": the genetic-causal-mechanistic and the synthetic-final-energic.[47] Once again he calls upon Kant for support:

> It is well known that Kant showed very clearly that the mechanistic and the teleological viewpoints are not *constituent* (objective) principles—as it were, qualities of the object—but that they are

> purely *regulative* (subjective) principles of thought, and, as such not mutually inconsistent. . .
>
> Obviously I consider both these points of view necessary, the causal as well as the final, but would at the same time stress that since Kant's time we have come to realize that the two viewpoints are not antagonistic if they are regarded as regulative principles of thought and not as constituent principles of the process of nature itself.[48]

Jung first came to see the importance of distinguishing the two points of view when struggling with two different, but related problems. On the one hand, he found himself faced with the phenomenon of two opposing psychological systems in the work of Freud and Adler—apparently incompatible with one another and yet each having its own truth. And on the other hand, he himself had developed a theory of "libido" that was at variance with Freud's and hence in need of some theoretical justification. The first problem he resolved in the context of his growing interest in typology, by suggesting that the "causal" perspective of Freud and the "finalistic" perspective of Adler were both, at least in part, the result of temperamental differences between the two thinkers.[49] A further analysis of these contrasting points of view led, happily, to the solution of the second problem as well.

Jung's description of the two models is straightforward and unhampered by philosophical scruples. The causal outlook, he says, is mechanistic, seeks to describe the interactions between substances that are stable, and argues from effects to causes. The energic viewpoint, on the other hand, is finalistic, seeks to describe phenomena as expressions of a basic, undifferentiated energy-potential, and argues from means to ends.[50] It was clear to Jung from his clinical experience that both approaches were needed to do justice to psychic phenomena, although there was never any doubt that he preferred the latter. Thus he described the causal point of view as *reductive,* inasmuch as it considered psychic products as mere *signs* that could be *analyzed* exhaustively for their association with the patient's past life, thereby establishing a chain of events that would explain his present condition mechanistically. The energic point of view, on the contrary, was *constructive,* viewing psychic products as symbols that needed to be *interpreted* as indications of an inner purpose, a striving for psychic wholeness. This implied critique of Freud and nineteenth-century materialism is present in fact throughout Jung's work, and occasionally surfaces in unmistakable form, as in the following passage:

> The reductive standpoint is the distinguishing feature of Freudian interpretation. It always leads back to the primitive and the elementary. The constructive standpoint, on the other hand, tries to synthesize, to build up, to direct one's gaze forward. It is less pessimistic than the other, which is always on the look-out for the morbid and thus tries to break down something complicated into something simple.[51]

While there is a great deal more to be said about the *practical* application of the energic viewpoint in Jung's method, its only remaining *methodological* consequences concern two subsidiary principles: synchronicity and opposition.

The principle of "synchronicity" (see above, Chap. 3, 1) can be said to represent Jung's most serious attempt to offer a philosophical basis to the energic-final standpoint.[52] The underlying concern of the argument is to free his psychological method from the demands of natural science for experimental verification through prediction. Such requirements, Jung contends, stem from the space-time-causality model of classical physics, which has long since abdicated its control over scientific method. Descriptive biology, atomic physics, and parapsychology, for example, have all had to seek alternative models. Jung intends to follow suit by showing how psychology must often dispense with the principle of causality.

In the natural sciences, he tells us, causes are statistical truths yielding laws of regularity. Chance deviations are dismissed as statistically meaningless; they may or may not indicate the presence of unknown causal factors. For the psychologist dealing with the individual case, however, the chance coincidence of a particular psychic state and an event in the physical world is often seen to carry meaning and importance. Here the search for causes by the use of testing and prediction is out of the question. What the principle of synchronicity states, quite simply, is that such instances need not be dismissed as "mere coincidences," but that the connecting bond of "meaning" is enough to confirm the coincidence as a piece of scientific datum.[53] If such data are then further sorted out according to whether they demonstrate the presence of archetypal motifs and patterns, the results can serve as evidence in support of a model that views the psyche in constructive, finalistic, synthetic terms.

Second, the principle of "opposition" is essential to Jung's energic point of view—although Jung *used* the principle, especially in his later work, more often than he *spoke* of it. What it means, in effect, is that the dynamism of the psyche (or "libido") is best described according to the first law of thermodynamics: energy demands two opposing forces.[54] The primary function of the principle appears in Jung's notion of a compensatory relationship between ego-consciousness and the unconscious.[55] It is then extended to the search for opposition in every aspect of psychic life: topology, archetypal imagery, values, and personal relationships.[56] No psychic state can be understood, according to Jung, until it has been seen as a tension of opposing factors. Indeed, even after talk of "energy" and "forces" had largely passed out of Jung's vocabulary, the principle of opposition remained behind as a tacit presupposition of his method.

The principle of opposition also provided Jung with a convenient argument in defense of the vagueness and ambiguity of his literary style: "We are surrounded by the opposites in psychology, so that the language we use should hold a double meaning."[57] The German language, with its heavily nuanced vocabulary and indefiniteness of expression serves this purpose better, Jung asserted, than English, with its precision of grammar and terminology.[58] On one occasion, he penned the following revealing lines:

> The language I speak must be ambiguous, must have two meanings in order to be fair to the dual aspect of the psyche's nature. I strive quite consciously and deliberately for ambiguity of expression, because it is superior to singleness of meaning and reflects the nature of life. My whole temperament inclines me to be very unequivocal indeed. That is not difficult, but it would be at the cost of truth.[59]

The statement is entirely appropriate and defensible as a methodological statement about the nature of psychological models and explanations. But when this "ambiguity of expression" finds its way into methodology as such, it needs a different sort of defense, and opens Jung to the criticisms that I shall specify in the following section.

3. Critical Comments on the Methodology

In spite of claims to the contrary by Jung himself, and by many of his followers,[60] there are serious theoretical difficulties with the methodology as outlined above. This is not to say that a good case cannot be made for the ambiguity that Jung found necessary in his psychological theory as such, nor that he was deceived in his intuition that the limits of "science" had to be extended to embrace the full reach of phenomena that he had discovered, but rather that Jung's talk about those issues did not offer so good a case for his methods as he had thought. In this section I shall restrict myself to certain basic philosophical problems, and save for the following chapter what has to be said regarding the God-image in particular.

Perhaps the most serious fault in Jung's methodological gridwork is his failure to clarify the relationship between fact and theory. He seems to have been aware of the problem in general terms, but he was largely unaware of its consequences for his own psychological method. He usually spoke of "experience" and "facts" as undeniably clear and distinct to the disinterested, unbiased, scientifically minded observer; and such data were then adduced as objective "evidence" for his hypothetical models of the psyche's structure. But at the same time he also acknowledged the inevitably theory-laden character of all observation, and the presence of limiting assumptions that disprove all claims for absolute objectivity. *What* these assumptions were and *how far* they relativized his own data and evidence were questions Jung saw no need to ask.[61]

This contradiction is best explained as a double standard at work in Jung's methodology. On the one hand, all psychic phenomena occurrent to the *patient* are open to interpretation as symbolic of deeper, unconscious processes. Dreams, fantasies, visions, emotions, obsessions, beliefs, artistic activity, indeed everything psychic is capable of being viewed, at leat in part, as expressive of subjective factors. Even where there is an apparent objective referent in the external world for a given perception or judgment, Jung would still claim that this referent is to be understood as projection.[62]

The *therapist,* on the other hand, is able to observe with no significant interference of his own. He enjoys a privileged position of objective detachment. Certainly Jung acknowledged the phenomenon of countertransference, and he saw the need for the therapist to undergo his own analysis to reduce the danger of such occurrences. Yet he did not permit this recognition to shake the fundamental acceptance of what Nietzsche once termed "the dogma of the immaculate perception." Hence Jung was indeed able to speak of a subjectively conditioned perception as an objective datum of observation, without recognizing the serious epistemological problems such a view involved.[63]

In his actual method—theory and practice—Jung treated therapy as a *Zusammenarbeit* in which both therapist and patient were subject to mutual processes of projection. But when he talked on the methodological plane of basic philosophical principles, he did not permit this insight its full scope.

A related methodological difficulty concerns a certain strain of arbitrariness in Jung's "energic-final" point of view. He treats it as an a priori assumption or "regulative principle," and as the conclusion to which he is driven by empirically grounded inference. Eager to defend himself philosophically and yet to maintain his reputation as a scientist, Jung argued in distinctly protean style. His use of the principles of synchronicity and enantiodromia typifies this ambivalence: at one moment he adopts them as quasi-axiomatic presuppositions; at the next he treats them as empirically cashable concepts. Not only was such inconsistency unresolved; there is no indication that Jung was even aware of it.[64]

Jung's claim to have contributed to the clarification of certain perennial problems in philosophy is equally insecurely based. I have already indicated the difficulties involved in his view that the archetypes may be seen as akin to and even as extensions of the Kantian categories. I focus attention now on two other claims, marked by similar flaws.

Jung evidently viewed his synchronicity principle as a necessary counterbalance to what he termed "the sacred dogma" of causality.[65] In fact, the positing of an acausal connecting principle in "meaningful coincidences" meant for him a step beyond Kant's *Kritik,* supported (he believed) by the findings of modern microphysics.[66] In the form in which Jung presents his case, however, the principle of synchronicity stands on very shaky philosophical foundations. His notion of causality, as H. H. Price has accurately pointed out, has more in common with the seventeenth-century rationalism against which Hume (whom Jung overlooks in this context) had rebelled than with the contemporary views of philosophers of science.[67] Accordingly, Jung's critique of the causal principle skips over two hundred years of controversy to direct itself to the admittedly naive cause-and-effect relationship that had dominated depth psychology up to that time. Further, the role of the archetypes in meaningful coincidences is unclear. In the weaker interpretation, the archetypes (as psychical realities) do not signify the missing causes of the actual *coincidences* (as objective occurrences in the physical world), but rather the way in which *meaning* is attributed to coincidental events.[68] Hence "causality" has reappeared here in a form that allows the whole argument to turn upon the internal mechanics of the mind.[69] In the stronger interpretation, mind and matter are presumed to share a common archetypal structure that appears clearly only in such chance coincidences.[70] Here the causal efficacy of the archetypes is considerably broadened to include the physical world, even though their ultimate intelligibility remains a purely psychic matter. Both interpretations follow from Jung's writings. In either case, however, synchronicity can be an "acausal" principle only if it stops short at the simple observation: coincidences occur. Unfortunately, then synchronicity ceases to be an explanatory concept and therefore loses the force that Jung intended for it.[71]

Second, Jung leads us to suspect that all philosophical problems are ultimately reducible to terms of depth-psychological questions.[72] He tried his hand at such analysis in *Types,* explaining the debate between nominalists and realists as a conflict of temperament.[73] We may, of course, insist that Jung was dealing *only* with a psychological problem inherent in a philosophical controversy. But we might also note that his reduction of the issue to psychological terms did not prevent him from slipping into the problem himself on the very philosophical plane that he meant to relativize. Such was the case, for example, in his methodological ambiguity regarding the archetypes, as was noted in the previous section.

Finally, we may turn to Jung's critique of metaphysics and faith, deliberately reserved for the conclusion to my general comments on his methodology. To be precise, I ought not speak here of a "critique" at all; Jung's antitheses (metaphysics vs. science, and knowledge vs. faith)[74] tended to be a mere shorthand for philosophical arguments that he felt unnecessary to elaborate. In fact, a careful study of Jung's actual use of these antitheses reveals that he attempted to settle the matter grammatically, by definition.

For Jung, *metaphysics* refers exclusively to philosophical speculation about the unknowable, and *faith* to theological speculation of the same sort. *Science* on the contrary addresses itself to the knowable, and *knowledge* is synonymous with the fruit of reflection on "experience." The conclusion that metaphysics and faith are scientifically and epistemologically sterile exercises is thus little more than a tautology.[75] What makes this rather loose and unconventional idiom intolerable, however, is that Jung extends it to cover virtually everything in the history of thought that has gone by the name of *metaphysics* and *theology*.[76] The mistake is so elementary that we are forced to look for a more plausible explanation than mere methodological imprecision.

We need look no farther than Jung's determined desire that depth psychology, and in particular his own analytical psychology, should achieve recognition as a science. Final judgment on this question must be reserved until we have examined the method itself. What interests us here is the prestige-value that Jung attached to the label *scientific*.[77] Since the defense of his work as science appears before and during the period of his collaboration with Freud, we cannot attribute his concern simply to the criticism he suffered as a result of their later break. It is more likely that Jung had begun taking part in the ongoing struggle of clinical depth psychology for an independence from medical science that would not throw it back under the aegis of academic philosophy. In time, as his own method took shape and established his reputation, Jung turned more and more to his own defense against the charges of psychologism, gnosticism, and mysticism that haunted him for nearly fifty years. As a result of both these factors, Jung was not only nonmetaphysical but actually *anti*metaphysical in his methodology.

Hence the only "truth" that Jung would acknowledge in metaphysical and religious beliefs was their "psychological truth":

such beliefs exist as facts that can often be linked to experiences of an archetypal and numinous nature. These beliefs are not the acceptance of certain propositions as corresponding to states of affairs in the objective world; they are empty of reference to any conceivable content; they are therefore purely speculative. In this way Jung dismissed the theoretical rights of metaphysics and theology, and defined their truth-claims exclusively in terms of the psychological states to which they sought to give expression.[78]

At this point we must return to see Jung's actual psychological method at work. Taken by itself, free of its wider context, the group of ideas discussed in this chapter shows only its weaknesses *as a methodology*. We need still to see the function that Jung himself intended it to play in his psychology as a whole, and that is the business of the concluding chapter.

5

Imago Dei: Fact and Interpretation

1. The Factual Material

It was Jung's opinion that the data upon which he constructed his psychological theory were gathered in an objective spirit of *wissenschaftliche Neutralität,* free of prejudice and preconceived expectations. Certain basic difficulties with this claim have been noted in the previous chapter. Let me now say something more specific concerning the actual heuristic principles that governed Jung's selection of relevant empirical data.

As I observed earlier, Jung's pioneering spirit was impatient with *methodological* nuance; this is equally true of the account he gives of the analytical techniques, the canons of selection, and the descriptive models that provided the factual basis of his *method.* Clearly there is no question of hoping to reproduce his clinical data in the sort of controlled situation familiar, for example, to the experimental chemist. The analytical setting is a long way removed from the objectivity of the laboratory, where cooperation among a number of persons acts as a further check against misinterpretation of results. In Jung's method the intuition and authority of the analyst appear to play so great a role as only to cast further doubt on the kind of "scientific" status he claimed for his observations.[1]

Of the actual *techniques* whereby Jung assembled data relevant to a case study, we know very little from his writings and lectures. He defends this omission on the same grounds as he defends the non-systematic character of his work in general: the relative infancy of psychological science, the inevitably unique correlation between a doctor and his method, the tendency of the individual case to overflow any framework of presuppositions.[2]

What we do know of his techniques, however, makes plain the general emphasis Jung placed on "unconscious material," namely, thoughts, images, feelings, and symptomatic behavior that appear to arise spontaneously from below the threshold of conscious control.[3] According to Jung, some of this material is gathered by having the patient concentrate on certain sorts of psychic phenomena (dreams, fantasies, visions). Again, the analyst may ask the patient to experiment with his mental processes in a more disciplined fashion (painting, sculpting, automatic writing, active imagination).[4] Finally, analyst and patient may cooperate in dialogue to unearth unconscious material (subjective amplification).[5] In none of these techniques, whatever Jung may say to the contrary, can consciousness be completely disregarded; in fact, its role seems to increase as we move from one to the next. This point, which is of crucial importance both for the characterization of certain data as "unconscious" and for the use of such data as evidence in support of a theory of the psyche, is largely overlooked in Jung's writings.[6] He seems to leave the decision in such matters to the discretion of the practicing analyst.

In dealing with the raw material thus assembled, Jung adopted certain *canons of selectivity* to isolate data relevant for purposes of analytical interpretation. Among the data selected are what he calls "God-images." Again we have no clear statement of his method for determining what will and what will not be counted as a God-image. We have to work backward and articulate what is only implicit in his writings; these canons can be formulated only from consideration of the many references to the *imago Dei* given in Part I of this book.

First, Jung accepts as a God-image whatever an individual claims to "experience as God." Consciously, one may entertain a single idea of God, however complex, and feel convinced of its self-consistency. But on the unconscious level, as a rule, numerous and often contradictory images, voices, or affective states are associated with the notion of God. Whatever shape and form these unconscious gods assume, whatever their relation to conscious beliefs, historical precedents, or dogmatic traditions, it is sufficient that memory or intuitive feeling identify them as images of God.[7] It is in this sense that Jung can speak of the experience of God as "absolute" for the individual subject.[8]

Second, it may happen that the patient mentions an unconscious fantasy identical with or strongly resembling some conception or image of God so familiar to him that memory ought to be enough to establish the connection at once, but it is not. Often a mere question from the analyst suffices to identify the *imago Dei* in the patient's mind. In such cases the "subjective amplification" clarifies what was only implicit in the original experience.

The use of these first two criteria as methods for abstracting God-images from the products of the unconscious raises little difficulty. Yet Jung wants to go much farther by offering two additional canons of selectivity unique to his own psychology of religion. Henceforth it is no longer the individual patient who acknowledges the *imago Dei,* but the therapist, who by his training is able to look beyond the patient's resistance or ignorance and dare to call certain psychic data images of God. Because Jung held this process to be preinterpretative, he was led to consider such data as objective in the same sense as the yield of the two preceding methods.

In the third place, then, Jung classified as an image of God any unconscious product that represented an individual's "highest value."[9] How such a canon worked in principle is vague. Suppose that this hierarchy of values is treated as a function of the patient's own habitual conscious judgments. Then the analyst merely designates as *imago Dei* whatever is thus felt to be of supreme value. In this sense we are driven to ask why the subjective experience of a "God" who is *not* simultaneously felt to represent the patient's highest value is also classed as a God-image. On the contrary, if it is the analyst's duty to determine whether some unconscious datum is a bearer of the patient's highest value, we want to know more of the general value-theory involved in such judgments. Jung seems to have used both approaches in his practice, thus widening the compass of the *imago Dei* and complicating the issue of the claim he made for the "scientific objectivity" of his factual material by the introduction of still more theoretical suppositions.

Fourth, Jung classified unconscious phenomena by reference to typical motifs encountered in the history of ideas, rituals, and artistic expression. In this context "God" has a place as a motif universally present among men of all times and places. The psychologist who is adequately trained in comparative religion, mythology, philosophy, imaginative literature, and art history can recognize an *imago Dei* wherever he meets it. By virtue of this expertise he notes the presence of this same motif in raw material provided from his patient's unconscious, even when the patient himself attaches no such sense to the imagery in question. The heuristic nets that Jung has cast to gather God-images are seen to be variously meshed and widely thrown, stretching beyond the limits of individual experience, beyond the limits of the therapeutic encounter. In fact, we find them cast into the whole ocean of human thought and language. As an unconscious element, the God-image is thus lodged in the collective experience of mankind, and nothing less is judged adequate to reveal its basic structure and meaning.

This fourfold method of selection represents the boundaries within which the constituents of Jung's pantheon were assembled. The "scientific" presentation of the factual material on which his theories rested was completed by one further procedure: the establishment of *descriptive models.* Jung had long since detached himself from concern with the relation between the God-images of psychology and the God of theology and metaphysics, but he recognized the need to adopt a rather unconventional taxonomy for his notion of the *imago Dei.*

Jung gives himself every latitude in defining the *imago Dei,* and we are hard put to come up with even one image[10] that could not in some context qualify as an instance of it.[11] Hence, to characterize "God-image" without losing himself in a seemingly endless swarm of "God-images," Jung hit upon the ingenious but very old formula that he had probably first met in his study of the Gnostics: he would describe the God-image as a *coincidentia oppositorum.*[12] Thenceforward all specific images would relate to this basic model much as Platonic particulars to their defining *eidos,* or paradigm.

Jung rejected the trinitarian structure as incapable of doing justice to the psychic experiences of God as evil and feminine, which by his methods of investigation he had tried to bring to light. The Trinity was in fact merely one God-image among others. In its place Jung opted for the quaternity, because it seemed to him to represent the *completion* of the Trinity, and because the numeral *4* seemed to him both the oldest and the most universal symbol of the union of opposites. Formally the quaternity was composed of two pairs of polar opposites whose precise content might vary according to the context (male-female, spirit-matter, good-evil, etc.). Thus Jung believed that he was not only able to order the entire plethora of God-images, but also at the same time to clarify the relationships among images that appeared in the case history of a particular patient.

If my description of Jung's heuristic method is fair, a number of serious objections arise to his persistent and unqualified claims for the "objectivity" of his factual material, and in particular of the phenomenon of the *imago Dei.* He did not attempt a systematic analysis of his method, and this alone makes us suspect that he was largely unaware of his own theoretical assumptions, or at least lacked the incentive required to ask the questions he needed to ask. As a result, the mass of allegedly unimpeachable empirical data that Jung treated as bedrock foundation for his psychological theory begins to assume the status of a vast construct born of other concerns than critical objectivity.

In expounding Jung's methods here in outline, I have sacrificed much to clarity of argument and to brevity. His own writings present a very different picture. There the techniques, the canons of selectivity, and the descriptive models form part of a larger organic whole. It is that whole which saves Jung from the simple criticism of having provided a potpourri with no connection between its haphazard items. Nonetheless, some organization of Jung's doctrine into an intelligible, coherent, logical structure—in which the premises on which his conclusions are based are clearly set out, the relations between premises and conclusions quickly discernible, and the principles involved in claiming such conclusions seen to follow from, or at least to be strongly supported by the now clearly stated premises—would be an important service to that whole. What follows is only a brief critical prolegomenon.

Consider first the raw material provided by the techniques where, it would appear, Jung's claims to scientific objectivity are strongest. Among this material Jung held up images occurrent in dreams as paradigms of all psychological data, since they were the product of psychic processes totally independent both of the patient's conscious control and of the analyst's interference. But this is very far from being, as Jung supposes, self-evident. He failed to distinguish properly between the dream as lived through and the dream as narrated.[13] Only the latter is a public datum; therefore the analyst must allow for uncontrollable distortions in memory and, through conscious reflection, even for deliberate untruth on the part of the patient. Further, it is far from clear why it is thought impossible that the patient's dreams should be affected by the therapeutic situation and by the analyst's views. Stekel's well-known comment that "patients dream in the dialect of whatever physician happens to be treating them"[14] must not be dismissed out of hand. The remaining techniques, employed as they are in states of greater self-awareness, seem to increase further the likelihood that the data provided by the patient will be affected qualitatively by his reactions to the analyst and by the latter's prejudices.

The problem of objectivity becomes still more acute when we turn to the canons employed in the selection of God-images from the initial data. When the patient himself identifies the image as a God-image, we may not here simply presume total independence of the analyst's influence. The patient may have previous knowledge of his therapist's methods and theoretical commitments. When the analyst is directing the patient in subjective amplification, it is still more probable that he will make positive suggestions. Jung was indifferent to such objections. In fact, he considered it his prescriptive right as a scientist to override the patient's judgment, if he thought it necessary, and appeal to his own definition of the God-image. Hence from the very outset Jung used the term *imago Dei* to describe two logically distinct sorts of datum. One was that supplied by what the patient said about his own psychic states (whatever the operative influences); the other was that supplied by what the analyst said about the patient's psychic states (in virtue of a determinate view of "God" as "highest value" or as a "typical motif" in myth and history).[15] Further, as a result of this confusion, when Jung classifies God-imagery of either sort according to the paradigm of polar opposition, he is similarly engaging a hypothetical model that can scarcely be referred to as the preinterpretative description of data as they are in themselves. It was for this latter that Jung strove, and yet this he cannot be said to have obtained.[16] When faced with charges against his objectivity, Jung's usual response was to point to data gathered in circumstances without his personal control. His prime example was a series of over 400 dreams and fantasies, 355 recorded by the subject himself, partially alone and partially under the direction of an analyst whom Jung characterized as "a beginner," knowing "very little" of his (Jung's) point of view. These data formed the basis of the first part of Jung's *Psychology and Alchemy.*[17] In fact, we now know that the analyst in question was Frau Erna Rosenbaum, one of the founders of the Society of Analytical Psychology in London and familiar with Jung's work since the early 1920s.[18] But even if we ignore such familiarity with Jung's psychology, we have no precise information on how she gathered the data.[19] We have no reason to claim that the same criticisms brought against Jung's confusion of the two sorts of evidence do not apply here as well. His own commentary on the dream-series, with its frequent references to motifs unknown to the dreamer, confirms this. Such complaints do not seem to have been met squarely by *any* of Jung's disciples, despite insistence by analysts of other schools that the mass of data to which archetypal psychology appeals is far from coincident with their own findings.

Finally, Jung's references to the *imago Dei* as an "unconscious" phenomenon suggest another objection, already hinted at earlier, against the objectivity of his factual material. Throughout Jung's writings the term *unconscious*—both as an adjective and as a substantive—tends to be used imprecisely. Reserving further comment on this tendency for later, I must still remark that even a charitable reading of those texts where Jung speaks of his primary data would seem to suggest the following simple formula: A psychic image is to be called "unconscious" if it arises in the mind spontaneously under conditions where one's conscious cognitive controls are so relaxed as to be virtually inoperative. The paradigm of such images for Jung was the dream-image. Yet he was not content to let the matter rest there. He proceeded to apply the term, by a series of presumably intuitively based steps, to data presented through the use of all of his techniques. Thus he blandly overlooked the theoretical bias involved in finding the threshold between conscious and unconscious processes that was crossed in such vivid experiences and activities as visions, painting, dancing, subjective amplification, the use of active imagination, and the like. In addition, therefore, to the previously indicated criticisms, Jung, in his further qualification of the *imago Dei* as an "unconscious datum," is guilty of a serious *petitio principii.*[20]

2. The Psychological Theory

We must refuse therefore to accept the claims to descriptive objectivity that Jung made on behalf of his method of gathering data, and this on grounds as clearly formulable as the mistakes, made explicit in the formulation, were relatively obvious. The theoretical structure of his hypothetical explanatory models presents a more engaging task. Again I shall concentrate on the *imago Dei,* deliberately restricting the field further to certain fundamental problems. This restriction should be remembered by the reader, and he must not suppose justice to be done to other themes and issues outlined in Part I of this work. The aim is modest, that of preparing the way for a proper methodological appraisal of analytical psychology by raising further difficulties in the way of accepting Jung's professed intention of fashioning his psychology after a "scientific" model.

According to Jung's view of the psyche, the *imago Dei* can be seen as *the unconscious projection of an archetype.* What Jung means by this doctrine and what consequences follow for his understanding of religion we have already seen in Part I. We must evaluate this thesis now as an explanation of the factual material that Jung classified as God-imagery.

The notion of *image* (or *imago*) in Jung's writings presents us with a first difficulty. The term has a wide range of uses, none of them defined so as to exclude the others. It seems clear that Jung's usage is intentionally ambiguous (and the German word *Bild* was helpful in maintaining his manifold of meanings), and so more poetical than philosophical.[21] Thus often the word *image* appears merely as a generalized synonym for *picture, likeness, or representation.* Elsewhere (and this seems to apply whenever the term is associated with "God"), it assumed a more technical sense. Here *image* must be understood as *apperception* of a psychic state, similar to apperception realized through perception of the material world by way of one's bodily senses.[22] Its defining characteristic is that, unlike the *idea* (of which it is said to be the ground), the image is nonrational, unreflective, spontaneously produced. As such, the image can be a pathological or a nonpathological manifestation: its origin may be in the personal or in the collective strata of the unconscious mind. Insofar as it is nonpathological and collective,[23] it may be seen as the "formal" aspect of the instincts whose content it presents to consciousness in symbolic form,[24] as an "archetypal" image.

In most cases the context supplies the necessary criteria for deciding how the expression is used. But the validity of the notion depended, for Jung, on the larger structure to which it was solely an appendix. The word *image* was an ordinary word that Jung had invested with new force by associating it with his developed theory of the unconscious. In no sense can Jung be said to have taken up a definite stance toward the complex philosophical problems involved in the analysis of the concept of apperception, in seeking the grounds of the alleged analogy between infrapsychic perception and perception of the world around us, in establishing the relation between image and that which it represents, or in determining the sense in which images can be regarded as now particular, now universal. Jung merely presumed that a nod in the direction of the Kantian critique would suffice. Yet Kant's profound analysis of these problems requires much more detailed attention, and their relevance to Jung's specific concerns much more detailed treatment than Jung gives. Instead, the fog only grows thicker as we pass on to the closely related notion of *projection*.

The importance of the notion of projection in Jung's psychology can hardly be overestimated.[25] It represents his attempt to remove the perennial issues raised by theological anthropomorphism from the realms of abstract philosophical and theological analysis and submit them to scientific scrutiny. Although it is nowadays usual to distinguish two moments in the treatment of projection, the genetic and the functional, Jung himself often failed to separate opinions on the "how" of projection from those on its "why," shifting his ground rather freely back and forth between the two in frequently confusing manner.

Jung did not trouble himself much over the actual mechanism of the projection process. When he did, he tried to avoid using the vocabulary of "causality." Yet the very fact that he spoke of certain psychic images as projections shows that he was attempting to say something about their psychogenesis.[26] In his use of the term *projection* we may distinguish four essential elements: the individual subject; the content of a particular psychic state of the subject; the object, real or imaginary, upon which the content is thrown by the subject; and the actual process of projection itself.[27]

The concepts of the experiencing subject and the individual psyche in Jung's psychology, for all the richness he gave them, reveal certain unfortunate biases inherited from older philosophies of mind. Most significant of these is Jung's adoption of a spatial metaphor that speaks of events happening "inside" and "outside" of the subject, as if the subject were a determinate, bounded, three-dimensional space. This metaphor also suggests that the psyche is a spatial volume distinct from all that is adjacent and external to it. Further, it is treated as the *locus* for what falls within it as a box and its contents, and we notice the influence of this aspect of this dangerous method of representation in Jung's discussion of projection.[28]

Similar looseness of language characterizes what Jung calls the "content" of the projection, in origin a particular unconscious state that is constellated within the psyche into the determinate form of a "complex."[29] A complex consists of a "feeling-toned group of representations" (again to speak metaphorically), clustered like electrons about a central nucleus. But this nucleus is one of *meaning,* unconscious and beyond the control of the will. The representations associated with this "nuclear" sense consist of elements stemming both from the personal and from the collective layers of the unconscious. The entire complex functions as a whole autonomously, set in opposition to the conscious ego. Since it is unconscious, it cannot be recognized immediately, but appears as a phenomenon that seems to assail the subject from without; it is thus that it operates as a projection that is reified and invested with causal properties, analogous to those found in an external threat—for example, flying debris, a mad dog, an infectious germ, and the like. The use of such imagery borrowed from both modern physics and from the field of identifiable threats to human well-being to describe what is essentially subjective, together with Jung's talk of "contents" and "representations," fetters the reader only too easily to a quasi-mythology of "entities" interacting in the "space" within the mind. The supposed relation between the sense-data (sights, sounds, pressures, tastes, smells) that in varying ways disclose to us the presence, behavior, and properties of material things, and the things in question on the one side, are on the other the relation between our feelings, occurrent images, and associations following in their trail, and the alleged strong psychological conditions that such experiential contents manifest are in Jung implied to be analogous. But the analogy is left utterly uncriticized.[30]

The subjective complex is said to be projected when the "content" appears manifested in an "object" that is experienced as external to the conscious ego. This may come about in several ways. Sometimes another person is viewed as the bearer of one's own complex: the clinical phenomenon of transference and the attitudes of the early Christians to Jesus are taken by Jung as comparable instances of this. Alternatively, material objects may be endowed with *mana* or spiritual power (which ultimately derives from the complex); this happens in the thinking of the alchemists and in what Jung called (following Lévy-Bruhl) the *participation mystique* of primitive man with nature. Again, the complex may engender its own imaginary object, which is then regarded as part of the furniture of the actual world: goblins, angels, demons, and gods are all examples of such projections. Finally, the complex may assume the form of a privately and "internally" perceived image, and this, of course, is what happens in dreams, fantasies, and visions. Now, Jung held that the psychologist must ignore all talk about the physical world as such; thus it is clear that *all* objective referents of such experiences (whether real or imagined) must themselves be seen as imagos or aspects of psychic apperception. Logically, we are led to think of projection building upon projection, and thus the argument ends in an infinite regress wherein the original distinction between "content" and "object" is dissolved. From this dilemma, it seems, Jung lacked the philosophical expertise to deliver himself.

Of the actual process of projection in which subjective content and the objective referent unite through the agency of unconscious forces to form a new image, Jung tells us nothing, except to advise us that it occurs. His explanation of the *imago Dei* as a projection, therefore, offers us very much less in the way of effective causal explanation than we were led to expect. In the end, all we learn is that every God-image is held to be the carrier of an unconscious complex of personal and/or collective origin.[31]

Persons, material objects, spiritual entities of the sorts mentioned, and dream figures are all equally capable of becoming God-images through projection. Hence, whatever the precise causal process involved, the entire meaning of any image identified as a God-image is to be located in an original complex, which it first adumbrates and then reveals. To decipher such meaning, Jung found it necessary to study the function of the God-image in the psyche.

At first Jung held that God-image may represent a complex of a strictly personal nature. Such projection either compensates for a conscious underevaluation of the objective referent divinized by the projection process or realizes dramatically the subject's actual system of values. In either case the projection was seen to present repressed feelings struggling, as it were, to become conscious. A relic of Jung's early Freudian tendencies in psychology of religion, this hypothesis quickly diminished in importance with the advent of his theory of the archetypes. Even where its validity was acknowledged, Jung turned his interest to the deeper, collective patterns of behavior that were activated by the personal complex.

Jung's usual way, therefore, of approaching the interpretation of a God-image, whether in a pathological situation or not, was to view it as a *symbolic compensation* for the conscious attitudes of the subject. As an *image* from the unconscious, it is able to represent repressed feelings responsible for psychic disorders in the subject; and as an image *of God,* it displays, in any case, a deeper and nonpathological significance: the spontaneous struggle of the psyche for its goal—the Self. In short, the complex that the God-image expresses contains elements from both the personal and the collective layers of the unconscious, the latter having the greater importance.

Now, the hypothetical relationship of symbol to symbolized that Jung sets up between the *imago Dei* and the Self is one of those deliberate ambiguities which are at once suggestive and frustrating. The notion of the Self as such vacillates between two meanings entertained by Jung on different occasions. It is sometimes used to signify the *actual composition of the psyche,* that is, the totality of conscious and unconscious processes. At other times, the Self is seen rather as the *potential goal of the process of individuation,* that is, as the successful understanding of those processes, conscious and unconscious, as they function in one's psyche. In the first sense, Jung felt obliged to postulate the Self as a hypothetical entity; in the second, to deny its actual existence in favor of a primordial, collectively shared, and innate drive in man to achieve wholeness and to find self-fulfillment.[32]

All other questions aside, what is common to both definitions of the Self is the emphasis on unconscious processes, and more particularly on those of a collective, impersonal nature.[33] This brings us at once to Jung's doctrine of the archetypes, upon which both the Self and the *imago Dei* depend for their meaning as psychological realities. Jung himself recognized this, and hence insisted vigorously not only on the empirical reality of the archetypes, but also on the validity of this concept as an indispensable constituent of any hypothesis concerned to treat, in a manner at once comprehensive, simple, and aesthetically satisfying, a vastly diverse range of psychological phenomena. Unfortunately, as his critics have been saying ever since he first introduced the notion, his insistence was stronger than his arguments. Now let me approach the problem again by raising first some questions concerning the seat of the archetypes, the collective unconscious.

Arguing inductively, Jung adduces as the grounds for the positing of a collective unconscious the continued appearance of typical motifs throughout human history and in the unconscious complexes of his patients. The actual analysis of the notion itself is not always clear. Under pressure, Jung admits that the name *collective unconscious* is merely a label for a class of psychically resemblant data, writing almost as a nominalist. Yet most of the time he speaks of the collective unconscious as an identifiable entity, a "part" of the psyche, understood with causal properties. And on some occasions he even extends the notion to cover all that is unknown in the universe![34]

Consider, for example, the following dream, which Jung cites in support of his notion of the collective unconscious:

> A young man dreamed of *a great snake that guarded a golden bowl in an underground vault.* To be sure, he had once seen a huge snake in a zoo, but otherwise he could suggest nothing that might have prompted such a dream, except perhaps the reminiscence of fairy tales. Judging by this unsatisfactory context the dream, which actually produced a very powerful affect, would have hardly any meaning. . . . In such a case we have to go back to mythology, where the combination of snake or dragon with treasure and cave represents an ordeal in the life of the hero. Then it becomes clear that we are dealing with a collective emotion, a typical situation full of affect, which is

> not primarily a personal experience but becomes one only secondarily.[35]

Whatever we may think of Jung's appeal to a recurrent mythological motif to interpret the meaning of the dream, a number of difficulties arise in connection with his conclusion that it originated in an innate pattern of emotional behavior, and not primarily from the subject's personal experience.

First, Jung did not satisfactorily disprove the possibility of cryptomnesia (hidden memory). Personally acquired "reminiscence of fairy-tales" may well have left memory traces capable of being reactivated in the patient's dreams. The high emotional tone of this dream in no way precludes this possibility any more than it proves the collective origins of the actual image. Such oversight demonstrates Jung's tendency toward facile generalization. He satisfied himself in a few cases that a certain unconsciously produced image could not be attributed to unrecognized or repressed memories; in consequence he grew more and more confident that such a possibility might properly be ignored in most future cases as well.[36]

Likewise, telepathic communication cannot be prematurely ruled out as an explanatory hypothesis. Jung's reasons for doing so are unclear, although his writings, lectures, and letters give ample evidence that he recognized the validity of some evidence for such phenomena. At any rate, such a view would have accorded with the facts of the case cited above equally well and, like the hypothesis of cryptomnesia, might have opened up avenues of possible empirical research of the sort the collective unconscious would not.[37]

Jung considered such explanations incompatible with his notion of the collective unconscious. It is obvious, therefore, that more is at stake in this issue than the status of a mere class of data. In fact, the hypothesis of the collective unconscious is being offered as a causal explanation, against which such concepts as cryptomnesia and thought-transference (as part of an alternative, complementary framework) were seen as a threat.

For Jung, the notion of the compensatory function of the unconscious verified the assumption of trust in the wisdom of the collective psyche, in its "healing and redeeming depths."[38] Again, his application of the principle "ontogeny recapitulates phylogeny"[39] to the psyche involves the notion of a gradual birth and emergence of conscious experience from the collective unconscious. Hence he insisted on the structural similarity between the "prelogical" thinking of primitives[40] and the thought of children. This connection prompted Jung to take a further step and to claim that the presence of mythical motifs in unconscious phenomena could not ultimately be explained by reference to cultural transmission or to the migration of symbols, but only by appeal to an inherited unconscious common to all men and so structured as necessarily to produce those motifs at all times and places.[41] Each of these adaptations of the theory of the collective unconscious encouraged his gradual reification of the collective unconscious. From a quasi-substance it became a cosmic principle,[42] although this latter extension served no assignable function in Jung's psychological theory. Rather, it must be viewed as a speculative flight, more indicative of the reverence in which he held the collective unconscious than of its actual theoretical content.

Even before questions of the scientific verification of its reality are raised, therefore, there is much in Jung's exposition of the collective unconscious that calls for clarification. On the face of it the concept is alternately too abstract and too concrete. On the one side, it is too remote from the data on which it rests and in terms of which it must partly be analyzed, and attains status as a necessary and sufficient condition only through elimination of intermediate conditions. Conversely, it reveals itself as a "fact" on the same ontological level as the "facts" it claims to explain.[43]

Jung's notion of the archetype is no less radically problematic, in that he invokes for the archetypes at least three different theoretical functions. (1) As models for classifying psychological data, such archetypes are used as offering *evidence* helping to suggest the hypothesis of a collective unconscious. (2) As specific innate patterns of psychic behavior, they function as the formal *causes* of the psychic phenomena that constitute the data. (3) As the primordial structures behind specific fantasy-images, they are said to embody the *meaning* of the processes of collective unconscious. Not only does Jung not draw these distinctions, but the vocabulary used to refer to each distinguishable function is unscrupulously applied to the others as well.[44] Needless to say, in conventional scientific discourse, logical universals, epistemic preconditions,[45] and hermeneutic principles[46] need to be carefully distinguished from one another. To Jung's failure to observe such distinctions is due much of the obscurity in his notion of the *imago Dei.*

In the previous section I attempted to show that it was impossible to offer a precise description of what constitutes an image of God for Jung, and that this is in large part because of an undefined method of gathering and classifying observations. In the present section it has been argued that the theoretical framework that Jung evolved to explain the psychic causes and functions of God-imagery is equally ambiguous. To conclude this section of the argument, I must add some final remarks on Jung's suspension of judgment whether or not God existed except as the content of psychic imagery.

One thing is clear: Jung did *not* at any time claim that as a psychologist he could "prove" or "disprove" the existence of a transcendent God.[47] The basis of conflicts of opinion concerning Jung's view on the reality of a transcendent God is to be found elsewhere—in the deep obscurity inherent in his model of the psyche.

There is no doubt that Jung comes dangerously close to implying that "God's" ontological status is that of an identifiable image produced by the unconscious. If we combine his occasional attacks on metaphysical speculation with his treatment of the archetypes as preconditions of knowledge, we must admit that those who call him an atheist are not without some justification. Likewise, if we read "*Sermo I*" of the *Septem sermones* in the light of Jung's pre-1916 libido theory, we seem to find an inference that the collective unconscious understood as a cosmic principle is to be identified with the transcendent God of theology. So a charge of pantheism finds some support. From Jung's work as a whole, however, it seems quite clear that, at least after 1920, he definitely discarded the possibility of drawing theistic, atheistic, or pantheistic conclusions from his premises. Because he had in fact never drawn such explicity, he had no need to recant, only to stress his scientific agnosticism; and this he did repeatedly.

If we were to ask Jung whether he regarded the collective unconscious as a necessary and sufficient condition for the presence of the *imago Dei* throughout human history, he could only answer no. Even from a strictly psychological point of view Jung refused to pronounce on the sufficiency of any causal explanation where religious phenomena were involved. The fact that he was not always aware of the causal models contained in his theories raises the question whether he *would* finally have opted for a pantheistic or atheistic stance if he had formulated his method more clearly and applied it with greater rigor. For myself, I think not. Indeed, his resistance to similar steps, when taken by critics or disciples, was resolute enough to make one suppose that their handling of the issue had touched nearer to the bone than he was willing to admit.[48]

Jung's personal views on a transcendent God remain largely matter for speculation. On the whole it seems that he saw God as an ultimately unknowable and uncontrollable power at work within, yet not coextensive with, the collective unconscious in its widest sense.[49] On such a metaphysical basis, Jung's claim that he himself did not need to *believe* in God because he *knew,* can be interpreted as meaning that the supposed forces of the unconscious had come to be as real and as much day-to-day empirical reality to him as the "experiences" they sought to explain; that these forces further represented man's deepest and most inviolable link to the energy that moved the universe; and that the *fides quaerens intellectum* of the theologian inevitably ended up by ignoring the paradoxical status of these forces and elaborating, on the basis of immediate experience, a theoretical construction vacuous in explanatory power.

3. Science and Therapy

With the material amassed in the previous sections spread out before us, some final critical questions toward which we have been steadily advancing may now be formulated. So far I have for the most part resisted the temptation to suggest ways of resolving the contradictions or dissipating the ambiguities constantly present in Jung's thinking. Thus the task has been almost too easy, and its completion may leave the reader with the suspicion that an injustice has been done somewhere.

In evaluating Jung's notion of the *imago Dei,* I took as basic reference point the claims that he himself made in his methodology. Admittedly I have brought forward some serious reservations regarding those claims and the way in which Jung argued them. At this stage it was uncertain whether this was due merely to his distaste for the details of philosophical logic and his perceived need for ambiguity of expression, or to some basic incommensurability between his method as a psychologist and his desire to defend his psychology as a science. But we then discovered that both the factual material and the explanatory models were so insecure that, even on Jung's problematic stance on "scientific" methodology, his actual methods stand condemned.

Before we draw final conclusions, it is necessary at this point to remove the inverted commas that I have been using all along to characterize Jung's notion of science. The fact is, Jung never succeeded in finding an established science to which he might refer as a paradigm of his own methods.[50] He liked to compare his model of the psyche to the atomic models used by physicists; yet he recognized the impossibility here of the controlled experimentation possible in physics. Alternatively, he noted the parallels with such descriptive sciences as comparative anatomy; yet he was not satisfied with this paradigm, because he believed that by his methods he could establish hypotheses by which he could both render the arcana of human behavior intelligible and—from these, conjoined with premises referring to the situation of a particular individual—predict the individual's responses to circumstances likely to involve him in the future. He saw himself as doing something much more than classifying observations. Finally, he likened his method to that of biology, with its teleological bias; yet here too he realized that many of his data were not publicly observable phenomena. Hence, without offering any definition of what constituted a "science," Jung defended his method as scientific because his data had affinities with those of several existing sciences that had successfully broken free of "philosophy." It was for a similar emancipation for psychology that he hoped and worked.

Of Jung's final failure to make his method scientifically respectable there seems little doubt.[51] Yet, if we stop there, we leave out of account an important and perhaps decisive aspect of his work—its origins in, and its needed verification through, the practice of psychotherapy. In spite of an increasing lack of interest in pathological, abnormal personalities,[52] Jung did not abandon the characteristic idiom of the therapist. To him the normal, healthy individual in search of a meaning to his life was often as much in need of the guidance that an analyst experienced in the interpretation of the psyche might offer, as was the neurotic or psychopathic individual.

Now admittedly, Jung did not pay sufficient attention to the effect of the therapeutic setting upon the status of the facts produced within it. Nor did he have a clear idea of what for him constituted proof, evidence, and verification.[53] Yet he did see that the "truth" of his theories was a function of their effectiveness in therapeutic practice.[54] Again, it is not clear what this claim amounts to, since Jung does not give us specific criteria for psychic health or "individuation"; nor does he seem to allow for a sense in which even repeated therapeutic failure can falsify a theory or decrease its probability; nor had he adequately allowed for the operation of factors other than use of his psychological theory that might be significant in any given cure (e.g., the passing of time, the personality of the therapist, the conditions external to the encounter of doctor and patient, etc.).

There is no denying that such complaints create still another objection to the prospect of Jung's psychology achieving the status of a science. We are left with the stubborn fact, however, that *applied as suggesting a method of therapy, Jung's psychology seems to "work."* Were that the only claim to be made for it, one might well side with those of Jung's critics who take his psychology for an esoteric form of religion or mysticism.[55] But the matter is not so simple.

Jung himself once noted that God-talk cannot be translated exhaustively and without remainder into psychological concepts, since it refers preeminently to unconscious processes for which science has yet to find the key. For this reason, he goes on, "we have the greatest difficulty, as scientists, in extricating ourselves at least so far from the language of metaphor as to reach the level of metaphor used by other sciences." Hence the conceptual hypotheses of psychological science merely create new symbols for an enigma that perplexed all ages before ours.[56] The passage is important, inasmuch as it points to the double function that Jung's theory of mind was meant to fulfill. On the one hand, it was meant as a hypothetical model to describe and explain the workings of the psyche; this is its properly theoretical function. But on the other hand, it was also meant as a critique of all theories of mind as but short advances beyond ancient mythical and religious models, and certainly inadequate to the richness of the psyche itself; this is its methodological function. In other words, two distinct cognitive levels are being conflated: Jung wants to use his own model of the psyche to perform more adequately the theoretical functions that he found lacking in other models, and at the same time to criticize all psychology as mere symbolic language. It was the therapeutic setting that provided Jung with the link between these two functions. There the individual was able to see, by means of Jung's theory, the way in which his psyche operated, and yet also to learn, by that same theory, a distrust of conceptual models. That is to say, the use of a single language to shift back and forth between explicit theoretical convictions and a critique of all theory—unacceptable from a philosophical point of view—may be justified as a therapeutic tool. The effectiveness of therapy, far from minimizing the correctness of Jung's model of the psyche or of his critique of psychological models in general, provided each of them with its fundamental frame of reference.

To take this ambiguity as essential to Jung's project is to suggest that we look at his psychology as primarily an abstraction from a therapeutic technique rather than as a scientific theory of mind for which supporting evidence could be found in psychotherapy. It is to hold Jung rigorously to his often-repeated assertion that his psychology had grown solely and exclusively out of his practice. It enables us to give better account, in my view, of the built-in limitations of Jung's work without gainsaying its brilliance or wide-reaching appeal. To illustrate the point, let us return to the *imago Dei*.

The defining characteristic of Jung's psychology of religion is his method of "objective amplification,"[57] which involves three stages: (1) the gathering of the primary data; (2) the search for parallels, analogies, and comparative material among the documents of history; and (3) the interpretation of the former in the light of the latter. Each stage requires its own rules of procedure, poses its own methodological questions and, to keep to our example, adds its own sense to the notion of the *imago Dei*.

Consider first the primary data. Although I have questioned the scientific objectivity Jung claimed for his factual material, it would be rash to conclude that the concept of the *imago Dei* is empty of *all* empirical cash value. However we may seek to negotiate the conditioning variables that intervene between the patient's discourse and the so-called unconscious processes of his psyche and the criteria that the observing analyst adopts to analyze that discourse into its component parts,[58] the fact remains that patients do refer to images of God that appear to them to arise spontaneously in dream and fantasy activity. And that is enough to provide the analyst with the basic text he needs to begin therapy. Hence, as a purely linguistic convention expressive of the self-reflection of the patient, the *imago Dei* can rightly be called an empirical datum.

The amassing of comparative material draws us beyond the immediate confines of the therapeutic setting. For in his appeal to mythology, folklore, literature, religious tradition, and so on, the psychologist must rely on the findings of a number of disciplines or, more precisely, on those scholars whom he accepts as significantly authoritative on such questions. Here the linguistic conventions that determine what is to count as an image of God are no longer of a subjective nature, but represent in one degree or another the conclusions of a community of scholarship. This stage of amplification takes three forms. First, we have the more or less precisely discoverable overlap of particular God-images in the patient's discourse and in the language of mythology.[59] Second, there is the identification of the patient's God-image through its classification as an instance of some pervasive God-type acknowledged as such by students of mythology. In these first two cases, the psychologist's work is preinterpretative, that is, insofar as he accepts the existence of the patient's personal discourse and the mythological references as empirically given. But when, third, he goes on to use the mythological God-type as a heuristic device for deciphering the content of a particular patient's God-image by reading its presence into the patient's statements, he is already engaged in interpretation based on notions derived from his own reflection and not from the patient's experience. In practice, then, this stage of objective amplification is not easily distinguished (especially in the second and third forms) from the final stage, with which it is almost entirely coincidental temporally.

The final and crowning task of the amplification is therefore the interpretation of the basic "text" by reference to comparative material. The fundamental hermeneutic principle governing this process is kerygmatic:[60] the discourse of the patient, insofar as it is characterized as "unconscious," contains a manifold of hidden meanings that are to be made manifest to the "conscious" ego and to become reflectively significant for his self-identification. Therapy consists in the combined efforts of doctor and patient to reconstruct the case history (its symptoms, etc.) as a symbolic expression of primordial needs, which are at bottom shared by all men and which define the horizons of human self-understanding. The *imago Dei,* as a universal mythological motif, provides a clue to this stubstratum of archetypal needs: the appearance of a particular God-image in the patient's speech suggests, either explicitly or implicitly, that it is possible to interpret that speech as revelation of a hitherto-unknown but innate relationship to a reality transcending both consciousness and, indeed, rational apprehension. In this work the languages of self-reflection and of mythology help each to interpret the other.[61] By amplifying the particular God-image of the subject with comparative material, a context is provided for what may originally have appeared to be a distortion or gloss; the attributes of the gods and the tales of their doings become metaphors descriptive of the struggles of the patient and indicative of the aims of his strivings. Conversely, the universality and importance of the mythical story is ascribed to the fact that it is itself a dramatization of the same archetypal human needs.

Interpreting Jung's psychology in the terms sketched would involve a significant shift from his own methodological premises. Such an interpretation suggests that archetypal psychology is best situated among the human rather than among the natural sciences.[62] More specifically with reference to the *imago Dei,* it suggests that the theory of projection may then be seen as a body of rules for interpreting God-talk symbolically as expressive of psychological needs. The theory of mind would then be viewed as a metaphorical model, subject to the canons of a hermeneutical critique but not to the verification procedures required of a theory in the natural sciences.[63]

The justification for such a reinterpretation of Jung on the methodological plane is twofold. Negatively, we are faced with the fact that his method and theories do not constitute a natural science. And positively, the hermeneutic standpoint seems to enable us to grasp adequately those processes of self-reflection which actually occur during psychotherapy. In short, inasmuch as Jung viewed therapeutic success as the final verification of his psychology, and inasmuch as he saw that such success did not require the patient's understanding of or agreement with the scientific claims of his doctrine, it is reasonable to argue that Jung's practical methods are better understood hermeneutically.[64] Experimental psychology and biology may still draw inspiration from his theory of mind for the construction of new hypotheses; cultural anthropologists, literary critics, historians, classicists, philosophers, and theologians may still find it of use in resolving the problems of their respective disciplines; but strictly in the context of Jung's thought, its sole defense seems to be as a practical and functional source for therapeutic interpretation.

The details of such a reconstruction of Jung's work on the level of hermeneutical discourse fall outside the scope of the present study, and one cannot pretend that the task will be an easy one. Many of the problems and ambiguities enumerated in the course of this evaluation will survive the shift of epistemological foundations, and where a particular criticism has vanished, a new one can be expected to emerge in its stead. Yet, whatever the prospects of such a venture, the challenge of Jung's psychology of religion remains—defiant, resilient, and clamoring for justice.

Notes

Introduction

1. Some years ago James Hillman argued convincingly for the term *archetypal psychology* to characterize Jung's approach (1970). It now seems better to retain the standard label *analytical* for Jung's own work, and to reserve *archetypal* for the continuing tradition to which it gave rise.

2. Schär, 1951, p. 8.

3. White, 1952a, p. 71. The phrase recalls a similar remark made by D. H. Lawrence some thirty years earlier regarding Freud and Jung (1971, p. 19).

4. Aniela Jaffé attributes this fact to Jung's awareness of the many sided enigma of the human psyche, his intuitive and nonsystematic approach, and "the impelling force of the creative daemon" that drove him on (1970, pp. 26-28). While the explanation is fair enough in general, honesty requires that we recognize certain occasions—notably in the story of his break with Freud—on which Jung was not above distorting the history of his work and thought.

5. Among the many brief and popular efforts to follow the growth of Jung's ideas, those of M. Fordham (1945, 1956), Lewis (1957), Lambert (1962), Harding (1965), and Bennet (1966) are probably the best. Ellenberger (1970, pp. 657-748) deserves special mention for his attention to source material usually overlooked, although his claims in this regard are rather exaggerated. The only attempt at a developmental study of Jung's psychology of religion was done by Raymond Hostie (1957). Elsewhere I have questioned the accuracy and adequacy of his report (1973b, p. 207). Part I of the present book should add further evidence in support of those complaints which, I might note, were shared by Jung himself (208, 1955, p. 7; letter to Hostie, 25 April 1955). (References having numbers before their dates, as here, are to the list of works by Jung.)

6. In English the most helpful are Jaffé (1970). F. Fordham (1968), and Bennet (1961). Jolande Jacobi's is still the most organized and structured synthesis of Jung's work available (1969), although, as she once admitted to me, many have criticized her for being oversystematic.

   It is worth noting that Jung himself never succeeded in presenting a clear résumé of his own ideas, though he did make an abortive attempt in a series of lectures given during 1933 and 1934 (100, Part I). A few years later he as much as admitted defeat when he wrote: "My endeavors in psychology have been essentially pioneer work, leaving me neither time nor opportunity to present them systematically" (142, 1939, p. ix; cf. 169, 1947, p. xi).

7. Part of the problem is the almost total lack of solid bibliographical research on secondary sources. *Psychological Abstracts* has never paid the Jungian tradition any particular attention; and the formidable five-volume index compiled under the auspices of the International Psychoanalytical Association complied with the wishes of its members (57% of the 62% who responded to a questionnaire) by excluding virtually all reference to Jung (Grinstein, 1957, vol. 1, introduction). What bibliographical work has been done is thin (Friedman and Goldstein, 1964; Clark, 1961). In an attempt partially to fill this gap I published a comprehensive study of source material on Jung's psychology of religion (1973b).

8. Hostie has emphasized this to the point of absurdity by asserting that repeated personal contact with Jung is "absolutely essential for a proper understanding of his actual writings" (1957, p. 5). In a less-flattering remark, Hans Prinzhorn once described Jung's psychology as "a philosophy which, for appreciation, requires esoteric association with the Master" (1932, p. 24).

9. Note Jacobi's comment: "Theoretic conceptions and explanations are adequate only up to a certain point for the comprehension of Jung's system, for in order to understand it completely, one must have experienced its vital workings within oneself" (1969, p. 60).

10. The editing of the *Collected Works,* which are appearing in Swiss, American, English, and most recently in Italian and French editions, should be completed shortly. The English translator, R. F. C. Hull, deserves the highest praise for producing work that is at once scrupulously accurate and of considerable literary merit in its own right. Although I have in each instance checked the translation against the original text, I quote Hull's version throughout this book with full confidence.

11. 101, 1934; 116, 1935.

12. 73, 1928-30; 100, 1933-40. Portions of Jung's seminar on Nietzsche (109, 1934-39) and on the interpretation of visions (84, 1930-34) have appeared periodically since 1960 in *Spring,* an annual journal of archetypal psychology published in Zurich.

13. A decision has been taken recently to publish these notes as a parallel series to the *Collected Works.* The project will take many years to complete. Meantime, it is with the kind permission of the Jung family that I quote occasionally from the notes, correcting only minor errors of grammar and spelling.

14. 13, 1906–61.

15. The interested reader is referred to an essay by G. Adler (1966, pp. 217-43). As perhaps the best single attempt that has appeared to date, its obvious inadequacies serve to point up the need for the hand of a critical historian detached from the internal wranglings of the movement.

Chapter 1 The Early Years (1902-1920)

1. To simplify things, I shall refer to the later and more accessible versions wherever no significant change in the relevant content is involved. In order to avoid unnecessarily encumbering the text, the respective dates of publication (or of completion, where known) will be included in the notes. Where a later revision has been used to quote an earlier article, both dates will be given.

2. A preliminary sketch of the material that appears in Part I was first published in 1971 (see bibliography).

3. Jung's reputation in the United States rested on his work with the word-association experiment and the psychogalvanic effect. Eschenbach (1967) and Meier (1959b, p. 7) claim that the discoveries Jung made in connection with his research on word-association can be seen to dominate in his later theories as well.

4. I am speaking here only of Jung's published work, but mention should also be made of four lectures he delivered to the Zofingia, a Swiss students' association, during his years at the University of Basel as a student. In those talks and the ensuing discussions recorded in the society's files, two themes of particular interest to the development of Jung's thought appear.

First, Jung argued vigorously against the "laughable materialistic world-view" of the times and its resultant spiritual poverty. To this he opposed a firm convicton in the reality of the soul (or "life-principle") which, although a metaphysical notion, could be treated empirically by studying such phenomena as hypnotism and somnabulism (1, 1896; 2, 1898). This view was already at work in Jung's earliest professional writings, though it did not become explicit until much later. In fact, if one compares Jung's short epilogue written in 1944 for a collection of his essays and lectures appearing in French translation, one finds that parts of it are almost identical with sections of his earlier Zofingia talks (159, 1944, pp. 333-34).

Second, Jung took up the case against Christian theology, claiming that it tended to underrate the mystical, experiential element that is essential to all religion. This in turn has led, he went on, to a pessimistic view of the individual and to a Christology that cuts people off from the possibility of direct contact with God (3, 1898; 4, 1899; cf. 237, 1961, pp. 97-98).

An interesting and useful firsthand account of Jung's student years has been provided by Gustav Steiner (1965).

5. 6, 1902, pp. 27, 29-31, 72-73, 79. We now know that the medium was in fact Helene Preiswerk, Jung's first cousin on his mother's side (see Ellenberger, 1970, p. 739 n. 25; Jung, 237, 1961, p. 296). A curious gloss to the story, mentioned in the notes from one of Jung's early seminar lectures, is the fact that, by Jung's own admission, his research was complicated by his discovery that in the course of his two-year study of her case the girl had fallen deeply in love with him (59, 1925, p. 4).

6. 6, 1902, pp. 16, 60, 69.

7. 7, 1903, pp. 126, 129.

8. 8, 1903, p. 186.
9. 10, 1905, pp. 219, 226.
10. 16, 1908, p. 163.
11. 14, 1907/1909, pp. 130-31.
12. 9, 1905, p. 99,
13. 12, 1906, pp. 117, 121, 134. Referring to the same patient, Jung says elsewhere of her delusional ideas: "Even the most absurd things are nothing other than symbols for thoughts which are not only understandable in human terms, but dwell in every human breast" (16, 1908, p. 178).
14. 16, 1908, pp. 158-59. It is worth noting that in the same year, upon completion of his house at Küsnacht, Jung had the following words carved in stone over the front door: *VOCATVS ATQVE NON VOCATVS DEVS ADERIT.* The phrase is a Latin translation (which Jung had discovered in the *Adagia* of Erasmus as a student of nineteen) of the reply of the Delphic oracle to the Spartans on the eve of their attack on Athens. Nearly fifty years later, Jung explained that he had those words inscribed because, as he said, "I always feel, in a way, *unsafe,* as if I'm in the presence of superior possibilities" (209, 1955, p. 147; see also his letter to E. Rolfe, 19 November 1960).
15. An exchange of letters between Freud and Karl Abraham in the spring of 1908 might seem to indicate the opposite. Freud had written that Jung "as a Christian and a pastor's son finds his way to me only against great inner resistances"; to which Abraham replied: "Jung seems to be reverting to his former spiritualistic inclinations" (Abraham, 1965, pp. 34, 44). But it was merely Jung's general interest in the occult, which Freud distrusted (cf., for example, Jung's letter to Freud dated 2 April 1909), and the lasting mutual antipathy between Abraham and Jung, which Freud was trying to soften (cf. Jung's letter to Freud of 7 May 1908, and Freud's to Jung of 26 and 30 December 1908) , that account for these comments. They refer to personal conversations and correspondence rather than to arguments derived from Jung's actual writings.
16. Jung tells us that he feared mentioning Freud in his work because of the stigma then attached to his name, even though he found that Freud's theory of repression coincided perfectly with his own word-association experiments (59, 1925, pp. 16-18). The article is a clear exception, however, and Wittels (1924, p. 131) has no grounds for denying that Jung had failed here to acknowledge his dependence on Freud.
17. 17, 1909, pp. 320-23. Particular attention should be paid the implied development of the God-concept from the Old Testament to the New: the God of Fear becomes the God of Love. This is an idea that Jung seems to have picked up somewhere in his reading and used frequently throughout his work. It can be traced back to the Gnostics' depreciation of the Old Testament, especially as worked out by Marcion, who exploited the Pauline distinction of Law and Gospel by using it to contrast the fearful justice of Yahweh with the compassionate love of the Father preached by Jesus.

18. Dated 11 February 1910. When a pupil quoted these passages to Jung some fifty years later, Jung wrote in reply: "For me it is an unfortunately inexpungeable reminder of the incredible folly that filled the days of my youth. The journey from cloud-cuckoo-land back to reality lasted a long time" (dated 9 April 1959).
19. 18, 1909, p. 28.
20. 20, 1910, p. 315.
21. 19, 1910, p. 380.
22. Cf. Jaffé, 1972, p. 168.
23. 12, 1906, p. 4. Cf. his letters to Freud dated 5 October 1906, 2 April 1909, and 25 December 1909. Freud was aware of this very early, as a letter to Jung dated 7 October 1906 makes clear.
24. 15, 1908, pp. 18-19.
25. Jung tells us in his autobiography that he began this study in 1909 (237, 1961, p. 131). But already, three years earlier, he had made the following brief remark at the end of a lengthy dream-analysis: "I have refrained from pointing out the numerous analogical connections, the similarities of imagery, the allegorical representations of phrases, etc. No one who carefully examines the material can fail to observe these characteristics of mythological thinking" (12, 1906, p. 62.) Again in 1908 in a similar context Jung praises Freud's use of sexual symbolism: "In my view he is really easiest to follow here, because this is just where mythology, expressing the fantasy-thinking of all races, has prepared the ground in the most instructive way. . . . No one who considers this material will be able to conceal from himself that there are uncommonly far-reaching and significant analogies . . . ." (15, 1908, p. 23).
26. Dated 25 December 1909. See also letter to Freud of 2 June 1910. In the first months of 1910 Jung delivered a series of six lectures to several scientific societies of students in which he tried to relate individual conflicts to mythical types. Reference is made to the fact in letters to Freud of 30 January and 24 May 1910, but the lectures seem to have been lost.
27. 21, 1910, p. 40.
28. 23, 1911, pp. 53-55.
29. Dated 12 June 1911.
30. On 29 October 1913 Jung wrote to Alphonse Maeder, a member of the Swiss Freudian group who was to remain loyal to Jung: "I consider it of no advantage to Freud to have sickened me off. . . I *won't* collaborate with Freud any longer. It will make a very bad impression all round. But inner successes count more with me than the howling of the mob." Freud's correspondence from a few months previous to that shows him still eager to reach agreement with Jung (S. Freud, 1963, p. 60); but, as Lou Salomé tells us, he was becoming increasingly hostile (1965, pp. 38-39). Soon thereafter his letters speak of "brutal, sanctimonious Jung" and refer to Jung as "crazy" and as a "system-builder." On 3 January 1913, Freud officially proposed to Jung that they abandon all personal relations, adding:

"I shall lose nothing by it for my emotional tie with you has long been a thin thread." To make matters complete, Freud wrote to Karl Abraham in March of 1914 to inform him that he had finally got rid of Jung's photograph (Abraham, 1965, pp. 141, 167, 186; Freud, 1966, p. 68)! For a brief account, strongly biased in Jung's favor, of the controversy excited by *Psychology of the Unconscious,* see Heyer-Grote, 1965.

31. 186, 1950, p. xxiii. Reactions at the time were not much different. Ferenczi wrote a devastating critique of it from a Freudian stance (1913). Reik found it "far-fetched" (1921, p. 88). Other reviewers referred to it as "a stimulating swindle" (Bloch, 1914); "impressively well-intentioned, enormously learned and extremely muddle-headed" (Anon., 1923); and "some 500-odd pages of incoherence and obscurity" (Fite, 1916). Lou Salomé, with customary perceptiveness, noted in her diary that the book seemed "a premature and hence quite sterile synthesis" (1965, p. 43). Even those who were favorable to Jung's pioneering spirit, such as Bleuler (1925), were careful to exclude approval of its inconsistencies and frequently faulty information. Jack London read the book when it appeared in English translation in 1916 and, according to McClintock, wrote a series of short stories in an attempt to assimilate Jung's ideas into his own (1970). Tansley, one of the few to adopt Jung's arguments on religion, does so only by treating the material as uncritically as Jung himself had (1920, pp. 163-64, 136-39).

32. In my view, Harding is quite correct when she asserts that "most of Jung's works deal with problems raised by this first book" (p. 2).

33. 24, 1911-12, p. viii.

34. The case was first described by Théodore Flournoy, whom Jung had met and who later wrote his approval of Jung's analysis (57, 1924, p. xxviii; 84, 1934, 11:188; 237, 1961, pp. 378-79).

35. 186, 1950, p. xxv. It also served him, as Jaffé points out, as a model for organizing his unsystematic study of mythology (1972, p. 169).

36. 59, 1925, pp. 33-34. He did admit, however, that it was the similarity of Miss Miller's fantasies to his own—namely, their mythic, impersonal quality—that first attracted him to them (ibid., p. 29).

37. 186, 1950, p. xxviii.

38. 24, 1911-12, p. 71. In fact, direct reference to "The Significance of the Father . . ." is made on four occasions. As Jung wrote later, *Psychology of the Unconscious* complemented the earlier article by showing how not only the father but also the mother has a determinative influence on the genesis of religious beliefs (63, 1926, p. 301).

39. 24, 1911-12, pp. 8-41. Despite the striking similarity to Hobbes's distinction between "regulated" and "unguided" thought (*Leviathan,* 1.3), it seems probable that Jung first got the idea from William James, with whose writings he was well acquainted.

40. Ibid., p. 427 n. 34.

41. Freud had mentioned this problem at the end of a series of criticisms sent to Jung regarding an earlier draft of the book, now apparently lost. See Freud's undated letter of ca. 22 June 1910.

42. Ibid., pp. 23, 147. The way in which he adopts Kantian language to demarcate the boundaries of psychological inquiry is best seen in the following passage from a lengthy note: "It is not to be forgotten that we are moving entirely in the territory of psychology, which in no way is allied to transcendentalism, either in positive or negative relation. It is a question of relentless fulfillment of the standpoint of the theory of cognition, established by Kant, not merely for the theory, but, what is more important, for the practice. . . . In the same measure that the true reality is merely a figurative interpretation of the appreciation of reality, the religious symbolic theory is merely a figurative interpretation of certain endopsychic apperceptions. But the one very essential difference is that a transcendental support, independent in duration and condition, is assured to the transsubjective reality through the best conceivable guarantees, while for the psychological phenomena a transcendental support of subject limitation and weakness must be recognized as a result of compelling empirical data. Therefore true reality is one that is relatively universally valid; the psychologic reality, on the contrary, is merely a functional phenomenon contained in an epoch of human civilization" (ibid., p. 529 n. 42).

43. Ibid., p. 31. Jung cites the interesting case of Abbé Oegger (p. 40).

44. Ibid., pp. 28, 35-36.

45. While Jung himself avoids these terms, his expressed concern with applying the laws of causation to the psyche seems to suggest their relevance here (ibid., p. 59; cf. 28, 1912, p. 1079).

46. "We know that, although individuals are widely separated by the differences in the contents of their consciousness, they are closely alike in their unconscious psychology. It is a significant impression for one working in practical psychoanalysis when he realizes how uniform are the typical unconscious complexes" (ibid., p. 198, cf. pp. 5, 7, 200-201). Jung intimates that he had already recognized this in his earlier research on his cousin the medium (p. 62), but I can find no textual evidence to support this claim.

47. At this time Jung was one of the staunchest defenders of this aspect of Freudian psychology (see, e.g., 25, 1911, pp. 60-73; 28, 1912, p. 107), even though Freud was not convinced of the fact (see Jung's letter to Freud of 29 July 1913).

48. 24, 1911-12, pp. 10, 12, 28, 135-36, 249.

49. Although Jung claims he had used this notion in "The Significance of the Father . . ." (ibid., p. 71), it is quite clear that he had deliberately avoided it there.

50. Ibid., pp. 250, 303, 463, 530 n.45. Jung discusses this point in a letter to Freud 7 May 1912 (see also 29, 1912, pp. 79-80; 27, 1911, p. 210). Later Jung was to compare his libido theory to Bergson's *élan vital,* a theme that was taken up and slightly expanded by the translator of *Psychology of the Unconscious* (Hinkle, 1919).

51. Some years later, reflecting on his break with Freud's sexual theory, Jung commented: "I hold that we undergo not so much a real transformation of the sex instinct as an alleviating of its power from the contents which don't belong to it. . . . Our biological side becomes more and more hollowed out, inasmuch as its specific spiritual contents are extracted" (84, 1931, 3:199).

52. 24, 1911-12, pp. 24-25, 30, 98.

53. Ibid., p. 479.

54. Ibid., pp. 75-76. For Jung it is a self-evident conclusion from postliberal theology, which claims only to be able to speak of the mythical reality of Christ while despairing of knowing anything certain about the historical Jesus, that Christ was the creation of psychic needs (see pp. 39, 200, 258-59).

55. Ibid., p. 427.

56. Ibid., p. 262.

57. Ibid., pp. 91, 260-61, 498 n. 3, 534 n. 107.

58: Ibid., p. 9.

59. The term *imago* is one that Jung had already used in earlier writings. It refers to the psychological fact that it is not the *real* father or mother who is the object of childhood transference, but only the child's *perception* of the parent, i.e., his imago. In an autobiographical aside during a lecture given several years later, Jung recalled that Freud had accepted this correction of his theory of childhood transference when Jung had confronted him with it (73, 1930, Part II, pp. 123-24).

60. 24, 1911-12, pp. 55-56; cf. p. 99.

61. Ibid., p. 96.

62. Ibid., pp. 200-201; cf. pp. 227, 505-6 n. 69.

63. Ibid., pp. 105-7.

64. Jung used Bleuler's word *ambitendency* to describe this tendency for every impulse to be accompanied by its opposite (ibid., p. 194; cf. 26, 1911, p. 197).

65. 24, 1911-12, p. 70. Later he notes: "The libido is God and Devil" (p. 120). See also pp. 116, 128.

66. Ibid., pp. 135, 403.

67. Ibid., p. 230. He explains this fact alternatively by referring to the "bisexual" character of the libido (p. 523 n. 67).

68. Ibid., p. 73.

69. Ibid., p. 23.

70. Ibid., pp. 30, 80.

71. Thus he writes regarding the identification of God and libido: "If it were not known how tremendously significant religion was, and is, this marvellous play with one's self would appear absurd" (ibid., p. 96). Elsewhere he speaks of religion as "the bridge to all the greatest achievements of humanity. . . .

of the greatest significance from the cultural point of view and of imperishable beauty from the aesthetic standpoint" (p. 262).

72. Ibid., pp. 100, 262.

73. Ibid., pp. 80, 258-59.

74. Ibid., p. 85. With reference to the Miller case, Jung states the principle in more general terms: "The phenomenon, well known to every psychoanalyst, of the unconscious transformation of an erotic conflict into religious activity is something *empirically wholly worthless,* and nothing but an hysterical production. Whoever, on the other hand, to his conscious sin just as consciously places religion in opposition, does something the greatness of which cannot be denied. This can be verified by a backwards glance over history. Such a procedure is sound religion. *The unconscious recasting of the erotic into something religious lays itself open to the reproach of a sentimental and ethically worthless pose*" (p. 82).

75. Gardner Murphy's comment on the book is near the mark: "Its method—it is no more than a friendly exaggeration to say this—is to argue that because A is somewhat like B, and B can, under certain circumstances, share something with C, and C has been known on occasion to have been suspected of being related to D, the conclusion in full-fledged logical form is that A = D" (1966, p. 424).

76. 237, 1961, pp. 170-99.

77. *The Psychoanalytic Review,* which printed these lectures, carried an opening letter in which Jung clearly pleads the cause of his new approach: "It is beyond the powers of the individual, more particularly of physicians, to master the manifold domains of the mental sciences which should throw some light upon the comparative anatomy of the mind. . . . We need not only the work of medical psychologists, but also that of philologists, historians, archaeologists, mythologists, folklore students, ethnologists, philosophers, theologians, pedagogues and biologists" (33, 1913, pp. 117-18).

78. 32, 1912, pp. 111-12, 115, 118-19. Jung brought this revised version of Freud's sexual theory to the United States in September of 1912, hoping to win converts for psychoanalysis, but only broadening the rift between himself and Freud (Freud, 1914, p. 58, and Jung's letter to Freud of 11 November 1912).

79. 32, 1912, pp. 140-41, 166-68. This view is not as yet satisfactorily worked out. Indeed, as late as 1919 Jung was to argue that most neuroses can be traced back to childhood causes (47, p. vi).

80. 32, 1912, pp. 155-56. This leads him logically to identify the mind of the child with that of the primitive, thus implying again the ontogeny-phylogeny model (p. 152).

81. Ibid., pp. 192-93; cf. 36, 1913, p. 284.

82. 46, 1918, p. 10. As early as 1916 Jung had spoken of a *collective psyche,* which term he frequently used in his letter writings as well (44, 1916, p. 275). Jung

often uses the unqualified substantive *unconscious* on its own, omitting any qualification (*personal, collective,* or both). That he never gave up this habit in his later work, despite continued criticism, suggests that his ambiguity was intentional.

83. 49, 1919, p. 133.

84. 38, 1914, pp. 309-10; 45, 1917, p. 295.

85. 30, 1912, p. 258; 46, 1918, pp. 12-13, 21.

86. 30, 1916, p. 406.

87. The clearest statement of this is to be found in two posthumously discovered papers written during this period (41, 1916, p. 173; 43, 1916, p. 174).

88. 35, 1913, pp. 241-42. Note also his criticism of the God of modern man, a God who has become "much too tolerant" (30, 1916, p. 371).

89. 46, 1918, pp. 19, 23-24.

90. After analyzing the conversion of St. Paul as an instance of the power of autonomous unconscious complexes with accompanying psychogenetic blindness, Jung adds the following remark: "Science does not, in a way that satisfies our intellectual conscience, allow us to explain the case of St. Paul on supernatural grounds. We should be compelled to do the same with many similar cases within our medical experience, which would lead to conclusions antagonistic both to our reason and our feeling" (50, 1919, p. 258).

91. 38, 1914, p. 310; 30, 1916, pp. 412-13.

92. 35, 1913, p. 237. Jung is harking back here to a view he had already expressed in 1901, in a lecture on Freud's *Die Traumdeutung* (5, p. 178).

93. From a letter to H. Schmid, 6 November 1915.

94. Cf. 38, 1914, pp. 307, 311; 39, 1916, p. 293.

95. 30, 1916, pp. 414-15, 431.

96. 50, 1919, p. 254.

97. Ibid., pp. 268-69.

98. That this approach can still be valid on occasion is especially clear from Jung's discussion of two cases: one where the appearance of "God" in a dream is analyzed as a reference to the patient's own father (38, 1914; p. 304; cf. 48, 1919, pp. 220-25) and the other where the patient's divinization of the analyst in his fantasies is seen as a regression to infantile transference (30, 1916, pp. 408-9; 38, 1914, p. 179).

99. 44, 1916, pp. 273-87. Adler had used the word to describe certain basic features of neurotic power psychology.

100. Cf. ibid., p. 287; 30, 1916, pp. 413-14. In a letter to H. Schmid (6 November 1915) he refers to passing to "the divinity within us."

101. 30, 1916, pp. 417, 434.

102. Cf. 44, 1916, p. 281. In an interview held in 1912 Jung is reported to have referred to God as "the greatest abstraction of all," as if it were a consciously devised concept (31). And in an unpublished paper dating from 1916 he notes: "The individual must now consolidate himself by cutting himself off from God and becoming wholly himself" (43, p. 175). Since it is clear that Jung is not counseling us to cut ourselves off from the collective unconscious, he can only be alluding again to the consciously elaborated notion of God. It is only in the light of his later work that this confusion can be cleared up. At this stage, one can only admit to a general ambiguity capable of several different interpretations.

103. 59, 1925, pp. 38-39, 58.

104. 237, 1961, pp. 189-91. See also Fodor, 1964.

105. Letter to Alphonse Maeder, 19 January 1917. Quispel has tried to point up similarities between Jung and the gnostic Basilides (1970).

106. 194, 1952, p. 468. As a matter of fact, apart from his autobiography Jung makes no reference to the work in the whole of his published work. Likewise no mention is made of it in any of his seminar lectures. (During one discussion, however, a participant did allude to it on a single occasion [84, 1933, 10:132].)

107. Around this same time Jung was writing his fantasies down in a number of notebooks. Later the entire collection, spanning some six years, was gathered together into one volume of roughly 600 typewritten pages, the so-called "Red Book." Although its private nature makes it unsuitable for publication, we can suppose from certain sections cited by Frau Jaffé, to whose hands Jung entrusted the manuscript, that many of the same early formulations of later theories appear in the "Red Book" as well (1972, pp. 174-76). Among Jung's available writings, however, the *Sermones* stand alone as a first systematic outline of the fundamental vision that lay behind ideas not to appear in his published works for many years to come.

108. Heisig, 1972.

109. Despite the crude state of his theory of the archetypes, Jung would already have encountered the usefulness of the "4" model in his researches on typology, which had begun in 1913. Moreover, the "Red Book" was full of mandala-sketches, and in 1916 Jung painted his first mandala, with the unmistakable quaternity structure. (A copy of this painting, which bears the title *Systema mundi totius,* appears as the frontpiece to vol. 9, no. 1 of his *Collected Works.*) Finally, the pattern of the three-plus-one had already appeared in an earlier allusion to a medieval interpretation of the story of the three young men in the fiery furnace, according to which the three form a Trinity out of which is produced a fourth who was "like the Son of God" (24, 1911-12, p. 184).

110. In an essay written during the same year as the *Sermones,* Jung coined the term *transcendent function* to describe this process of cooperation between the ego and the unconscious, which he held was essential for the birth of the differentiated or "individuated" man (42, 1916). Not without good reason Sborowitz has called this notion "the crowning point" of Jung's psychology (1951, p. 283).

111. 32, p. 140.

112. Abraham, 1955, p. 110; 1914, pp. 72, 82; see also Eitingon, 1914, p. 104: Lippman, 1916.

113. Jones, 1948, p. 136.

114. Anon., 1918, p. 35.

115. Baynes, 1923, p. i. At the time Baynes was not alone in this view. (Cf. Van der Hoop, 1923, p. 138.)

116. One reviewer, although very favorable to Jung, suggested that his argument becomes clearer if one reads the book backward, beginning with the last chapter and going on to the first (Sinclair, 1923, p. 436)!

117. From now on Jung refers to his work exclusively as "psychology," reserving the name "psychoanalysis" for Freud's approach.

118. 51, 1920/1960, pp. 243, 408. In one place Jung even ventures to equate the term *metaphysical* and *unconscious* (p. 143). Again, he suggests that certain metaphysical debates in the history of philosophy could be solved by moving them to the psychological plane whence they arose in the first instance. He gives as an illustration the scholastic dispute over the problem of "universals" (pp. 38-46, 488). Hostie's criticism of Jung is convincing here, although he tends to dismiss the entire problem of differences of philosophical temperament along with Jung's particular arguments (1957, pp. 88-101). Urban is more sympathetic to Jung, but firmly and intelligently rejects his conclusions (1949, pp. 119-21).

119. In what follows, I am in full accord with critics who viewed *Types* basically as "an argument for the religion of the unconscious," not as a phenomenon to be observed but as "an experience to be lived" (Kantor, 1923, p. 637; Thorburn, 1924, p. 99).

120. 51, 1920/1960, p. 168. Despite his use of the phrase *the unconscious,* Jung makes it clear that he is dealing only with a certain class of contents or processes that have a determinative power over psychic life but are not related to the ego in any perceptible way. He rejects any "metaphysical" hypostatization of the concept: "On epistemological grounds, we are at present quite unable to make any valid statement about the objective reality of the complex psychological phenomenon we call the unconscious, just as we are in no position to say anything valid about the essential nature of real things, for this lies beyond our psychological ken" (p. 168; cf. pp. 483-84).

The same loosely Kantian position is held concerning the notion of "libido," which, Jung insists in reply to his critics, is not a reification of a general psychic energy, but merely a convenient way of speaking about degrees of intensity of determining power expressed in definite psychic effects (pp. 455-56). Shortly after completing *Psychology of the Unconscious,* Jung framed a paper to clarify his ambiguous use of the term (69). Although the paper was not published until 1928, its influence on *Types* is unmistakable.

121. 51, 1920/1960, pp. 431-33, 485.

122. Ibid., pp. 168, 298, 376, 486. Earlier Jung had called the archetypes modes of "intuition" (49, 1919, p. 133), but his new theory of intuition as one of the psychic functions (replacing what he had once called "fantasy thinking") led him to abandon that usage. Still, both terminologically and theoretically, Jung's archetype theory was only in its first beginnings. The much-needed historical study of the growth of this theory remains to be written. Meanwhile, one can hardly do better than Jacobi's competent essay on the subject (1959).

123. "I myself am so profoundly convinced of the uniformity of the psyche that I have even summed it up in the concept of the collective unconscious, as a universal and homogeneous substratum whose uniformity is such that one finds the same myth and fairytale motifs in all corners of the earth, with the result that an uneducated American Negro dreams of motifs from Greek mythology and a Swiss clerk reexperiences in his psychosis the vision of an Egyptian Gnostic" (51, 1920/1960, p. 491).

Elsewhere he writes these words: "What Kant demonstrated in respect of logical thinking is true of the whole range of the psyche. The psyche is no more *tabula rasa* to begin with than is the mind proper (the thinking area). Naturally the concrete contents are lacking, but the potential contents are given *a priori* by the inherited and preformed functional disposition" (p. 304; cf. pp. 374-75). A fuller account of Jung's ideas, spanning the whole range of his writings, will be given in Part II.

124. 51, 1920/1960, p. 338.

125. Jung also appeals to the term *constructive* to distinguished his method from what he calls the "causal-reductive" method: ". . . A fantasy needs to be understood both causally and purposively. Causally interpreted, it seems like a *symptom* of a physiological or personal state, the outcome of antecedent events. Purposively interpreted, it seems like a *symbol,* seeking to characterize a definite goal with the help of the material at hand, or trace out a line of future psychological development" (ibid., p. 432; cf. p. 422).

126. Ibid., pp. 413, 423.

127. 51, 1920, p. 150. (This phrase occurs in a sentence omitted from the later revision.)

128. 51, 1920/1960, pp. 448-50, 115, 126, 480. These ideas first appear in three unpublished essays written in 1916 (41, 42, 43).

129. Ibid., pp. 125, 259-62, 264-65.

130. Not too much importance should be laid on this particular phrase, which appears only three times in the book and whose meaning is far from precise. Jung seems to have intended it only as a *façon de parler,* and therefore omits to mention it in his chapter of definitions. It is useful only as a means of focusing attention on the positive role of religion in psychic well-being.

131. Jung makes this statement in opposition to William James's contention that the idealists can be characterized as having a religious attitude, while the empiricists

have an irreligious outlook. Jung goes on: "The tough-minded indeed have their empiricistic religion, just as the tender-minded have an idealistic one. . ." (51, 1920/1960, p. 315).

132. 51, 1920/1960, pp. 91, 248.

133. Ibid., p. 185. ". . . The religion of the last two thousand years is a psychological attitude, a definite form and manner of adaptation to the world without and within. . ." (ibid.). "Collective ideas always have a religious character. . . . Their religious character derives from the fact that they express the realities of the collective unconscious and are thus able to release its latent energies" (p. 220).

134. Ibid., p. 315. The allusion to primitive psychology was a blend of conventional anthropological opinion and Jung's own conviction that the structures of the psyche can give us a model for explaining its actual origins.

135. Ibid., pp. 13-14, 18. Victor White has praised Jung's interpretation here, and briefly explains the phrase in the wider context of Tertullian's thought (1952a pp. 61-63, 79). This he does as a revision of his previous criticism of Jung for having misunderstood Tertullian's meaning (1942, pp. 35-36).

136. 51, 1920/1960, p. 53; cf. pp. 244, 249-50. The argument owes its apparent circularity to the fact that Jung is trying to do several things with the same terminology: (1) to redefine *religion* in psychological terms; (2) to evaluate psychologically what is called "religion" in ordinary language (i.e., the major religious traditions: Christianity, Buddhism, Islam, etc.); (3) to discourage all forms of "religion" that are psychologically damaging; and thereby (4) to understand the nature and contents of the unconscious mind from which all "religious" phenomena spring. While Jung's intentions in any given context can usually be discerned, his failure to draw such distinctions as these resulted in some inevitable theoretical vagueness.

137. Ibid., pp. 141, 141 n. 242.

138. Ibid., pp. 192; cf. pp. 139, 418-20.

139. Ibid., p. 53. See also his comments on St. Paul (pp. 428-31).

140. Ibid.

141. Ibid., p. 73. He briefly treats the opposition to Gnosticism in the early Church and in the ninth-century debate over the dogma of transubstantiation as examples of this trait of organized religion. What "salutory effects" he does find in institutionalized belief are at best temporary and opportunistic in balancing a one-sided spirit of the age. It is clear, however, that such benefits are no longer possible for the "modern mind" (pp. 11, 24-25). Hence the charge leveled against him at this time that his psychology is a refuge for "spiritual aristocrats" (Isham, 1923, p. 16).

142. 51, 1920/1960, p. 213.

143. Ibid., p. 248. Jung does not use the word *soul* in the accepted Christian sense, which he finds too narrow. Instead, he understands the soul as a Janus-faced "personification" of the subject. Insofar as the subject is viewed in terms of

its relations to the "outer world" of objects, it is called the *persona* (the Latin name for masks worn by actors in antiquity); and viewed in terms of its relations to the "inner world" of unconscious contents, the subject is termed the *anima* or *animus* (according to whether the subject is masculine or feminine) (pp. 247, 463-70). This idea had already appeared, in somewhat different form, in Jung's previous writings (cf. 44, 1916, pp. 298-99).

Soul is a translation of the German word *Seele,* whose connotations are not easily rendered in English. In some contexts it has been translated as "psyche" or "mind." Consistency would betray Jung's meaning. For several years he wavered between describing the object of psychology as *Seele* and as *Psyche,* eventually settling for the latter after 1933. I refer the reader to the extended comment of R. F. C. Hull, whose conventions I am following (CW, 8:300). I find no support in Jung's writings for Mann's identification of *Seele* and *Ichbewusstsein* (1971, p. 12).

144. 51, 1920/1960, p. 184. "It is well known that the unconscious, when not realized, is ever at work casting a false glamor over everything, a false appearance: *it appears to us always on objects,* because everything unconscious is projected. Hence, when we can apprehend the unconscious as such, we strip away the false appearance from objects, and this can only promote truth" (p. 129).

145. "The ontological argument is neither argument nor proof, but merely the psychological demonstration of the fact that there is a class of men for whom a definite idea has efficacy and reality—a reality that even rivals the world of perception" (ibid., p. 41). As noted above concerning the term *religion* (n. 136 above), so too *reality* is used ambiguously by Jung. For instance, this shows up blatantly when he speaks of archaic images (and, by implication, images of God as well): "Although, as a rule, no reality-value attaches to the image, this can at times actually increase its importance for psychic life, since it then has a greater *psychological* value, representing an inner reality which often far outweighs the importance of external reality. In this case the *orientation* of the individual is concerned less with adaptation to reality than with adaptation to inner demands" (p. 442).

146. 51, 1920/1960, pp. 46, 110, 253.

147. Ibid., p. 243.

148. Ibid., p. 124; cf. pp. 38, 473. Jung's advance beyond the position assumed in "The Significance of the Father. . ." is clear. Indeed, no reference is made to this article in the whole of *Types.* A failure to acknowledge this development led one critic to accuse Jung at this time of "subjectivism" and "religious psychologism" because he had reduced religion to the status of a symptom of the Oedipus complex (Macintosh, 1940, pp. 70-73).

149. 51, 1920/1960, p. 243. It is best to read this section as an outline of Jung's own views rather than as the commentary on Eckhart that it pretends to be. As J. Clark has shown, Jung's reading of Eckhart is highly suspect. He uses isolated passages to judge the whole, and makes use of uncritical texts known to contain spurious material. For these reasons and others, Clark concludes that

modern scholarship cannot support Jung's apparent discovery of a "purely relativistic conception of God and of his relation to man" (1959). A. Vetter criticizes Jung for an imprecision in his use of the term *function*. Moreover, he finds the adoption of a mechanical term in theological discourse out of place and, in any case, quite against the spirit of what Eckhart was saying (1936, p. 224).

150. 51, 1920/1960. p. 243.

151. Ibid. In the original edition of *Types* Jung referred to the absolute God as the belief of "orthodoxy" (ibid., 1920, p. 301). In a later revision he substituted the term *metaphysics* (51, 1949/1960, p. 243).

In speaking of the primitive mentality Jung adopts Lévy-Bruhl's term *participation mystique,* which he says "consists in the fact that the subject cannot clearly distinguish himself from the object but is bound to it by a direct relationship which amounts to partial *identity*" (51, 1920/1960, p. 456; cf. pp. 244, 255).

152. 51, 1920/1960, pp. 253-55. The passages in the first three of the *Septem sermones* (40, 1916) dealing with Pleroma and Creatura show a marked resemblance to this interpretation of Eckhart's thought (cf. Heisig, 1972, pp. 209-12).

153. Cf. 51, 1920/1960, p. 376, and index under "Self." I capitalize the term in accordance with conventional usage among Jungians, even where the translator prefers the lower case.

154. Ibid., p. 265.

155. Sandy had already advanced such a theory in 1910, and seems to have been the first to do so. Note his two propositions for a modern 'Christology: (1) "that the proper seat or *locus* of all divine indwelling, or divine action upon the human soul, is the subliminal consciousness;" and (2) "That the same, or the corresponding, subliminal consciousness is the proper seat or *locus* of the Deity of the incarnate Christ" (1910, p. 159).

156. Perhaps the clearest reference is Jung's observation that the notions of "Self" in Buddhism and "God" in Christianity perform similar psychic functions (51, 1920/1960, pp. 221, 199 ff.). Again, inconsistency in terminology makes it impossible to establish Jung's views on the basis of the text alone. "Self," "subject," "Soul," and "personality" are all possible psychological equivalents of "God" in *Types*. Furthermore, the relation between anima-figures and God had not yet been resolved at this time, as Jung was to disclose some years later (59, 1925, p. 61).

Chapter 2 The Middle Years (1921-1949)

1. In fact, his practice still absorbed most of his time and effort. By his own reckoning, he had analyzed some 50,000 dreams during the first twenty-five years of practice (71, 1928, p. 10; 73, 1928, Part I, p. 18).

2. 82, 1930/1950, p. 84. Cf. 79, 1930/1931, p. 389; 81, 1930, p. 324; 112, 1935, p. iii.

3. Charles Baudouin presents an interesting portrait of Jung in his seminar lectures, based on selections from personal diaries (1963, pp. 19-37). Note also a comment made by J. L. Brunneton in 1933: "C. G. Jung is one of those intellectual phenomena, a veritable genius of work; he is aided by a power of concentration and a memory that are incomparable. He reads everything that he gets his hands on and ceaselessly returns to the sources" (1933, p. 683).

4. Ernesto Buonaiuti mentions this fact in his memoirs of the Eranos meetings (1964, p. 293). For a brief history of the beginning and development of the meetings, see Corti, 1955; and for a treatment of Jung's influence in them up to 1935, Baumann, 1935.

5. It is not surprising, therefore, to find a summary of Jung's thought, published by one of his students in 1929, that makes no reference at all to his views on religion (Corrie, 1929). More generally speaking, Jung did not take kindly to criticisms of theoretical confusion, as a letter to E. Sabott of 3 February 1933 makes clear: "And in later years I have gradually come to the conclusion that the muddle is not located in my head but in the heads of others, and that besides me there are a whole lot of people who still possess an uncontorted intelligence and can therefore think straight."

6. 60, 1925, p. 87.

7. 59, 1925, p. 24; 74, 1929, pp. 339-40; 81, 1930, p. 326. Jung was, of course, totally opposed to Freud's own critique of religion as it had appeared in *The Future of an Illusion* (cf. 74, 1929, p. 335; 91, 1932, p. 35; 102, 1934, p. 172).

8. 44, 1928, p. 204; 88, 1931/1934, pp. 340-41; 103, 1934, p. 537; 116, 1935, p. 185; 118, 1936, p. 190; 121, 1936, p. 15.

9. The "isms" of today, Jung writes, are "only a modern variant of the denominational religions. A man may be convinced in all good faith that he has no religious ideas, but. . . his very materialism, atheism, communism, socialism, liberalism, intellectualism, existentialism, or what not, testifies against his innocence" (120, 1936/1954, p. 62. Cf. 84, 1930, 1:111 and 1932, 6: 155-56).

10. 65, 1931, pp. 376-81; 116, 1935, p. 142; 129, 1937.

11. 73, 1929, Part II, p. 95; 75, 1929/1938, p. 48; 81, 1930, p. 327; 84, 1931, 3: 20; 92, 1932, pp. 335, 344; 102, 1934, p. 172; 107, 1934, pp. 25, 180; 110, 1935, p. 555; 115, 1935, p. 16; 116, 1935, p. 181. In one place Jung admits, untypically, that psychology can deal only with "the emotions and symbols which constitute the phenomenology of religion, but which do not touch upon its essential nature" (52, 1922, p. 65).

12. "My attitude to all religions is therefore a positive one. In their symbolism I recognize those figures which I have met with in the dreams and fantasies of my patients. . . . Ceremonial ritual, initiation rites, and ascetic practices, in all their forms and variations, interest me profoundly as many techniques for bringing about a proper relation to those forces (of psychic life)"

(74, 1929, p. 337. Cf. 30, 1925/ 1942, pp. 105, 107; 59, 1925, p. 127; 61, 1925, pp. 159, 161; 79, 1930/1931, p. 399; 87, 1931, p. 67: 124, 1936, 1: 202; 125, 1936, p. 79).

13. 66, 1927, p. 132; 69, 1928, p. 20; 95, 1932, p. 172. It is also worth mentioning here that frequent mention is made of the Christian missionary effort, which Jung viewed with extreme skepticism (cf. 70, 1928/1931, p. 89; 73, 1929, Part II, pp. 35, 50; 73, 1930, p. 133; 77, 1929, p. 52; 84, 1933, 9: 25-26, 38; 84, 1934, 11: 180; 109, 1934, 2: 79, 130; 117, 1935, p. 187; 124, 1937, 2: 127-28).

14. There is considerable development in Jung's views during the period under discussion, although he did not at this time assume a definite position. Because this would take us too far afield, I refer the interested reader to the following important passages: 59, 1925, p. 73; 68, 1928; 69, 1928, p. 59; 84, 1933, 9: 56; 9, 1934, 11: 133; 92, 1932, pp. 333-35, 347; 94, 1932, p. 44*; 109, 1934, 2: 174; 119, 1936, pp. 530-32, 534, 537; 124, 1936, 1: 83; letters to Frau V., 15 December 1933; to H. Oberhänsli, 16 December 1933; to W. Laiblin, 19 March 1934; and to J. Jacobi, 24 June 1935. Kiesow has studied these questions in some detail, through he did not make use of Jung's seminar notes (1962, 452). A perusal of the relevant texts makes it clear that to claim that Jung is closer to Catholicism, and Freud to Protestantism, as some have suggested (Dillistone, 1959, pp. 158-60; Schmidt, 1954, p. 702), is altogether too facile a conclusion.

15. For example, in the revision of an earlier article, Jung omits entirely one such reference to the end of the Christian age (cf. 30, 1916, p. 406 and 30, 1925, pp. 61-62).

16. 123, 1936, p. 272; 92, 1932, p. 337; 84, 1930, 1: 230; letter to R. Corti, 12 September 1929.

17. 108, 1934/1954, pp. 14-15. Cf. ibid., pp. 7-8, 22; 30, 1925, p. 81; 59, 1925, p. 110; 62, 1926, p. 336; 69, 1928, pp. 58-59; 70, 1928/1931, pp. 83-84, 87-91: 71, 1928, p. 36; 73, 1929, Part II, pp. 33-34; 81, 1930, p. 326; 84, 1930, 1: 80, 230-31; ibid., 1932, 6: 168; 101, 1934, pp. 324-25; 107, 1934, pp. 180-82; 109, 1935, 3: 65; 117, 1935, pp. 128-29; 119, 1936, p. 531; letter to M. Patzelt, 29 November 1935. This is not to say that Jung was uninformed in such disciplines. His interest in Oriental religions, for example, was strong at this time, and remained with him until his very deathbed, where he was reading Charles Luk's *C'han and Zen Teachings* and is reported to have remarked that he wished he could have said in his work what he was reading in the thought of Hsu Yun (see Smith, 1966, p. xi).

While Jung freely admitted that he was not the churchgoing sort (73, 1930, Part II, p. 41), his struggle with Christianity was nevertheless intensely personal and important to him, as he makes clear on several occasions. In one seminar talk we find these works: "My problem is to wrestle with the big monster of the historical past, the great snake of the centuries, the burden of the human mind, the problem of Christianity" (116, 1935, p. 142; cf. 67, 1927; 103, 1934). Note also his oft-cited statement: "Among all my patients in the second half of life—that is to say, over thirty-five—there has not been one whose problem in the last resort was not that of finding a religious outlook on life" (92, 1932, p. 334).

18. 44, 1928, p. 239. Elsewhere Jung refers to "certain idiots who have thought my conception of God was nothing but a human emotion" (109, 1936, 7: 12). On the basis of Jung's earlier writings, as we saw in the previous chapter, such idiocy was not altogether without its foundation (cf. 98, 1933, pp. 316-17).

19. 62, 1926, p. 328. Cf. 53, 1922, p. 97; 73, 1928, Part I, p. 207; 84, 1931, 2: 230; 108, 1934/1954, p. 22; 109, 1935, 3: 15-16; 109, 1937, 8: 74; 130, 1937/1954, p. 108.

20. 97, 1934, p. 155.

21. 75, 1929/1938, p. 54. In a revision of an earlier passage where he had referred to the problem of God's existence as "fatuous" and "absurd" (30, 1916, p. 415), Jung adjusts his phrasing and refers to the problem as merely "superfluous" (ibid., 1925/1942, p. 71). Cf. 38, 1928/1948, pp. 278-79 (only the short phrase repudiating the "metaphysical" and its accompanying footnote were added to the 1948 revision of this paragraph); 44, 1928, p. 235; 73, 1930, Part II, pp. 159-60; 84, 1931, 2: 227-28, 232; 84, 1934, 11: 157; 88, 1931/1934, pp. 351-52; 109, 1934, 1: 46, 143; 109, 1936, 7: 10, 87-88; 109, 1938, 8:2; 114, 1935/1953, p. 511.

22. Cf. 109, 1936, 7: 23; 124, 1936, 1: 83, 202; 84 1931, 2: 205. See also Jung's letters to H. Langenegger, 20 November 1930; to Pastour Damour, 15 August 1932; to F. Pfäfflin, 5 July 1935.

23. 117, 1935, p. 116.

24. 92, 1932, p. 347. Cf. 30, 1925/1942, pp. 116-17.

25. 81, 1930, p. 327. Cf. 79, 1930/1931, p. 402; 84, 1933, 8: 66; 87, 1931, pp. 67-68; 109, 1934, 1: 115. In one of his seminar talks he remarks *ad rem*: "You should not cheat people, even for their own good. I do not want to cheat people out of their mistaken faith" (116, 1935, p. 107). And in a letter to W. Laiblin, 19 March 1934, he writes: "So long as the Church does not practice restraint of conscience it can safely be kept alive for all those, the weak ones, to whom no offense should be given. . . . A renewal of religious beliefs has no form at present, so that the weak and those who are dependent on forms should not be prematurely precipitated into formlessness" (cf. also letters to F. Pfäfflin, 5 July 1935 and 30 August 1937). Again, Jung remarked in a seminar talk: "I am quite convinced that there are a number of persons who are not meant to be "I,' " and who, therefore, belong under the protection of the Church (109, 1935, 5: 70).

26. 74, 1929, p. 339.

27. 69, 1928, p. 59. Cf. 44, 1928, p. 235 n. 6; 54, 1923, pp. 16-27; 70, 1931, pp. 83-85; 75, 1929/1938, pp. 49-51; 81, 1930, pp. 324-25; 83, 1930, 1: 12; 84, 1931, 2: 205; 84, 1933, 10: 161; 108, 1934, p. 59 (the relevant passage is omitted in the 1954 revision); 109, 1934, 1: 144; 109, 1934, 2: 143; letters to Anon., 7 September 1935; to W. Uhsadel, 18 August 1936.

28. He writes in a letter at this time: "Can anyone say 'credo' when he stands *amidst* his experience. . . when he knows how superfluous 'belief' is, when he

more than just 'knows,' when the experience has even pressed him to the wall? . . . Now it is not merely my 'credo' but the greatest and most incisive experience of my life that this door, a highly inconspicuous side-door on an unsuspicious-looking and easily overlooked footpath—narrow and indistinct because only a few have set foot on it—leads to the secret of transformation and renewal" (to B. Baur-Celio, 30 January 1934). Cf. 73, 1928, Part I, p. 135; 98, 1933, p. 321; letters to J. Schattauer, 20 February 1933; to P. Maag, 20 June 1933.

29. 84, 1932, 5: 16-17. Cf. 59, 1925, p. 123; 109, 1936, 6: 75. He interprets Jacob's fight with the angel as a struggle against such inflation (84, 1934, 2: 115).

30. 44, 1928, p. 133. Here Jung is referring back to an earlier case (see chap. 1, §1 and 2, also n. 11 above), but it is impossible to determine whether this later interpretation is entirely new or was merely suppressed in his earlier account. A similar instance of a change of interpretation occurs in 120, 1936/1954, p. 62; 122, 1936, pp. 51-52. (Cf. 24, 1911-12, pp. 108-9.)

In a 1932 address to a conference of Alsatian pastors, Jung made a strong appeal in favor of the "religious function" of the psyche (92). Cf. also 74, 1929, p. 339; 75, 1929/1938, pp. 36-38; 83, 1931, 2: 28; 84, 1930, 1: 191; 104, 1934, p. 409; 117, 1935, pp. 114-15.

31. 56, 1924/1946, p. 83; 79, 1931, pp. 401-2; 88, 1934, p. 356; 95. 1932, p. 175.

32. Dated 30 April 1929; cf. 73, 1930, 2: 234.

33. 44, 1928, pp. 160, 204; 73, 1928, Part I, p. 132; 94, 1932, p. 196; 108, 1934/1954, p. 7; 116, 1935, pp. 153-54; 123, 1936, p. 212; 127, 1937, p. 328; letter to K. Plachte, 10 January 1929.

34. 64, 1927/1931, p. 155; 65, 1927/1931, pp. 369-70.

35. 64, 1927/1931, p. 156; 86, 1931, p. 45.

36. 44, 1928, p. 204; 73, 1928, Part I, p. 134.

37. "Every person who possesses even a modicum of intelligence and the necessary educational urge will, after thorough reflection on his experiences during the analytical treatment of his neurosis, hit upon trains of thought which agree in a remarkable way with the religious ideas of all times and peoples" (letter to Anon., 19 November 1932; cf. 56, 1923/1946, pp. 116-17).

38. 65, 1927/1931, p. 375; 95, 1932, p. 177; 125, 1936, p. 76.

39. 84, 1933, 8: 103. Cf. 44, 1928, p. 238; 60, 1925, p. 87; 73, 1928, 1: 210; 73, 1932, 7: 36. This is also the sense of Jung's association of "God" and "mana" (cf. 69, 1928, p. 65-66; 73, 1930, Part II, p. 163). Elsewhere he refers to the image of the Wise Old Man, "the archetype of meaning" (108, 1934/1954, p. 37) as a "personification of God" (109, 1934, 2: 207).

40. Cf. 106, 1934, p. 439; letter to K. Plachte, 10 January 1929.

41. 108, 1934/1954, pp. 13, 23-24.

42. 73, 1930, Part II, pp. 215-16.

43. 118, 1936, p. 185.

44. 120, 1936/1954, p. 59. Cf. 44, 1928, pp. 233-36; 59, 1925, p. 80; 73, 1928, Part I, pp. 132-34; 73, 1930, Part II, pp. 159-60; 75, 1929/1938, pp. 36-38, 45, 51 and 51 n.; 84, 1930, 1; 126; 84, 1931, 2: 3-4, 88, 1931/1934, pp. 351-52; 99, 1933, 1: p. 86.

45. The term *transcendent function* falls into disuse at this time, and is usually replaced by references to the process of *individuation*.

46. Jung's use of the term *Self* was multifunctional from the start and hence full of ambiguities. It remained so throughout his writings, as M. Fordham has shown (1962a, 1963; cf. Abenheimer, 1968). It suffices to mention here that, as with "God," Jung preferred to maintain silence concerning the actual nature of the "Self" *in se,* and to deal with the archetype of the Self as it expressed itself symbolically (117, 1935, pp. 198-200).

47. Literally, *mandala* is the Sanscrit word for "circle." As Jung points out, "most mandalas take the form of a flower, cross, or wheel, and show a distinct tendency towards a quaternity structure . . ." (75, 1929, p. 22). Jung first discovered the mandala in his study of Tantric Buddhism in 1918, and first made reference to it in the article just cited, which concluded with a collection of ten "European mandalas." (The third mandala in the series was painted by Jung himself, as he afterward disclosed (94, 1932, p. 116).) Three years later he showed a collection of mandalas during a lecture to the Natural Science Society of Zurich (90, 1932, p. v.). He tells us in his autobiography that he had himself drawn mandalas in 1916 without knowing what they were at the time (237, 1961, p. 334). He also claimed that as early as his study of the fifteen-year-old medium who was the subject of his doctoral dissertation he had met with the mandala figure, again unable to recognize it at the time (100, 1933, Part I, p. 42; 6, 1902, pp. 39-40).

48. 84, 1932, 2: 156.

49. 73, 1928, Part I, p. 90; 99, 1933, p. 105; 117, 1935/1944, p. 129.

50. 44, 1928, p. 238; 117, 1935, p. 136.

51. 84, 1934, 11: 95, 166-67; 109, 1936, 6: 15; 109, 1936, 7: 112; 126, 1937, pp. 10-15; letter to K. Plachte, 10 January 1929.

52. 84, 1934, 11: 39; 109, 1936, 1: 44; 109, 1936, 7: 81. At other times he seems to suggest the identity of "God" and "the unconscious," although the relevant passages are neither too clear nor too forceful (84, 1933, 9: 109; letter to A. Vetter, 8 April 1932).

53. Here we leave mandala symbolism to one side. Although Jung does refer to the fact that Christ is the center of the typical medieval Christian mandala (75, 1929/1938, p. 22; 116, 1935, p. 138), little more is made of the observation at this time, except for one place where he refers in passing to the Christian mandala as a "plain anticipation of the idea of the Self" (117, 1935, p. 192).

54. 84, 1933, 10: 16; 84, 1933, 11:124; 109, 1934, 1: 16, 117; 109, 1934, 2: 145. Jung is also reported to have made the suggestion that "Mary is really the

symbol of individuation . . . for woman as Christ is the symbol of individuation for man" (84, 1933, 10: 22). The ideal appears only once again, several years later (105, 1950, p. 333).

55. 73, 1928, 1: 96-97, 192. Cf. 84, 1932, 6: 121-22; 109, 1934, 2: 61-63; 109, 1935, 3: 13, 17; 109, 1936, 7: 29-30; 124, 1937, 2: 117.

56. 75, 1929/1938, pp. 52-54; 92, 1932, p. 340; 95, 1932, pp. 180-81. Jung also expresses his opposition to attempts to dehumanize the figure of Christ, falsifying him and draining him of his archetypal significance for modern man (73, 1930, 2: 166-67; 84, 1932, 5: 143-44; 109, 1934, 2: 77-78). In one context, reminiscent of his early writings, Jung intimates that Jesus suffered from an inflation of his conscious ego (44, 1928, p. 229).

57. 83, 1932, 2: 116; 84, 1931, 2: 86; 84, 1931, 3: 178; 84, 1931, 4: 56; 84, 1932, 5: 123: 84, 1932, 6: 113, 120-22; 84, 1933, 9: 47; 94, 1932, p. 212; 124, 1936, 1: 40-41, 87. Some connection can perhaps be supposed as well between this view of Christ and a vision Jung recounts as occurring to him in December of 1931. A figure named Salome appeared to him and he asked her, "Why do you worship me?" to which her reply was, "Because you are Christ" (59, 1925, p. 133).

58. 73, 1930, Part II, pp. 209, 214; 84, 1933, 8: 13; letter to A. Vetter, 8 April 1932.

59. 84, 1930, 1: 203; 109, 1934, 2: 75; 124, 1937, 2: 58. For a simplified account of Jung's general use of number symbolism, see Bertrand, 1955.

60. See especially his remarks on the "heretical" visions of the Swiss mystic, Brother Niklaus von der Flüe (98, 1933, pp. 320-23; 108, 1934, pp. 58-59). Jung also alludes to the mandala of Jacob Böhme, which divided the God-image into a light and a dark side (108, 1934, p. 59) and to the writings of the sixteenth-century alchemical philosopher, Gerhard Dorn (105, 1934, p. 48).

61. 69, 1928, pp. 54-55; 73, 1930, Part II, pp. 158, 161; 84, 1930, 1: 19-20, 125, 220; 84, 1931, 2: 69; 84, 1932, 7: 13, 75, 106; 84, 1934, 11: 75-76; 109, 1934, 2: 141, 170; 109, 1935, 4: 97; 109, 1936, 6: 71; 109, 1936, 7: 14, 34-35. In several of these references the theologian Friedrick Gogarten is the object of Jung's attack on the theological notion of the *summum bonum*.

Jung also draws a distinction between "perfection" (*Vollkommenheit*) and "completeness" (*Volständigkeit*) at this time, but does not yet apply it explicitly to the God-image (cf. 99, 1933, 1: 157; 116, 1935, pp. 109-10, 149; 117, 1935, p. 163; 84, 1932, 5: 129). He also states his dissatisfaction on one occasion with the scholastic definition of evil as a *privatio boni* (84, 1932, 5: 89). Both of these themes will receive fuller treatment in his later writings.

62. This is a symptom, according to Jung, of the definite masculine bias of the Christian religion as a whole (84, 1932, 5: 8; 109, 1935, 4: 69). It is worth noting that nowhere does Jung distinguish traits of *sex* (biological) from traits of *gender* (historico-cultural) in speaking of God-imagery, but seems to conflate the two in a third category, which Ulanov has called the *symbolic* (1971, pp. 140-41).

63. 75, 1929/1938, pp. 26-27; 98, 1933, p. 323; 117, 1935, pp. 156, 192-95; 120, 1934/1954, pp. 64-65. At times the anima-figure is also named as the missing feminine in the Godhead (cf. 120, 1934/1954, p. 29).

64. 64, 1927/1931, p. 156; 73, 1930, 2: 155; 109, 1937, 8: 35; 116, 1935, p. 111; 122, 1936, p. 45; 125, 1936, pp. 11, 33. In *Psychology of the Unconscious* Jung had already acknowledged the feminine qualities of the Holy Ghost in Gnostic literature, though he did not take any particular notice at the time (24, 1911-12, pp. 147-48).

65. 84, 1934, 11: 1; 109, 1937, 5: 133; 109, 1937, 8: 39; 125, 1936, p. 48.

66. 237, 1961, p. 204. Cf. 44, 1928, pp. 219-20; 69, 1928, pp. 46-47; 84, 1931, 2: 156-57; 130, 1937/1954, p. 105; letter to E. Neumann, 22 December 1935.

67. See, for example, 123, 1936, pp. 223-24, 230-37, 250-51.

68. Later, when the book was translated into German by two of Jung's disciples, he took the opportunity of revising it and making some additions to the text before its publication in 1940. Since several of the interpolations are considerable (one of them running nearly ten pages), it has been necessary to refer at times to the original edition. Where there is no significant change in the text, however, I have used the retranslation of the 1940 text, which has corrected much of the linguistic clumsiness of the original one.

69. He also makes brief mention of two other dreams in this series, as well as of two dreams of another patient. Jung had first dealt with these dreams in an article in 1935 (117), and he took them up again in two courses of seminar lectures in America, one of which followed immediately upon his deliverance of the Terry Lectures (124).

70. Jung's apologia for these excursions is explicitly stated: "Close parallels to the symbolism of dreams can be found in the old alchemical treatises. . . . The symbolic statements of the old alchemists issue from the same unconscious as modern dreams and are just as much the voice of nature" (128, 1937/1940, p. 61).

71. Jung is using here what is in fact the accepted etymology of the word *religio*. Later, however, he opted for the derivation from *religare* (= linking back) (145, 1940/1951, p. 161). Later still he returned to his original view (30, 1942, p. 101; 186, 1950, p. 429 and 429 n.; letters to E. Böhler, 14 December 1955; to G. Wittwer, 10 October 1959).

72. 128, 1937/1940, pp. 7-8; cf. p. 81. No further indication is given of how far Jung might be willing to go with Otto's analysis of the *numinosum* (neither here nor elsewhere), despite the fact that there are certain striking parallels. A long reference to the unconscious as the "*tremendum*" is made later on (ibid., 1937, p. 104), but was omitted from the 1940 revision. Two other brief references in earlier seminars to Otto's *The Idea of the Holy* indicate that Jung considered the notion of the numinous as a functional equivalent of that of *mana* (84, 1932, 7: 106-7; 1933, 10: 117).

73. 128, 1937/1940, pp. 104-5; cf. p. 65. This attitude led one reviewer of the

lectures to conclude rather hastily that Jung was encouraging us "to abandon reason and embrace superstition and blind loyalties and hates" (Josey, 1938).

74. 128, 1937/1940, p. 62.

75. Ibid., pp. 9, 32, 42.

76. Ibid., 1937, pp. 103-5; 1937/1940, pp. 21-23, 43-44, 83.

77. 128, 1937/1940, pp. 45-46; cf. p. 50.

78. Ibid., p. 45; cf. pp. 9, 77, 104-5; 1937, pp. 93-94. Note also that these lectures are full of references to the comparative merits of Protestantism and Catholicism, all in conformity with his earlier views on the basis of these same arguments. Operating on the principle that "every religion is a spontaneous expression of a certain predominant psychological condition" (p. 97), Jung makes some suggestive, if historically suspect, remarks about the psychological origins and history of Christianity (pp. 96-97 et passim).

79. 128, 1937/1940, p. 81.

80. Ibid., p. 59. This expression occurs only once; Jung seems to prefer the term *natural symbol,* also coined in these lectures. The *idea* of the God-image as an archetype is, of course, nothing new to Jung.

The same argument stands behind Jung's observation concerning the supreme authority that the unconscious seems to enjoy, its superior clarity and intelligence over against ego-consciousness, which makes it fitting that it should be experienced as the *vox Dei* (pp. 18-19, 39, 41).

81. The one significant difference here is that Jung omits any reference to Christ in this regard, except for one casual remark about the "blasphemous" nature of those products of the modern psyche which seem to indicate man's share in the homoousia of Christ (128, 1937/1940, p. 61).

82. 128, 1937/1940, p. 79; cf. pp. 37-38, 55-57; ibid., 1937, pp. 73-74.

83. 128, 1937/1940, pp. 57-58, 80.

84. Ibid., p. 82; cf. pp. 61, 72.

85. Ibid., p. 96.

86. Ibid., pp. 29-30, 61-63, 72-73.

87. Ibid., p. 61.

88. I am paraphrasing here Jaffé's eyewitness account (1970, pp. 7-8). She tells us, further, that the stenogram of the lecture proved almost ready for publication; only some supplementary material was inserted. Eight years later Jung took up the entire text and added still more material, increasing its length more than fourfold and breaking up the original line of argument in the process. In this final version he also omitted all references to Speiser's paper.

At the meeting of the previous year, 1939, Jung had similarly surprised the Eranos assembly with two spontaneous lectures on the notion of rebirth (144).

89. Jung states this explicitly in a letter to H. G. Baynes of 27 May 1941.

90. 30, 1942, pp. 101-2; 109, 1938, 9: 33-34; 10: 13; 128, 1940, pp. 86-87;

134, 1939, p. 525; 140, 1939/1955, p. 488; letter to W. Y. Evans-Wentz, 9 February 1939. In a letter to Josef Goldbrunner dated 8 February 1941, Jung rejected the former's criticism that he had "psychologized" God out of existence (1940, pp. 21-23). In a later book Goldbrunner only slightly modified his views, accusing Jung, instead, of a "positivistic, agnostic renunciation of all metaphysics," which in fact has the effect of reducing God to psychic factors (1964, pp. 160-62). Once again Jung replied, repeating his earlier criticisms of such an interpretation (letter, 14 May 1950; cf. 215, 1956-58, p. 17).

91. 136, 1939, p. 249; 139, 1939, pp. 15, 25, 28, 30; 145, 1940/1951, pp. 154, 162-63, 168-69; 150, 1941/1954, pp. 250-51; 151, 1941, pp. 97-104. Jung is reported to have said at the conclusion of the 10th International Medical Congress for Psychotherapy, held in Oxford in 1938, that the "growing tendency to insanity was due to the neglect of the religious order of life" (Gregory, 1939, p. 437). Further, in a memorial article written on the occasion of Freud's death, he attacked the latter for his ignorance of philosophy and his total misunderstanding of what religion was all about (138, 1939, p. 45).

Jung's interest in the relative merits of Protestantism and Catholicism appears much less frequently at this time. See, however: 139, 1939, pp. 5, 8, 10-11; 30, 1942, pp. 77-78.

92. 128, 1940, p. 85. Of course, Jung continues to press the point that the withdrawl of *all* projections is impossible (100, 1941, Part III, p. 67; 109, 1939, 10: 143).

93. 100, 1939, Part II, pp. 17, 127-28; 135, 1939, p. 554; 140, 1939/1958, pp. 483, 500.

94. 153, 1942, p. 79; cf. 137, 1939, p. 518. In the light of his general views on religion, we can only conclude that this phrase is to be read as a mere figure of speech. Contrast, for example, the following remarks: "I do not expect any believing Christian to pursue these thoughts of mine any further, for they will probably seem to him absurd. I am not, however, addressing myself to the happy possessors of faith, but to those many people for whom the light has gone out, the mystery has faded, and God is dead. For most of them there is no going back, and one does not know either whether going back is always the better way. To gain an understanding of religious matters, probably all that is left us today is the psychological approach" (128, 1940, p. 89. These lines were a later insertion into the original text of *Psychology and Religion*. Cf. 109, 1939, 10: 142).

Jung expresses himself similarly regarding religious rituals and icons. In one talk he remarks that our churches should not be excessively "cleaned up" and that our rituals should be closely observed, only to add soon thereafter that he himself was no longer able to attend the Mass "because I know too much about it" (139, 1939, pp. 9, 13, 15). In another lecture he is reported to have said: "True faith seems nonsense to me; the experience exists or it does not exist . . ." (100, 1941, Part III, pp. 142-43. In actual fact, this citation is misplaced in the 1960 printing of these lectures, which I am using here; it belongs to vol. 4, Lecture 9 of the original seminar notes, and hence to the year 1940, not 1941).

95. 146, 1940, pp. 31-33, 50 n. 1.

96. Ibid., pp. 33-36, 39. Here Jung is taking issue with Speiser's argument that the Christian Trinity has its origins in the Platonic formula, by insisting that he had failed to make certain essential distinctins here drawn (Speiser, 1942).

97. 146, 1940, pp. 37-38.

98. Ibid., pp. 35, 42 n.

99. Jung does not himself use this phrase, though the context and insertions in the later revision of the article seem to justify its use here (cf. ibid., 1948, pp. 180-85).

100. 146, 1940, pp. 39-43. Evans seems to me in error in his interpretation of Jung's Trinity article inasmuch as he ignores the fact that Jung is speaking not only of the development of consciousness, but also of the way in which changing God-images reflect that process (1956).

An alternative model for viewing the development of consciousness via the history of God-images was presented by Jung two years later. It shows the following stages: (1) unity of man, God, and nature (= wholly unconscious); (2) differentiation of man and nature (= of consciousness and the unconscious); (3) conflict between a good God and his evil adversary (= superiority of consciousness over the unconscious); (4) rejection of all gods as mere unconscious projections (= rational enlightenment and its consequent dismissal of the problem of good and evil); and (5) recognition of the "reality" of the gods (= of the importance of the unconscious and of the problem of good and evil) (152, 1942/1947, pp. 200-201; Cf. 150, 1941, pp. 120-21).

Jung's notion of the three "worlds" bears a striking resemblance to the "three ages of the Spirit" in Hegel's *Phenomenology of Mind* (1967, "On Revealed Religion," pp. 750-85). While Jung does not mention this fact, it is not unlikely that he had met these ideas in his brief and frustrating encounter with Hegel (167, 1946/1954, p. 170; 237, 1961, p. 61; letter to J. Rychlak, 27 April 1959). In a later book Jung will refer to Joachim of Flora's notion of the "Age of the Spirit" in such a way as to suggest comparison with the present theory (184, 1950, pp. 82-87). although it does not seem that this accounts for the original idea. The question remains moot.

Among contemporary thinkers, the notion of the three stages of God's evolution as symbolized in the trinitarian dogma appears again in the American theologian Thomas Altizer, sire of the "death-of-God" current in theological thought. In spite of his constant allusions to Hegel, it seems to me that a good deal of unacknowledged Jungian inspiration lies at the basis of his theory, and in particular of his notion of the "third age of the Spirit" (1966). (Altizer, it is to be noted, had done his doctoral research on Jung's thought.) In stating this, I mean to modify my previous position on Altizer's relation to Hegel (1970).

Finally, we should recall that it is during this period that Jung returns to his early idea of the transformation of the God of Wrath in the Old Testament to the God of Love in the New Testament (150, 1941/1954, pp. 236, 270-71).

101. 146, 1940, pp. 43-50.

102. "The ideal of completeness is, of course, the circle or sphere, but its natural

minimal division is a quaternity" (ibid., p. 52).

103. 146, 1940, p. 53. Cf. 100, 1940, Part III, p. 11. Earlier mention of this occurs in 84, 1932, 5: 89.

104. 146, 1940, p. 54. Cf. 152, 1942/1947, p. 236; 140, 1939/1958, pp. 495-96.

105. 146, 1940, pp. 50, 54-55.

106. Ibid., pp. 55-56.

107. Ibid., p. 56. Earlier allusions to the theme of Christ and Antichrist as hostile brothers appear in the seminar notes (73, 1929, Part II, p. 98; 84, 1931, 2: 69). The notion of "synchronicity" is discussed in chap. 3, § 1 above.

108. 146, 1940, p. 57. Cf. 100, 1939, Part II, pp. 190, 194; 128, 1940, pp. 59-60; 132, 1938, pp. 438-39; 143, 1940, pp. 96, 106-9; 152, 1942/1947, pp. 209-10; 148, 1941, p. 183 n. 18.

109. 146, 1940, pp. 61-62; cf. pp. 53-54, 63; 128, 1940, p. 80 n. 26. The only reference to the "missing feminine" in Jung's lecture is made with regard to the attempt of certain Gnostics to identify the Holy Ghost with the Mother of God. While the pattern Father-Mother-Son is more logical and rational, Jung rejects it, both because the Mother belongs naturally in the second (not in the third) place, and because it means a return to a primitive polytheism that ignores the meaning of the Holy Ghost as he had developed it. Behind the Gnostics' attempt to introduce the feminine into the Trinity, however, Jung sees a fundamental need for the participation of humanity in the Trinity, for whom Mary as woman and as *Mater Dei,* is the archetypal image (146, 1940, pp. 45-49).

It is indeed surprising that Jung does not take up further the problem of the feminine in God (either as *Sophia* or as related to the Devil) in connection with his quaternity theory, especially since the notion had appeared so frequently in his works since 1930. In fact, the theme is given very little attention at all during the period 1938-43 (cf. 100, 1939, Part II, p. 203; 128, 1940, p. 73 n. 16 (the last sentence does not appear in the 1937 version); 145, 1940/1951, pp. 173-74, 175-76; 152, 1942/1947, p. 229).

110. 146, 1940, p. 63.

111. Ibid., pp. 63-64; cf. pp. 44-46. The theme of relativizing meaning to personal experience (or "gnosis," as he often calls it at this time), and the concomitant critique of ecclesiastical dogmatism, is a frequent one (cf. 100, 1939, Part II, pp. 171, 196; 1940, Part III, p. 14; 128, 1940, pp. 74, 105; 133, 1938, p. 2; 135, 1939, p. 553; 139, 1939, pp. 29-30; 143, 1939, p. 17; letters to W. E. Hocking, 5 May 1939; to H. G. Baynes, 22 January 1942). Concerning the specific problem of "faith" and "experience" in Hermetic philosophy, see: 148, 1941, pp. 127-28, 157-58, 159-60, 185.

112. 100, 1939, Part II, pp. 161-63; 150, 1941/1954, pp. 207, 222-23, 267-68.

113. 100, 1941, Part III, p. 81; 148, 1941, pp. 167, 179, 189; 149, 1941, p. 110. See also his analysis of the Spirit Mercurius in fairy-tales and alchemy (152, 1942/1947, pp. 229, 237).

114. 100, 1938-40, Part II, vols. 3 and 4.

115. 100, 1939, Part II, pp. 113, 128, 189, 1940, pp. 88-89, 90; 140, 1939/1955, p. 477; 144, 1940/1950, pp. 121, 128 (the last phrase of paragraph 229 was added in 1950); 145, 1940/1951, p. 166; 150, 1941, pp. 88-89, 91; letter to A. Zarine, 3 May 1939. In a rather complicated comparison of Paracelsus with other alchemists, the same theme of the identify of Christ and Self makes a frequent appearance (148, 1941, pp. 126-27, 132, 136, 139).

As several of the above references will show, Christ is not the only possible symbol of the Self, even though it provides Jung with his most common reference-point. An attempt to develop the mythical figure of the Kore as a Self-symbol (147, 1941/1951) was later acknowledged by Jung to have been unsuccessful (see Kerényi, 1967, pp. xxvii-xxxii).

116. The seminar notes reflect this confusion. For example, in contrast to his many references to Christ as an image of the Self (see the previous note), Jung also takes "God" as the "Self-image" (143, 1940, pp. 116-17, 120-21; 100, 1939, Part II, p. 113) and yet elsewhere calls "God" the symbol of the "unconscious" (100, 1940, Part II, p. 260).

117. 1 February 1945. Cf. his letter to Eleanor Bertine, 17 April 1947, in which he attributes his illness to "the terrific conflict between practical work with patients and my creative scientific work."

118. 156, 1943, pp. 3-37.

119. Ibid., p. 7.

120. Ibid., pp. 7-8, 11 n. 6.

121. 174, 1948, pp. 290-91; letters to Anon., 6 January 1943; to V. White, 5 October 1945; to Fritz Buri, 10 December 1945. This is also called the "religious function" or "religious instinct." Jacobi (1949) has studied this latter term in Jung's work up till 1949.

122. 156, 1943, pp. 10-11; 162, 1945, pp. 211, 214-15; 166, 1945, p. 231; 146, 1948, pp. 188-89; 158, 1944/1948, pp. 296-97; 176, 1949, pp. x-xi; letter to H. Meyer, 30 January 1946. An ambiguous remark of Jung's concerning the link between the horrors of Nazism and the reappearance of the religious need is reported in an interview that took place in 1945 (164, p. 3). It is hard to interpret the passage by itself; in fact a letter of Jung's (to H. Ullmann, 25 May 1945), which criticizes the interviewer for poor reporting, gives us sufficient reason to ignore it altogether.

123. There is some occasional ambiguity in Jung's writings concerning the term *imago Dei,* which he uses both for the God-archetype as such and for a particular archetypal symbol (cf. his letter to M. Frischknecht, 8 February 1946, and 165, 1945/1947, p. 246).

124. 156, 1943, p. 17. Cf., p. 14; 50, 1948, p. 318 n. 15; 146, 1948, pp. 180, 163 n. 16, 183 n. 4, 199-200; 168, 1947; 172, 1948, pp. 7-8; 174, 1948/1950, pp. 34-35; letters to H. Irminger, 22 September 1944; to M. Frischknecht, 7 April 1945 and 17 July 1945; to V. White, 5 October 1945.

125. 156, 1943, p. 17; cf. p. 13, also 166, 1945, pp. 193, 196; 176, 1949, p. xii; letters to V. White, 5 October 1945 and 13 April 1946; to H. Wegmann, 20 November 1945.

Jung's "comparative method" of relating unconscious phenomena to mythological and religious themes is the basis of his claim to empiricism (cf. 154, 1943, p. 574; 175, 1948; 177, 1949). For a survey of the community of scholars whom Jung held to be part of this interdisciplinary venture, see his unpublished lecture of 1948 (170).

126. 146, 1948, p. 199.

127. 165, 1945/1947, pp. 211-12, 252.

128. "Cases are not unknown where the rigorous exercises and proselytizing of the Catholics, and a certain type of Protestant education that is always sniffing out sin, have brought about psychic damage that leads not to the Kingdom of Heaven but to the consulting room of the doctor" (156, 1943, p. 20; cf. 155, 1943, p. 135; 165, 1945/1947, p. 254; 166, 1945, pp. 193-97; 167, 1946/1954, p. 221; 174, 1948/1950, p. 294. Allusions to the relative psychological value of Catholicism and Protestantism can be found in: 146, 1948, p. 192; 166, 1945, p. 194; letters to H. Wegmann, 19 December 1943 and 6 December 1945; to H. Irminger, 22 September 1944; to P. Métraux, 23 May 1945.

129. 156, 1943, p. 15, Cf. pp. 12, 13, 16, 27, 29, 33; 176, 1949, p. ix; 165, 1945/1947, pp. 212-14; 167, 1946/1954, p. 205. Jung continues to oppose the adoption of oriental philosophies and religions by Western man as a solution to his spiritual crisis (154, 1943, pp. 568, 571; 180, 1949, p. 9; letters to H. Berger, 12 July 1947; to V. White, 31 December 1949.

130. 156, 1943, pp. 12, 14, 25, 32, 35; 174, 1948/1950, p. 33; 166, 1945, p. 172; letter to P. W. Martin, 20 August 1945. Note also the following comment from a letter to Max Frischknecht dated 17 July 1945: "The theologian today must *know* a bit more about the human soul if he wants to address it. I once told Archbishop Temple (William Temple, Archbishop of Canterbury): 'Send me an intelligent young theologian. I will lead him into the night of the soul so that one of them at least may know what he is actually dealing with.' But nobody came. Naturally they knew it all already, and much better. That is why the light has gone out."

131. 156, 1943, p. 34. Commenting on this theme, which was the subject of *Psychology and Alchemy,* Jung later remarked in his autobiography: "Thus I had at least reached the ground which underlay my own experiences of the years 1913 to 1917; for the process through which I had passed at that time corresponded to the process of alchemical transformation discussed in that book" (237, 1961, p. 209).

132. According to a letter to Victor White, dated 6 November 1946, it was late in that year that Jung first set down to the work of revision. In introducing his revision of the lecture, Jung admits that he is still bothered by "the uncomfortable feeling that there is much in my exposition that still needs improvement" (156, 1943, p. 111).

133. 156, 1943, pp. 112-17, 119-27. Jung's argument on the *Timaeus* is an unusual one and raises a number of problems that cannot be dealt with here. In any case, it is hardly any more necessary to his basic position than is his concluding comment on the psychological link between Plato's triadic, wholly masculine God-image and his lifelong bachelorhood!

134. 156, 1943, pp. 138-47.

135. Ibid., pp. 150-51, 160, 183, 194. Cf. 166, 1945, p. 214.

136. 146, 1948, pp. 152-53. Jung cites D. F. Strauss as an example of the "enlightened" view of dogma that he rejects.

137. 146, 1948, pp. 193-94.

138. Ibid., p. 183.

139. Ibid., p. 185. The same basic idea lies behind Jung's revision of his 1909 article, "The Significance of the Father in the Destiny of the Individual." While in 1926 he had remarked that "there is nothing in it that is actually wrong—merely too simple, too naive" (63, p. 301), by 1948 his view had altered too radically to permit a third edition to appear uncorrected. Hence the earlier Freudian passage (see above, nn. 3 and 4 of chap. 1) is completely deleted and supplanted with later and more mature ideas on the archetypal origins of religious belief (30, 1948, pp. 319-31; cf. also 56, 1946, pp. 85-86).

Note also the reference to the "Wise Old Man," the father-image, as an *imago Dei* (165, 1945/1947, pp. 215-16, 225).

140. Cf. 156, 1943, pp. 19, 26-27, 96, 124, 193, 205, 323; 165, 1945/1947, p. 234; 166, 1945, pp. 207-8, 318-19, 323; 167, 1946/1954, p. 199; 174, 1948/1950, pp. 31-32.

141. These notions, present in essence in previous writings, get more attention at this time. Cf. 146, 1948, pp. 168-70, 195-97; 156, 1943, pp. 20-21, 25, 31, 371, 464; 157, 1944, p. 584; 163, 1945, p. 79; 165, 1946/1947, pp. 213, 248; 166, 1945, pp. 192, 315; 178, 1949, p. 18; also letters to A. Kesser, 18 June 1949; to V. White, 31 December 1949.

142. Letter to H. Wegmann, 19 December 1943.

143. Jung's interest in the parallel was supported by a vision he had sometime around 1939 of a greenish-gold Christ, which he later associated with the alchemists' search for the *aurum non vulgi*—the central symbol of the art (237, 1961, pp. 210-11).

144. 146, 1948, pp. 153-54.

145. Ibid., p. 156. This same psychological insight, according to Jung, was implicit in alchemical thought, through it never reached the light of consciousness (156, 1943, pp. 354-55).

As Jung further notes, theology might want to reverse the insight and take the Self as an allegory of Christ—a step forbidden to the psychologist (156, 1943, pp. 18-19). Among those who have taken up the suggestion, Zacharias's study is the most ambitious (1954), although Jung was highly critical of it (letter to W. Lachat, 29 June 1955). In general, however, Jung stands opposed to those who would accent the historicity of Christ at the expense of his symbolic meaning (cf. 156, 1943, p. 185. The pertinent passage is an interpolation in the later revision.).

146. 146, 1948, pp. 156-57. Cf. 166, 1945, p. 262.

147. 156, 1943, p. 19. As this statement implies, there are a number of possible Self images from a number of different religious traditions (pp. 17-18; 174, 1948/1950, p. 30). In alchemy as well "sulphur" appears as such an image of totality (173, 1948/1954, pp. 120-23) and is therefore often compared explicitly with Christ.

148. 146, 1948, p. 190; 156, 1943, p. 19. In the last half of an Eranos lecture entitled "Über das Selbst," Jung repeats and summarizes his position on the Christ-archetype. It concludes with two quaternity structures. In the first the opposites are polarized as Unitemporal vs. Eternal and Unique vs. Universal; and in the second as Good vs. Evil and Spiritual vs. Chthonic. The former describes how Christ, as a union of the opposites (historical man and transcendent God) is a fitting symbol for the Self, which is both individual and archetypal. The latter includes the Antichrist and, as the text implies, represents a compensation for the completely good and "light" view of the Self given in the former (174, 1948, pp. 304-15. The editors of the *Collected Works* neglected to point out that this material formed the basis of chapter 5 of vol. 9, no. 2. I have cited the original, however, because of the frequent revisions incorporated in the final version, especially regarding the question of evil as *privatio boni.*). Elsewhere Jung characterizes the mythical and alchemical figure of Mercurius as a symbolic counterpart of Christ, i.e., as the "shadow side" of the Self (152, 1947, pp. 235-36, 241-42, 244-47).

149. 146, 1948, pp. 156, 160, 194; 157, 1944, pp. 580-81; 174, 1948/1950, p. 31; letters to A. Jaffé, 3 September 1943; to H. Irminger, 22 September 1944; to G. Frei, 13 January 1948.

150. Edinger suggests a somewhat similar interpretation of the difference between the "3" and the "4" in Jung's theory (1964).

151. 166, 1945, p. 200. See also Edinger, 1966, where the notion of Christ as a paradigm of the individuating ego is developed. My only complaint against his analysis is the identification of God the Father with the Self. This is justifiable only in terms of Jung's occasional use of the term "Self" to refer to an unconscious archetype; but in no sense can the Father be an image for the actual goal of individuation, which involves consciousness.

152. 146, 1948, p. 132; 156, 1943, p. 22.

153. 146, 1948, pp. 161-62; 156, 1943, pp. 23-24. Jung also makes a passing reference to the *Mundus Symbolicus* of Philippus Picinelli (1687), in which Mary is depicted as the taming influence who helped to transform the Old Testament God of Fear into he New Testament God of Love (146, 1948, p. 443). No reference is made to the notion of the quaternity.

154. 156, 1943, pp. 19, 22, 464-65; 166, 1945, p. 308.

155. 146, 1948, p. 171 n. 13. Later Jung expressly refers to Mary as a "goddess" and adds that her "divinity" may also be deduced as a *"conclusio probabilis"* of Christian doctrine (p. 171 and 171 n. 15).

156. 146, 1948, pp. 170-72. In the course of an earlier seminar lecture, Jung took a contrary position, arguing that it was impossible for the Catholic Church to acknowledge Mary as a goddess inasmuch as this would entail the introduction of imperfection into the Godhead (109, 1937, 8: 39-41).

Chapter 3 The Late Years (1950-1961)

1. Whereas the 1909 essay, "The Significance of the Father in the Destiny of the Individual" was cited several times in the original version, the 1950 revision omits all reference to it, even in the form of its 1948 edition (see above, n. 139 of chap. 2)

2. Exceptions to this lie in Jung's continued insistence on the therapeutic value of religion (188, 1951, pp. 21, 117; 199, 1953, pp. 301, 347 (Jung completed this manuscript in 1953, according to a letter of his to J. Kirsch, dated 29 January 1953)); on the archetypal origins of religious myths (195, 1952, pp. 300-301); and on the role of psychology in providing a link to the unconscious for those who find themselves estranged from existing forms of religion (188, 1951, pp. 122-23; 194, 1952, p. 472). References to *Aion* and *Answer to Job* are omitted here.

3. 105, 1950, pp. 324-25, 337, 354; 181, 1950, pp. 357, 382 et passim; 193, 1952/1955, pp. 456-57; 199, 1953, pp. 262-63, 281, 282, 332, 336-37; letter to Adolf Keller, 26 March 1951.

4. 105, 1950, p. 330; 191, 1951, pp. 312-14.

5. 181, 1950, p. 367; 199, 1953, pp. 283, 335-36; letter to W. Niederer, 26 March 1951.

6. 184, 1950, p. x; 239, n.d., p. 68. It is possible that Jung had begun working on *Aion* as early as 1946 (see his letter to V. White, 13 February 1946).

7. Although a small portion of the material had appeared in 1948 (171, 174) and has already been mentioned in the previous chapter, I shall refer frequently to it again here, since the overall context and the revision of that material make it preferable to treat *Aion* as a whole. Unaltered passages are indicated, as elsewhere, by the dating.

8. 184, 1948/1950, pp. 36-37; ibid., 1950, pp. 67, 176.

9. 184, 1950, pp. 67-68, 194-95 n. 32, 198.

10. Buber, 1953a. Oddly, Buber cites only Jung's *Septem Sermones ad Mortuos* in support of his claims.

11. 194, 1952, pp. 470-71; cf. pp. 467-68.

12. Buber, 1953a, p. 175. Jung remarked later in a letter to Eric Neumann (30 January 1954): "That Buber has a bad conscience is evident from the fact that he copies his own letter and doesn't grant me any fair representation, since I'm a pure Gnostic. . . ."

13. Cf. 195, 1952, pp. 303, 309; 199, 1953, pp. 300, 345-46; letters to H. Haberlandt, 23 April 1952; to L. Stehli, 31 October 1952; to W. Niederer, 1 October 1953.

In the course of his reply to Buber, Jung makes a curious exception to this principle and engages in the "poetics" of transcendent speculation, writing: "God has, it is true, made an image of himself, without man's assistance, that is at once inconceivably sublime and mysteriously contradictory. This image he has placed in man's unconscious as an archetype, an *archetypon phos,* not in order that theologians of all times and places might come to blows, but in order that without pretensions and in the stillness of his soul man might catch a glimpse of an image related to him and built out of the stuff of his own spirit, an image which contains everything that he will ever imagine concerning his gods or the ground of his soul. This archetype, whose presence is verified not only in human history but also in the psychic experience of individual man, is wholly sufficient for me" (194, 1952, p. 471).

14. 184, 1950, pp. 176-77.

15. Ibid., p. 178; cf. pp. 169, 178 n. 5; 105, 1950, p. 350.

16. 184, 1950, p. 182; cf. pp. 67, 189.

17. Ibid., pp. 182, 183. See also Jung's comments on his intentions in *Aion* as given in his autobiography (237, 1961, pp. 211-12, 220-21).

18. 184, 1950, p. 269.

19. Ibid., 1948/1950, pp. 31-32; 184, 1950, pp. 134-35, 190, 204, 219, 224, 233-34, 241.

20. Ibid., pp. 37-40.

21. In a letter to Upton Sinclair commenting on his book *A Personal Jesus,* Jung wrote: "What we call Jesus Christ is—I am afraid—much less a biographical problem than a social, i.e. collective, phenomenon, created by the coincidence of an ill-defined yet remarkable personality, with a highly popular *zeitgeist,* that has its own no less remarkable psychology" (196, 3 November 1952, p. 19; cf. 184, 1950, pp. 68, 178-79; letters to Anon., 17 March 1951; to A. Keller, 20 March 1951; to Anon., 30 August 1951; to Upton Sinclair, 24 November 1952; to W. Bremi, 11 December 1953).

Jung goes on to assert that the loss of the image of the personal Jesus of history represents an advance of consciousness: "Objections have always been made to this dissolution of Christ's personality, but what has not been realized is that it represents at the same time an assimilation and integration of Christ into the human psyche. The result is seen in the growth of the human personality and in the development of consciousness" (184, 1950, p. 221).

22. To be precise, we should note that in an earlier seminar Jung had alluded to the relation between the astrological symbolism of the Pisces and the Christ-Antichrist opposition (84, 1932, 4: 49-50). Brief reference also occurs, later, in his article on the Trinity (146, 1940, p. 174). But *Aion* is the first extensive treatment of the theme.

23. 184, 1950, pp. 89-90.

24. Ibid., pp. 111, 114.

25. 184, 1948/1950, p. 43. In presenting his analysis, Jung draws on a number of different traditions from the Middle Ages onward, all of which had made use of astrological theory to describe the course of Christianity's evolution (ibid., 1950, pp. 71-102).

26. Ibid., 184, 1948/1950 p. 87; cf. p. 94 n. 84.

27. Note, for example, the apparently post-Christian adaptation of the pictoral representation of the two fishes swimming in opposite directions—symbolizing Christ and the Antichrist—in place of the usual astrological imagery, which puts the two fishes at right angles to one another (ibid., pp. 91-92).

28. Ibid., pp. 85, 92-93, 149-50, 184, 258.

29. The earliest reference I have been able to trace occurs in a comment made in a 1928 seminar: "Synchronicity is the prejudice of the East, causality of the West" (71, p. 29). While the report is a particularly poor one, it is unlikely that the secretary had invented the word. As Jung says (193, 1952/1955, p. 452 n. 59), he first used the word in print in 1930 (80, p. 56). Later the word appears on occasion in the seminar notes (e.g., 84, 1933, 9: 168) and in his published work (e.g., 146, 1940, p. 56), though never with sufficient explanation. It is little wonder, therefore, that the translator of Jung's 1936 lecture on the notion of redemption in alchemy erred in rendering "durch ein 'synchronistisches' Geschehen" (123, 1936, p. 51) as "by a certain 'synchronism' of events" (ibid., p. 233).

30. 189, 1959; 193, 1952. Cf. Jung's lengthy letter on the subject to J. R. Smythies, 29 February 1952.

31. 193, 1952/1955, p. 441.

32. 105, 1950, p. 344 and 344 n. 168; 182, 1950, p. 11. Jung used the principle of synchronicity in his 1950 commentary on the *I Ching* (185), despite his earlier hesitation expressed in a letter to Wilfred Lay, dated 20 April 1946: "I once had the immodest and rather foolish fantasy of writing a commentary on the *I Ching*, but I soon recognized the enormity of such a task and the absolute inadequacy of my equipment." His only previous remarks on the book appeared in 1930 (80, pp. 54-59), though by his own admission he had begun consulting the oracle already in 1923 (237, 1961, p. 373).

As testimony to his own growing interest in parapsychology in general, Jung wrote a lengthy report of his personal experiences in a "haunted house" in England (183, 1950).

33. 193, 1952/1955, pp. 440, 481, 490-93. The application of the principle in

this regard becomes explicit only in Jung's later work, as we shall see farther on in this chapter. In any case, the claim that the principle of synchronicity represents an excursion into theological metaphysics quite misses the point of Jung's intentions (Cox, 1959, p. 11).

34. 184, 1950, pp. 69-70, 110-11. See also the motto at the beginning of the book and Jung's explanation of it (p. 64).

35. Ibid., pp. 40-41, 61, 62 n. 75, 68-69.

36. Ibid., pp. 72-73. The source for this idea, Jung claims, is to be found both in Middle and Near Eastern myths and in astrological theory (p. 74). Symbolically, the fish, the *lapis philosophorum,* and Christ are all related to the hermetic drive for a return to a primitive *imago Dei,* i.e., to the Self (pp. 126 ff., 134-40).

37. 184, 1950, pp. 41, 57-58, 110, 147, 230. "The splitting of the Messiah into two is an expression of an inner disquiet with regard to the character of Yahweh" (p. 108; cf. pp. 58-60 for examples of this in Jewish literature).

38. Ibid., pp. 40, 42-44, 145, 148-49; letter to V. White, 24 November 1953.

39. 184, 1950, p. 87; cf. pp. 27, 224-25, 267-68; 1948/1950, p. 22.

40. Ibid., pp. 41, 45-53.

41. Ibid., p. 110, Hence Jung refers favorably to Gnostic doctrines of God as the author of good and evil alike (pp. 54-56).

42. ". . . We do not know what good and evil are in themselves. It must therefore be supposed that they spring from a need of human consciousness and that for this reason they lose their validity outside the human sphere. That is to say, a hypostasis of good and evil as metaphysical entities is inadmissible because it would deprive these terms of meaning. If we call everything that God does or allows 'good,' then evil is good too, and 'good' becomes meaningless. But suffering, whether it be Christ's passion or the suffering of the world, remains the same as before. Stupidity, sin, sickness, old age, and death continue to form the dark foil that sets off the joyful splendor of life" (ibid., p. 267; cf. pp. 47, 53, 54, 61.

43. Ibid., pp. 28-29. This is the sense in which Jung's characterization of the "shadow" or "absolute evil" is to be taken (p. 10).

44. Ibid., pp. 52, 54. All of the basic arguments that Jung brought to bear against the *privatio boni* theory reappear in his correspondence with Victor White after 1949 (cf. letters dated 9-14 April 1952, 30 April 1952, 30 June 1952). In *Aion* as well, Jung resists White's accusation that he had slipped into a Manichaean world-view by insisting on the reality of evil (184, 1950, p. 61 n. 74. The reference is to White, 603; cf. also p. 610). During one of his several prolonged visits to Bollingen—17 to 27 July 1952—White discussed the matter at length with Jung and the two even consulted the *I Ching* concerning their disagreement (cf. Jung's postcard to White, 7 August 1952). The results of the debate were, however, "unsatisfying" (cf. letter to B. Roff, 19 November 1952) and, as later events were to show, estranging.

In his foreword to a collection of essays by White on archetypal psychology and theology, Jung also alludes to this problem of the *privatio boni* (195, 1952, pp. 304-06) and observes further that he can find no "archetypal basis" for the theory, despite the fact that in one of his letters to White (dated 9-14 April 1952) he admits to such a basis in the archetype of the Absolute Being who is a *summum bonum*.

45. 184, 1950, pp. 194, 195.

46. Jung incorrectly refers to this as "the traditional Christian view" (ibid., p. 192).

47. Jung's researches into Gnostic symbols of the Self in *Aion* operate from the same framework as his study of astrological parallels to the Christian era. However, inasmuch as he finds in Gnosticism a sort of telescoping or prefiguration of later developments within Christianity, his interest in historical questions slackens in the last third of the book and he turns to an examination of the more timeless and unconscious symbols of wholeness.

48. 184, 1950, p. 109; cf. pp. 23, 198; 184, 1948/1950, pp. 18-19. In a letter to a theological critic Jung writes: "I am completely of your opinion that a man only lives, and lives ever completely, if he is related to God, who stands over against him and defines him" (to D. Hoch, 28 May 1952).

49. Letter to Anon., 17 March 1951.

50. According to Eleanor Bertine, Jung kept the manuscript locked in his desk for a long time, uncertain what to do with it (1960, p. 32).

51. Letter dated 17 July 1951. For some reason, this particular letter does not appear in his published correspondence, but is cited by Jaffé (1970, p. 108).

52. Letter to J. Amstutz, 28 March 1953. Cf. letter to E. Evans, 17 February 1954. R. F. C. Hull comments: "You should see the manuscript of *Antwort auf Hiob;* the thing poured out of him, the writing contains hardly any corrections and the printed text is almost identical. Pages of foolscap were obviously written in a torrential rush, and, most amazing of all, this book. . . was released under the pressure of illness and written in about ten days, when he had a high fever" (from a personal letter dated 27 September 1971). See also Jung's letters to A. Jaffé, 29 May 1951; to Anon., 30 August 1951.

53. Prior to this, Jung had sent copies of the manuscript to a number of colleagues; the theologians among them were, in Jung's words, "shocked," while "many young people were positively impressed" (letter to W. Uhsadel, 6 February 1952).

54. Wildberger, 1954, p. 443.

55. Michaëlis, 1954, p. 372.

56. Watkin, 1955, p. 239.

57. Van den Bergh, 1953, pp. 34, 36. Jung replied to these criticisms in a letter to Van den Bergh dated 13 February 1954.

58. White, 1956, pp. 207, 208. Oddly enough, this comment, made in 1956, contrasts sharply with White's first reaction communicated to Jung in a letter on 5 April 1952: "(*Job*) is the most exciting and moving book I have read in

years: and somehow it arouses tremendous bonds of sympathy between us. . ." (Jung had sent him a copy of the book with the inscription *Inter antiquissima novum*). See also Jung's letter to White, 2 April 1955.

59. Typical of the comments appearing in his correspondence at this time are the following: "It is really not easy to talk with theologians: they don't listen to the other person (who is wrong from the start) but only to themselves (and call this the Word of God)" "The book has let loose an avalanche of prejudices, misunderstandings and above all frightful stupidities" (to H. Corbin, 4 May 1953). See also his letter to W. Bernet, whose book, with its appendix on *Job,* Jung criticizes severely (13 June 1955).

Acting on the advice of his publishers, Jung had the English translation appear first in England, apparently fearful of pressure from the U. S. Committee investigating "unamerican activities" (cf. letters to J. B. Priestly, 8 November 1954; to U. Sinclair, 25 February 1955).

60. 210, 1955, p. 358.

61. "I would have liked to avoid sarcasm and ridicule, but I could not, since I felt that way. If I had not spoken so, it would have been concealed therein, which is worse still. . . . Of course, sarcasm is not a nice quality, but I was compelled to make use also of means one would have preferred to leave aside, in order to be able to free myself from the Father. . . . Sarcasm is the means one adopts to hide from himself feelings that have been stirred up. So you can see how much the understanding of God has offended me and how much I would have preferred to remain as a child under fatherly protection and to have avoided the problem of the opposites" (from a letter to H. Schär, 16 November 1951).

It is interesting to recall here Karl Barth's little-known comment on the book. He found it, he said, a "humanly very gripping document, exceedingly instructive as to the psychology of the professional psychologists. As a contribution to the interpretation of the biblical Job, however, and above all of the Bible, it suffers hopelessly from the fact that the author, according to his own interpretation, has given the Word over unabashedly and recklessly to his very remarkable affect, which inhibited him from reading and pondering what lay before him in a state of calm. In this sense, his work has become completely unprofitable" (cited by Thurneysen, 1963, p. 164).

62. In saying this, I do not mean to agree with those who ignore the naiveté in matters of theology and Christian dogmatics, which Jung was careful to confess —e.g., with someone who could write that *Job* "could conceivably be the very first time that the whole of the Old Testament was illuminated and made comprehensible to a scientific mind" (McLeish, 1961, p. 315).

63. It would be unnecessary to repeat these ideas—stated continually throughout Jung's letters, writings, and lectures for more than thirty years—were it not for the fact that so many able critics of the book seem to have overlooked them altogether. Dry, for instance, writes that "In *Answer to Job* the biblical accounts of God in his dealings with man are interpreted not as though *man's ideas* of

God had undergone a process of moral development, but as though the conception were that the process of development has occurred within the nature of God himself" (1961, p. 203). Bernet makes the equally strange claim that here for the first time Jung has identified the Self and God ontically: "Insofar as Jung thereby goes beyond his original definition of the God-concept to say something of an objective, metaphysical God, he has unhappily overstepped his bounds" (1955, pp. 190-91). Mann concurs, calling the book a "psychotheological study" and a clear digression into metaphysics (1965, p. 190). Michaëlis errs similarly in attributing Jung's comments about the biblical image of Yahweh to God rather than to the God-image (1953, p. 194).

Jung's letters at this time give ample expression to the frustration he felt at being so misunderstood on this point. See his letters to E. Neumann, 5 January 1952; to F. Buri, 5 May 1952 (in reply to the latter's criticisms, 1952); to D. Hoch, 28 May 1952 and 3 July 1952. See also the letters to M. L. Ainsworth, 23 December 1959; to J. Rudin, 30 April 1960; to H. Kiener, 1 June 1956.

64. 190, 1951, pp. 360, 464. This distinction is obviously offered as a substitute for the earlier distinction of *Psychology of the Unconscious* between "literal" and "psychological" truth, which was since abandoned and eventually omitted from the 1950 revision of the book.

65. 190, 1951, pp. 360-61, 363.

66. Ibid., pp. 403, 452, 454, 463-64, 468-70. Jung claimed later that he wrote the book for the "unbelieving" (letter to B. Martin, 7 December 1954).

67. 190, 1951, p. 409; cf. pp. 400, 406-9, 440-41, 446; letters to D. Hoch, 3 July 1952, 23 September 1952 and 30 April 1953.

68. The phrase is Michel Fordham's (1955, p. 273).

69. If we study Jung's allusions to Job in his earlier work we find the same thing stated clearly on several occasions. The first such passage occurs in *Psychology of the Unconscious* (24, 1911-12, pp. 70-71), and was modified considerably in the later revision (186, 1950, pp 54-57), which leads one to suspect that this may have directly prompted Jung to choose the Book of Job as his *point de départ*. The theme appears later in the seminar lectures (84, 1932, 7:106; 1933, 9: 35; 109, 1935, 5:114; 1936, 7:24; 1937, 8:13), and in several places in his recent published writings (cf. 17, 1948, p. 321; 146, 1948, p. 169; 184, 1950, pp. 42, 58). A letter to Pastor Wegmann of 6 December 1945 defends Job against Yahweh in a manner similar to that of *Answer to Job*.

70. 190, 1951, pp. 365-66.

71. The quote comes from 2 Samuel 1:26. In the original German edition, Jung had erroneously cited its source as 2 Kings. After a critic had called his attention to the mistake (Anon., 1952, p. 23), it was emended in later editions (cf. also Jung's letter to E. Neumann, 5 January 1952). Jung wrote later that the quotation was meant as an apology to those whom he might shock, though this seems to have been more an afterthought (letter to B. Martin, 7 December 1954).

72. As we have already seen from the previous chapter, Jung takes Satan, the

Devil, Lucifer, and the Antichrist as psychologically identical. The same is true in *Job,* where no importance is given to distinctions between Scripture and legend, nor even to the internal exegetical evidence of the Bible itself.

73. 190, 1951, pp. 380, 390-91.

74. Ibid., p. 378.

75. Ibid., p. 372.

76. Ibid., pp. 367-86, 415, 419-29, 430. Naturally, Jung's opposition to the notion of the *privatio boni* continues here (pp. 357-58, 383).

77. Ibid., pp. 376-77, 381, 384-85; letters to P. Billeter, 3 May 1952; to E. Metzger, 7 January 1953; to J. Rudin, 14 March 1953.

78. Jung dates the Book of Job between the seventh and fourth centuries B. C., and Proverbs—where the idea of Sophia as the personfication of the *Sapientia Dei* first arises—between the fourth and third centuries. Modern scholarship would date them even closer together.

   Corbin (1953) has shown the sense in which the role of Sophia in *Job* can be viewed as the key to Jung's whole enterprise. His essay, the most intelligent favorable response to the book that I know, also goes into considerable detail to relate the themes of Job to hermetic philosophy. Jung himself accepted the article with the highest of praise (see his letter to Corbin, 4 May 1953).

79. 190, 1951, p. 391.

80. Ibid., pp. 386-97.

81. Ibid., pp. 375-76.

82. Ibid., p. 405; cf. p. 418; letter to E. Neumann, 5 January 1952.

83. 190, 1951, p. 399.

84. Ibid., pp. 432-33.

85. Ibid., p. 434. In contradiction to then current exegetical opinion, Jung held that the psychological evidence pointed to the identity of the author of the Apocalypse and of the Epistles of John, and that the Apocalypse was based on a series of visions had by its author.

86. "The purpose of the apocalyptic visions is not to tell John, as an ordinary human being, how much shadow he hides beneath his human nature, but to open the seer's eyes to the immensity of God, for he who loves God will know God. . . . Like Job, he saw the fierce and terrible side of Yahweh. For this reason he felt his gospel of love to be onesided, and he supplemented it with the gospel of fear: *God can be loved but must be feared*" (Ibid., p. 450).

87. 190, 1951, pp. 436-37. In a letter to E. Evans of 17 February 1954, Jung resists the criticism that his image of the scriptural Christ is identical with the all-light, dogmatic, and traditional Christ.

88. Ibid., p. 470. The term *Christification* occurs only this once in *Job.* and only one other place in Jung's work, to my knowledge, namely, in a rather ambiguous reference to the conversion of St. Paul (30, 1916, p. 384). The idea

that it represents, however, is present in his work ever since the 1940 lecture on the Trinity.

89. Ibid., p. 456. Cf. pp. 412-17, 431-32, 455, 460, 467; letter to J. Amstutz, 28 March 1953. This idea, the key to the entire second half of *Job,* was extremely important to Jung, and he was therefore unhappy with those who got stuck in the first half of the book, missing its climax (see his letter to A. Jaffé, 18 July 1951).

90. 190, 1951, p. 456.

91. Ibid., pp. 413, 416-17, 461.

92. Ibid., pp. 462-66. Jung had already expressed the same thing in a letter to V. White dated 25 November 1950 (see also his letters to Anon., 17 March 1951; to A. Keller, 20 March 1951; and to D. Hoch, 28 May 1952) together with other initial reactions to the proclamation of the dogma.

93. 190, 1951, pp. 398, 461-69; cf. 191, 1951, p. x.

94. 190, 1951, p. 444.

95. In August of 1955 he wrote to M. Bancroft: "My name enjoys an almost independent existence on its own. My true self is chopping wood in Bollingen and cooking meals, trying to forget the plagues of an eightieth birthday." Cf. his letter to G. Schmaltz, 30 May 1937. For an interesting personal account of Jung's last years, see Jaffé, 1971.

96. A letter to V. White of 9 April 1952 indicates that he had completed the work in 1952; yet it seems that he continued to work on the manuscript for some time thereafter, finishing it only in 1954, in his eightieth year (see the editorial note to vol. 14 of the *Collected Works*).

97. In fairness to Jung, it should be noted that this title, chosen by his American publishers for the original *Gegenwart and Zukunft,* did not particularly please him. As he wrote in a letter to H. E. Bowman on 18 July 1958: "It was not my idea, since the Self is not really discovered but only ignored or misunderstood."

98. Despite his professed "love" for the Gnostics, Jung rejected the assertion that his work smacked of Gnosticism merely because he had found their writings of great psychological interest. Cf. his letter to D. Cox, 25 September 1957 (215, pp. 237-39); 208, 1955, p. 7; letters to E. Neumann, 30 January 1954; to M. Oakes, 11 February 1956.

Again and again in *Mysterium Conjectionis* Jung repeats his denial of metaphysical interests (203, 1954, pp. 208, 325-26, 390, 454-55, 547-53; cf. also 214, 1956, pp. 293-94; 215, 1956-58, p. 248; letters to R. Corti, 2 May 1955; to Anon., 17 August 1957; to C. E. Scanlan, 5 November 1959).

Perhaps the best summary of his late remarks on the above topics is to be found in those letters dealing with his earlier debate with Martin Buber (to B. Lang, 8 and 14 June, 1957; to R. C. Smith, 29 June 1960).

99. In a letter replying to E. Thornton's claim that "one would have thought that the theologians would have acquiesced in the fact that there now exists something in

the nature of an experimentally proven natural theology [namely, Jung's psychology]" (1965, p. 138), Jung rejected any such assertion for his own work, insisting that it can deal only with man's *image* of God (220, 1958, p. 142; cf. also 215, 1956-58, pp. 2, 221; letters to J. Amstutz, 23 May 1955; to Walter Bernet, 13 June 1955; to P. A. Hilty, 25 October 1955; to Anon., 2 January 1957; to V. Brooke, 16 November 1959).

At times he reveals a still deeper rejection of talk about the transcendent God as it occurs in theological discourse: "I know much less about God, since everything that can be said about the highest Unknown is in my eyes arrogant anthropomorphism" (letter to Anon., 7 May 1960; cf. 215, 1956-58, p. 248; 221, 1958, p. 328 n. 12).

100. It is because religious experiences are real in their own right that Jung proclaims it the duty of the psychologist to come to terms with them (222, 1958, pp. 444-45: letters to Calvin S. Hall, 6 October 1954; to P. Cogo, 21 September 1955).

In matters like miraculous cures, the psychologist must acknowledge the facts and seek to discover the accompanying psychological conditions, without necessarily trying to "explain away" the apparent miracle (227, 1959, pp. 7-9; letter to J. E. Schulte, 24 May 1958). Concerning the metaphysical insights achieved under the influence of drugs, on the other hand, Jung was more skeptical and insistent on the need for a purely psychological explanation (see his letter to A. M. Hubbard, 15 May 1955). In any case, Jung was consistently opposed to all attempts to reduce philosophy or theology to psychology (150, 1954, pp. 247-48, 296; 215, 1956-58, pp. 253-54; 225, 1959, p. 475; letters to V. White, 2 April 1955; to T. Bovet, 9 November 1955; to I. Moon, 23 February 1960).

101. 207, 1955, p. 19; 221, 1958, p. 349; letters to A. R. Eickoff, 7 May 1956; to O. Nisse, 2 July 1960.

102. 206, 1955, Part V, p. 6. Given this statement, the title of the interview, "I Believe in God," seems particuarly poor. Some years later the interviewer, Frederick Sands, published an account of a talk he had with Jung just four days before the latter's death, and unscrupulously included the above passage, nearly verbatim (236, 1961, p. 139).

103. 234, 1960, p. 133. A report of the interview appears in 229, 1959, pp. 722-25. Cf. also 226, 1959, pp. 458-59; letter to L. W. Wulf, 25 July 1959.

104. 215, 1956-58, pp. 15-16. See the similar remarks in other letters to P. A. Hilty, 25 October 1955; to H. J. Barrett, 12 October 1956; to Pastor Tanner, 12 February 1959; to G. Wittwer, 10 October 1959; to V. Brooke, 16 November 1959; to Leonhard, 5 December 1959.

105. Cf. 206, 1955; 208, 1955, p. 7; 214, 1956, pp. 259, 261; 216, 1957, p. 19; 238, 1961, pp. 45, 89; letters to B. A. Snowdon, 7 May 1955; to Anon., 8 February 1957; to R. Topping, 12 November 1959; to K. G. Lafleur, 11 June 1960; to Rev. David, 11 February 1961.

106. 203, 1954, p. 256; cf. 150, 1954, p. 293; 211, 1955, pp. 691, 693.

107. "A creed gives expression to a definite collective belief, whereas the word *religion* expresses a subjective relationship to certain metaphysical, extramundane factors" (214, 1956, p. 256. Cf. also 215, 1956-58, pp. 232-33, 236; 221, 1958, p. 345; letters to B. G. Eisner, 12 August 1957; Anon., 2 October 1954; Tanner, 12 February 1959; V. White, 10 April 1954.

108. In *The Undiscovered Self,* a book replete with religious overtones, the relation of the individual to society is a dominant theme; in this context Jung goes on to assert that the spirit of collectivism is even anti-Christian at its roots (214, 1956, pp. 265, 271, 275-76, 292; cf. his letter to W. Bernet, 13 June 1955).

109. 200, 1954, p. 256; 203, 1954, pp. 199-200, 216-17, 301, 346-47, 348, 366, 418, 523-24, 547; 208, 1955, p. 7; 213, 1956, p. v; 214, 1956, pp. 292-93; 215, 1956-58, p. 13; 233, 1960, pp. v-vi; letters to P. Cogo, 21 September 1955; to K. W. Bash, 12 December 1958.

110. 234, 1960; letters to P. A. Hilty, 25 October 1955: to H. Burnett, 5 December 1959; to O. Nisse, 2 July 1960. Jung, of course, knew he was a "heretic" and even took a kind of good-humored delight in the appellation (cf. Jacobi, 1956, p. 18: W. Meyer, 1961).

Jung's position is stated unequivocally at this time. Concluding a commentary on problems within Christianity, he writes: "This is not to say that Christianity is finished. I am, on the contrary, convinced that it is not Christianity, but our conception and interpretation of it, that has become antiquated in the face of the present world situation. The Christian symbol is a living thing that carries in itself the seeds of further development" (214, 1956, pp. 279, 280, 304; 203, 1954, pp. 200, 321, 370; 221, 1958, p. 328; 235, 1960, pp. 56-58).

111. From a letter to A. Gerstner-Hirzel, September 1957. Cf. 206, 1955; 208, 1955, p. 7; 221, 1958, p. 361; 230, 1960, p. 85; 238, 1961, pp. 82, 101; letters to V. Brooke, 16 November 1959, and to P. Cogo, 21 September 1955. The God-archetype demonstrates three qualities: it is numinous, autonomous, and authoritative (222, 1958, pp. 446, 449-50, 453).

112. To Lucas Menz, 28 March 1955. Cf. the comment that E. B. Howes attributes to Jung: "Why do I have to talk about God? Because he is everywhere; I am only the spoon in his kitchen" (1961, p. 24). It is hard to understand how a critic like Renée Hayes could write in 1956 of him: "Professor Jung is allergic to the word 'God,' which spiritually reduces him, as a paper rose can reduce an asthmatic, to a choking, strangling struggle for breath" (1956, p. 134). To judge from her later reviews of Jung's work, she seems to have taken Jung's resentment of his Protestant Calvinistic upbringing far too seriously.

113. Jung's emphasis on the coincidence of good and evil in the Old Testament figure of Yahweh and his consequent rejection of the notion of the *summum bonum* follow along the lines of *Job* (cf. 132, 1954, pp. 102-3; 200, 1954, p. 256; 203, 1954, pp. 30, 170, 185, 187, 196-97, 253; 215, 1956-58, pp. 19-21, 217, 222, 228, 235, 241, 251; 239, n.d., p. 40; 221, 1958, pp. 337-38, 358; 222, 1958, pp. 447-49; letters to L. Menz, 28 March 1955; to Anon., 28 June 1956; to E. Kotschnig, 30 June 1956; to M. Esther Harding, 30 May 1957; to M. Kelsey,

27 December 1958; to C. E. Scanlan, 5 November 1959; to Anon., 7 May 1960; to Wilhelm Bitter, 7 December 1960; to A. Ledeen, 19 January 1961).

Similarly, Jung's repudiation of the metaphysical definition of evil as a *privatio boni* is a repetition of his earlier argument (cf. 203, 1954, pp. 79, 167; 215, 1956-58, pp 18-19, 212, 215, 221, 234-35; 226, 1959, pp. 456-58; letters to H. Kiener, 14 May 1955; to L. Menz, 29 June 1955; to E. Neumann, 3 June 1957; to Anon., 17 August 1957; to J. Gibb, 1 October 1958.

His debate with Victor White on this matter continued; but even after lying dormant for three years, its revival only led to the same stalemate as before (see Jung's letters to White of 10 April 1954, 19 January 1955, 2 April 1955, 25 March 1960; letter to A. Jaffé, 6 April 1954). The late Dr. Jolande Jacobi once told me of her efforts to bring the two together again during these final years by suggesting that White was speaking on a "metaphysical" plane, while Jung on a "practical" plane—but to no avail. A still more confused exchange on the problem of evil with Howard Philp (1958) produced even less clarity.

114. As a perusal of his comments on the feminine in God shows, the dogma of the Assumption still holds a place of special importance for Jung as a complement to the Christian Trinity (cf. 130, 1954, p. 96; 132, 1954, pp. 107-10; 203, 1954, pp. 170-71 n. 354, 186-88, 361, 466-67, 469; 215, 1956-58, pp. 219, 241, 252; letters to H. Philp, 10 March 1958; to V. White, 2 April 1955).

115. 203, 1954, pp. 101-2, 185-86; 204, 1955, p. 388; 215, 1956-58, pp. 216-21: letter to M. Imboden, 30 January 1958. Writing to W. P. Witcutt on 24 August 1960, Jung adds the following clarification: "The whole question of the quaternity is not at all a theory, but a phenomenon. There exists a large number of symbols of the Godhead with a quaternity-structure, and that is a fact, not a theory. I would not commit such a sin against epistemology. Here lies the stumbling block which has tripped up Victor White, along with others."

116. 204, 1955, p. 389; 219; 1957, p. 63; 150, 1954, p. 276; 203, 1954, pp. 207-8, 546; 215, 1956-58, p. 225, 243; 221, 1958, p. 339; letters to L. Menz, 28 March 1955; to H. Amstutz, 23 May 1955; to H. Kiener, 15 June 1955; to R. Dietrich, 27 May 1956; to E. Kotschnig, 30 June 1956. In writing a definition of the "Self" for a revision of *Types* Jung surprisingly failed to give more than the vaguest intimation of the relationship between Self and God, which he had been speaking of for nearly twenty years (224, 1958, pp. 460-61).

Consistent with his methodological premises, Jung was careful not to offer the Self as a theological or philosophical equivalent of God: "It is a misunderstanding to accuse me of having made out of this (the Self) an 'immanent God' or a 'God-substitute'. . . . Such misunderstandings arise from the assumption that I am an irreligious man who does not believe in God and just needs to be shown the way to belief" (226, 1959, p. 463; cf. his letter to W. Bernet, 13 June 1955).

As for those passages where God is identified with the unconscious (215, 1956-58, p. 245; 228, 1959, p. 16), they seem best able to be explained, however little we appreciate the looseness of terminology, according to the scheme devised earlier (chap. 2, §4)

117. "Living in the West, I would have to say Christ instead of 'Self,' in the

Near East, it would be Khidr, in the Far East atman or Tao or the Buddha, in the Far West maybe a hare or Mandamin, and in cabalism it would be Tifereth" (221, 1958, p. 410).

118. 215, 1956-58, pp. 223-24, 227, 230-31, 233, 239-40, 245, 253; 230, 1959, p. 56; ibid., 1960, p. 101; 239, n.d., p. 14; letters to V. White, 10 April 1954; to M. Kelsey, 27 December 1958. The alchemists represent one nondogmatic attempt to redress the balance by incorporating principles of evil and feminity into the image of Christ (cf. 203, 1954, pp. 184-85, 372-74, 379, 393, 404).

119. 132, 1954, pp. 104-5; 201, 1954, p. 31; 203, 1954, pp. 361, 364; 205, 1955, pp. 30-31; 212, 1956, p. 75; 214, 1956, p. 285; 223, 1958, p. 30; 238, 1961, pp. 72-73, 89; letters to V. White, 10 April 1954; to U. Sinclair, 20 January 1955; to P. A. Hilty, 25 October 1955; to H. Kiener, 1 June 1956; to Anon., 2 January 1957; to B. von der Heydt, 13 February 1958; to Herr Tanner, 12 February 1959; to A. Jung, 21 December 1960.

120. Four years before writing *Flying Saucers,* Jung took part in an opinion survey on this question; his views were then published in a popular Zurich newspaper (202, 1954). This provoked critical comments that were probably responsible for the writing of this book, although he had been collecting and reading books on UFO's since 1947 (cf. 221, 1958, p. 387; letters to B. Hinkle, 6 February 1951; to Fowler McCormick, 22 February 1951).

121. 221, 1958, pp. 416-17; letter to C. B. Harnett, 12 December 1957; 239, n.d., p. 64.

122. Jung took a similar attitude to ghost stories and other parapsychological phenomena (217, 1957, pp. vi-viii). In fact, he goes to great lengths in very many of his letters in these later years to defend and to clarify his concept of synchronicity, a notion he considered indispensable for the psychologist.

123. 221, 1958, pp. 311-12.

124. Ibid., pp. 327-28. The same point appears in the analysis of several of the dreams he cites in the book (pp. 337, 339, 354) and in his interpretation of certain paintings (pp. 386, 394).

125. This point is unclear in Jung's treatise on the UFO's, aside from a passing reference (ibid., p. 334) to Christ's saying "Ye are gods" (John 10: 34), which he had already cited in his article on the Trinity (and elsewhere) to refer to the Age of the Holy Ghost (146, 1940/1948, p. 158).

126. 130, 1954, pp. 95-96; 203, 1954, pp. 34, 216, 318, 375-76, 450-51, 454, 494, 524, 541; 215, 1956-58, pp. 225, 244-45; letters to E. Kotschnig, 30 June 1956; to M. Kelsey, 3 May 1958; to E. Neumann, 10 March 1959, Note also that in the revision of his study on the Mass, Jung added a long section expanding on his view that the Mass can be seen as "the rite of the individuation process." For insofar as Christ serves as an image of the Self, the union with Christ and the transformation into Christ celebrated in the Mass symbolizes the process of coming to psychic wholeness (150, 1954, pp. 273-96). A fine critique of the whole article, which pays particular attention to Jung's often dubious use of historical and symbolic parallels, was done by Gaffney (1963).

127. Cf. 203, 1954, p. 221 and n., 555, 318, 460, 481, 499, 505, 517.

128. Letter to W. Kinney, 26 May 1956. Cf. 214, 1956, p. 305; 238, 1961, p. 102; 215, 1956-58, p. 221. A 1955 article in *Time* magazine reports Jung as saying: "Yes, I've attained individuation—thank heavens! Otherwise I would be very neurotic, you know." Because of Jung's understanding of the Self as a goal that constantly eludes man, I suspect the quotation of being spurious, or at least carelessly doctored.

129. Letter to A. P. Savides, 13 January 1948. Cf. his letter to H. Flournoy, 12 February 1953.

130. Letter to E. von Pelet, 6 January 1960. Cf. letter to W. Niehus, 5 April 1960.

131. Alm (1963) has argued this point at considerable length, singling out the religious experiences that Jung includes in *Memories,* in replying to certain of Jung's critics.

132. 237, 1961, pp. 4-5. Ellenberger argues that "there are wide gaps, and contradictions between certain of Jung's assertions and the version given by other sources" (1970, p. 663). Yet neither he nor anyone else has, to my knowledge, gone into any detail on these questions.

133. 237, 1961, pp. 356-57. Cf. letter to Jaffé, 9 July 1957. Jung was particularly fond of the word *daimon* to express his inner self, inasmuch as it was freer of the connotations of good and evil that *God* and *Devil* carry (84, 1930, 1: 221-22, 231-32), and yet expressed the dynamic and numinous quality of fate better than "the unconscious" did (237, 1961, p. 347).

For many years Jung wore a Gnostic ring with a snake on it called the *agathodaimon,* remarking of it on one occasion: "It gives me a special satisfaction to wear such a historical thing. . . . It appeals to my nocturnal side particularly, it expresses something unconscious, and so it is thoroughly alive and full of mana" (84, 1932, 5: 169).

134. It is not impossible that Jung got the device of no. 1 and no. 2 personality from Herman Hesse's *Demian.* Shortly after reading the book in 1919, Jung wrote to Hesse on 3 December of that year that he had always known Demian and that the book had touched him in a deep and personal way. For his part, Hesse was already acquainted with Jung's work from 1915, and kept up his interest (1934, pp. 325-26). He met with Jung first in 1916. At the time he was undergoing analysis under Dr. J. B. Lang, a colleague and pupil of Jung's (cf. letter to E. Maier, 24 March 1950). Later, in 1921, Hesse had several analytical sessions with Jung himself. As Dahrendorf has masterfully demonstrated, the influence of Jung's thought on Demian is profound (1958). Unfortunately, he did not realize that not only Jung's *Psychology of the Unconscious* had fallen into Hesse's hands, but also the *Septem sermones ad mortuos.*

135. 237, 1961, p. 140.

136. Broad, 1953, p. 192. Note Jung's remark: "A vision as such is nothing unusual for me, for I frequently see extremely vivid hypnagogic images" (237, 1961, p. 210).

For a more complete account of the role of such phenomena in Jung's life and work, see Jaffé, 1971, pp. 1-16.

137. As M. Fordham has pointed out, it was the "religious idiom of his parents' belief and thought" that shaped Jung's interest in religion and that lay behind his imaginative encounters with Christianity, however much he may have rebelled against his paternal influence (1971, p. 80). Looser (1966) gives us deeper insight into the patterns of word association at work in Jung's early religious notions. Winnicott (1964) analyzes these and other remarks of Jung's about his childhood as symptoms of "infantile psychosis" already visible by the time Jung had the strength to transform this "schizophrenia" into personal insight.

138. 237, 1961, p. 13.

139. Ibid., p. 42. Both the phallus-dream, as well as the manikin and stone, were charged with a feeling of strict taboo during Jung's childhood. Indeed, it was not until the age of sixty-five that he ever mentioned the former to anyone (p. 41)—first to his wife and then to a medical colleague (see Bennet, 1961, p. 10).

140. Ibid., p. 39.

141. Ibid., p. 59. See also the earlier references to this boyhood doubt given in the seminar notes (73, 1930, Part II, p. 217; 84, 1934, 11: 95; 109, 1939, 10: 28).

142. 237, 1961, p. 59.

143. In addition, there were six pastors on his mother's side of the family and two more on his father's side.

144. Letter to D. Hoch, 28 May 1952. Cf. the letter to W. Bernet, 13 June 1955; 237, 1961, pp. 43, 73, 93-94, 141. Granjel's claim that Jung's father was a "humanistic pastor" and an extreme leftwing Protestant seems to me wholly without foundation (1949, p. 283).

145. 237, 1961, p. 56.

146. Ibid., p. 62, 66-67.

147. Ibid., p. 331.

148. Ibid., pp. 301-2, 311. Several commentators, such as D. Hoch (1963, p. 66), have seen, and rightly so, a certain messianic-prophetic tone to *Memories* in arguments such as these.

149. 237, 1961, p. 319.

150. Ibid., p. 340.

151. We know from a letter of Freud to K. Abraham (dated 3 May 1908) that he attributed Jung's resistance to the sexual theory and his attraction to religion to his upbringing as a pastor's son (Abraham, 1965, p. 34).

152. 237, 1961, pp. 151-52.

153. Ibid., p. 4; cf. pp. 341-42, 352-53.

154. Ibid., pp. 67, 91. Elsewhere he notes that not only men, but all of nature, partakes of this "divinity" (p. 45).

155. Ibid., pp. 280, 321, 333-34, 338.

156. Ibid., p. 354; cf. pp. 347-48.

157. Ibid., p. 42.

158. Ibid., pp. 358-59.

Chapter 4 On Style and Methodology

1. The most extensive treatment I know of appears in a short chapter (a mere two-and-a-half pages) by Jaffé (1970, pp. 26-28). Her approach is very general and, unfortunately, of not much help in the questions I am posing in this section. Cf. also Hellens, 1955.

2. Dry notes that even in Jung's earliest publication "traces appear of a more poetical approach than Freud permitted himself" (1961, p. 43). While this is clearly so, we cannot fail to acknowledge the radical break with the past that *Psychology of the Unconscious* effected.

3. A look around Jung's library at Küsnacht is far more instructive for appreciating the extent of his reading than is a mere study of the indexes and bibliographies of his published writings. To a short essay on Jung's library, von Franz (1963) has added some interesting remarks on his reading habits.

   One critic went so far as to claim that Jung's interdisciplinary efforts show the workings of a "schizoid intelligence" (Mrowka, 1968, pp. 128-30). Such nonsense is as unfounded as its opposite extreme; for example: "Jung has taken account not only of the established churches and generally accepted doctrines, but also of *all the possible sects and esoteric traditions. . .*" (Schär, 1951, p. 74. Emphasis added). Fairer is Jung's own comment, half joking, in a 1960 interview: "I have been the worst specialist in the world" (231).

4. In a letter to W. R. Corti, dated 30 April 1929, Jung diagnoses in himself a "hypertrophy of intellectual intuition." In two seminar lectures we find similar allusions to himself as an "introverted" and "thinking" type for whom "feeling" is relatively undifferentiated (59, 1925, pp. 30, 39-41, 127; 84, 1934, 2: 24). Again, in discussing a case of transference, he indirectly refers to himself as an intuitive type (105, 1950, p. 303). By piecing together the above information, we arrive at the conclusion stated above in the text. In support of this position, Frau Jaffé tells me that Jung wavered between defining himself as thinking-intuitive and as intuitve-thinking. Even this ambiguity is adequate for our purposes here.

5. 51, 1920, pp. 381, 400, 402.

6. 59, p. 29; cf. 237, 1961, p. 192. I am speaking here of general characteristics to which there are, of course, exceptions in Jung's work. I consider it an unfair appraisal of his work, however, to assert—as Schär does in comparing him to C. G. Carus, the nineteenth-century German philosopher: "Carus came to his ideas

intuitively—Jung investigates the unconscious with all the scientific equipment of the modern physician" (1951, p. 34). No less unsatisfactory is Vestdijck's contrasting view: "Jung isn't a thinker in the proper sense. He's a dreamer who carries himself with the sureness of a sleepwalker" (1955, p. 232).

7. The following passge by Michael Fordham is most instructive: "He (Jung) moves from one topic to another not because there is a logical connection but because there is an association either in his own mind or in the mind of his subject; indeed the apposition of two apparently unconnected ideas in a single text can be enough to assume a connection between them. How far this sometimes went I may perhaps illustrate by a personal reminiscence. I could not make out any reason at all for a footnote in *Psychology and Alchemy* and thought it might be removed. In my capacity as coeditor of the *Collected Works* I asked Jung about it: 'Oh, I just thought of it,' he said, and that was enough for it to be left in" (1962, pp. 11-12).

8. See Jacobi, 1967, p. vii, where the author cites a letter from Jung of 24 September 1948. (This letter does not appear in the pulished correspondence.) There is, of course, a touch of hyperbole in Jung's humility at his disorganization, which is more than balanced by his general attitude toward his critics.

9. 30, 1942, pp. 118-19; 56, 1946, pp. 106-7; 75, 1929/1938, p. 9; 132, 1938/1954, p. 94. Cf. Mueller, 1970, pp. 105-21. Note also the comment by Jean Piaget: "Jung is a force of nature. . . . The rational Latin spirit that is looking for proof and demands logical coherence gets lost and occasionally impatient with him. But the seeker who craves ideas and delights in explaining them in the light of fundamental insights drawn from lived experience will find in C. G. Jung as much as he desires" (1945, p. 170).

10. The hostility Jung was capable of showing toward those in disagreement with him seems only to have hardened his convictions nad made him increasingly impervious to criticism. Such claims, for instance, as that the East was better able to appreciate his ideas than the West (209, 1955, p. 150), and that most of his critics either did not bother to read his works or were too stupid to understand them (213, 1956, p. x; 231, 1960) are symptoms of the occasional unfairness and intolerance that were as much a part of Jung as were his generosity and intellectual honesty.

11. Von Weizäcker's claim that Jung moved only in circles interested in the humanities (1958, p. 74) is patently false. Yet there is no doubt that *anthropology,* in the widest sense of that term, had a far greater influence on his work than did the natural sciences.

12. The predisposition of the reader may also be an important factor in the formation of attitudes, perhaps equally as important as that of the writer. The point is often made by critics and followers of Jung alike. Bennet observes: "With the best will in the world, the extravert . . . will find Jung's books hard going" (1961, p. 18). One researcher found that approximately 75 percent of a tested sample of Jungian analysts corresponded to the "introverted-intuitive" type (Bradway, 1964, pp. 129-35). Others have pointed out the predominance of women and introvert

patients attracted to Jungian thought and therapy (cf. Sykes, 1962, pp. 71, 97; Jacobs, 1961, p. 100 n.1). Until such time as the subjective factor receives further clarificaton, however, it seems preferable to work exclusively from a more objective and impersonal critical base.

13. Kunzli, 1955, p. 942.

14. Huxley, 1956, p. 172. Anthropologist Peter Munz claimed that Jung's "artistic sensitivity" ran away with him, dulling his critical faculties (1961, p. 9). E. Carstens, a Danish playwright, made this theme the subject of an attack on Jung, marred by cynicism and poor taste (1964, especially Act 1, scene 3).

15. Von Weizäcker claimed, for example, that Jung's work was lacking in the "classical" quality of Freud's. He continues: "His style is uneven and rather impersonal, and that seems to point to a lack of depth in his thinking and of decisive clarity at the base of his character . . ." (1958, p. 73).

16. Stern, 1953, p. 230.

17. Cf. Perrot, 1970; Eliade, 1962, pp. 199-204.

18. Jung had first read *Zarathustra* at twenty-three or twenty-four (59, 1925, p. 6; 109, 1935, 3: 87), but he returned to read it "with consciousness" when he was thirty-nine (109, 1934, 2: 137). Prinzhorn's claim that Jung had a "bourgeois aversion to Nietzsche" is given the lie by the seminars, although certain of Jung's earlier writings might suggest such a view (1932, p. 174).

19. 109, 1935, 4:16. Midway through the discussions there was a debate among the participants as to whether they ought to continue, so far had they moved from the original text of Nietzsche's book and become absorbed in comparative material.

20. This is also the sense of Thiry's complaint about Jung's "psychological imperialism" (1957, p. 349), and Victor White's comment on Jung's tendency to "omnicompetence" (1952b, p. 242). Jantz, a Goethean scholar, has attacked Jung's interpretation of *Faust* (a frequent theme in Jung's writings) on similar grounds. The appeal to esoteric literature in blatant neglect of the accepted classical origins of Goethe's ideas puts Jung at a safe remove from professional interest and criticism, according to Jantz, but only at the expense of a misinterpretation of Goethe (1962).

21. 171, 1948, p. 13.

22. 218, 1957, p. xii.

23. For his part, Jung saw another danger, about which I shall have more to say in the following chapter: "Neologisms tend not only to hypostatise themselves to an amazing degree, but actually to replace the reality they were originally intended to express" (150, 1954, p. 290).

24. In this regard it is worth noting Mircea Eliade's estimation of Jung's non-systematic style: "Jung does not claim to handle a subject exhaustively, to present a complete and definitive description of a spiritual phenomenon; he pursues the analysis of a certain aspect which, at the time, seems salient to him. But years later he returns and puts himself to the task of evaluating still other aspects.

This lively manner of approaching spiritual phenomena explains perhaps the 'charm' of certain of Jung's writings, the extraordinary attraction that they exercise on the unprepared reader" (1955, pp. 103-4).

Another complicating element to be considered is the fact that psychological explanations also have a therapeutic function which, Jung felt, was better served by ambiguity than by univocal, operational definitions.

25. In composing these remarks I have made use freely of the work done by Hostie, 1957, pp. 101-8; Stein, 1958; Christou, 1963; and Toni Wolff, 1935, whose attempt to support Jung's psychological method by recourse to the philosophy of science was the first undertaken by any of his disciples and earned Jung's personal approval (156, 1943, p. 43 n. 3; 56, 1946, p. 90 n. 8; letter to E. Jahn, 7 September 1935).

26. There is no need to trouble ourselves over tracing the historical development of Jung's methodological opinions. In any case, there is little significant change after 1912 (recalling that it was then that his paper "On Psychic Energy" (69) was first drafted), but only constant repetition and paraphrase of a few seminal and unelaborated ideas.

Moreover, in concentrating on Jung's epistemological views, I am deliberately avoiding the question of an implicit moral philosophy underlying Jung's psychology. That such principles are at work is obvious. Kaune (1967) has done an admirably thorough job of teasing them out and evaluating them in the light of his own position, which is fundamentally Kantian. It is hard to know how Jung would have reacted to such criticism; but his general avoidance of theoretical ethics—as well as a passing comment in a letter to G. Senn of 13 October 1941 linking Kant's categorical imperative to his relationship to his mother (!)—make it unlikely that he would have given the matter much attention.

27. This view is supported by Herbert Spiegelberg (1972, pp. 130-31). Hostie gives a false impression in attributing to Jung certain views of the Husserlean school (1957, pp. 102-4), for even prior to his adoption of the term *phenomenology,* Jung subscribed to the views that he later encapsulated in the word. What is more, we have no evidence that he had ever read or encountered the teachings of the phenomenological movement. Progoff's claim that Jung's phenomenology is equivalent to the "pragmatism" of William James is far too facile and would hardly stand up to close scrutiny (1953, pp. 73, 167). Baudouin, observing that Husserl had distinguished empiricism from phenomenology in a way that Jung does not, recommends the term *phenology* to describe Jung's interest in description without philosophical prejudices (1963, pp. 298-99). The title of a 1947 essay of Jung's, "The Phenomenology of the Spirit in Fairy Tales" (165), leads us to suspect a Hegelian connotation to the word. But as Corbin has noted, Jung's phenomenology cannot properly be compared to Hegel's inasmuch as it replaces chronological progress with an ontological process that is wholly immanent and ahistorical (1953, p. 13).

28. Jung remarks of his phenomenological stance: "It is concerned with occurrences, events, experiences—in a word, with facts. Its truth is a fact and not a judgment"

(128, 1927, p. 6; cf. 56, 1946, p. 86; 72, 1928, p. 527; 147, 1941/1951, pp. 182-83; 179, 1949, pp. 3-4; 231, 1960, p. 8).

29. 30, 1916/1942, p. 95; 77, 1929, pp. 251-52; 84, 1930, 1:276; 92, 1932, p. 343 and 243 n. 4; 93, 1932, pp. 382-84; 154, 1943, p. 560.

30. 62, 1926, p. 320; cf. also 30, 1942, p. 117; 112, 1935, p. iv; 199, 1953, p. 328; 217, 1957, p. 11: letter to C. Hall, 6 October 1954.

Nearly all of his allusions to William James occur in this vein (e.g., 32, 1912, p. 86). Jung's sole meeting with James, during his 1909 visit to America, had confirmed the deep and lasting impression the latter's writings had made on him (cf. letters to V. Payne, 23 July 1949; to K. Wolff, 17 June 1958).

31. 174, 1948/1950, pp. 33-34; 193, 1952/1955, p. 449. He had first used the analogy in reference to those who refused to acknowledge Freud's work (12, 1906, pp. 3-4). See also 58, 1925, p. 200; 142, 1939, p. ix; 156, 1943, pp. 3-4; letter to K. Plachte, 10 January 1929.

C. A. Meier draws out what is implied in the above-mentioned passages: that Jung first applied all of his psychological findings and theories on himself, only later making them part of his method (1959b, p. 6). Rudin wisely notes two underlying motives to Jung's a priori commitment to the primacy of experience: (a) a mistrust of theory vis-à-vis the mysterious depths of the psyche; and (b) a recognition of the gripping and numinous quality of inner experiences (1964, pp. 238-39).

32. 108, 1934/1954, p. 70; cf. 113, 1935, p. 548; 131, 1938, p. 7.

33. For instance, even where it is obvious that Jung means to attack the dogmatism of Freud's sexual theory, he often does so with principles Freud himself championed, leaving his criticisms to suggest a subtle untruth—as in the following passage: "I have never wearied of emphasizing that onesidedness and dogmatism harbor in themselves the gravest dangers precisely in the domain of psychology. . . . The phenomenology of the psyche is so colorful, so variegated in form and meaning, that we cannot possibly reflect all its riches in *one* mirror" (82, 1930/1950, p. 85).

34. 203, 1954, p. 105. Cf. 76, 1929, p. 71; 102, 1934, p. 163. Jung also recognized the dangers inherent in this approach: "The psychotherapist should realize that so long as he believes in a theory and in a definite method he is likely to be fooled by certain cases, namely by those clever enough to select a safe hiding-place for themselves behind the trappings of the theory" (56, 1946, p. 112). But despite these problems and the occasional demand to suspend one's hypothesis, Jung still clung to the demand for verification in the clinical setting, rejecting "the current prejudice that I produce nothing but theories. My so-called 'theories' are not figments, but facts that can be verified" (198, 1953, p. vii; cf. letter to J. Jacobi, 13 March 1956).

35. 158, 1944/1948, pp. 281-82; 193, 1952/1955, p. 451. Note however, that in his early work with the word-association test, Jung relied a good deal more on experimental psychology, as he states explicitly on one occasion (11, 1906, p. 145).

36. Note Ivar Alm's interesting criticisms against the Jungians in this regard (1936, pp. 102-3). For his part, Jung was not above an occasional exaggeration

concerning his understanding of Kant. The following remark, from a letter to B. Lang dated June 1957, was provoked by Buber's accusations of "gnosticism": "On this threshold are minds divided: namely, those who have understood Kant and those who are not able to follow him."

37. 74, 1929, p. 340. This is not the same as a commitment to a *Weltanschauung* (a conceptualized attitude toward the world), which science does not possess, or rather ought to avoid. Indeed Jung's call for a new *Weltanschauung* looks very much like an argument for the supremacy of the psychological point of view. The very Kantian principles we are here discussing are evident throughout his arguments on this question (65, 1931, pp. 377-81).

38. "The limitation of the material is obviously an arbitrary proceeding, in accordance with Kant's principle that to 'comprehend' a thing is to 'cognize it to the extent necessary for our purpose' " (38, 1914/1948, pp. 240-41; cf. 37, 1914, p. 181; 96, 1933, p. 639).

39. The mistake is not the translator's but Jung's own. He frequently confuses the terms *transcendental* and *transcendent* in his references to Kant—an elementary error regarding a distinction that appears in the opening pages of the *Critique of Pure Reason.* (Cf. 75, 1929/1938, p. 54; 24, 1911-1912, p. 529 n. 42 (partially cited above, p. 19 n. 43).) In his defense, we might note that Kant himself was not always perfectly consistent in his use of these terms.

40. 32, 1912, p. 177; 188, 1950, p. 124; 192, 1952; letter to M. Fierz, 7 May 1945.

41. 120, 1936/1954, p. 57. Cf. 167, 1946/1954, pp. 228-29; letter to H. Murray, 10 September 1935; to V. Brooke, 16 November 1959. Contradictions on this question abound in Jung's writings. In one context, for example, he asserts that the subjectivistic dilemma is not a problem for natural science, which *has* its "Archimedean point," but only for psychology (165, 1945/1947, p. 207). Elsewhere he observes that the real world of the exact sciences is a fiction, an "anthropomorphism" to which psychology gives the lie (62, 1926, p. 327; cf. also letter to C. Kaufmann, 30 April 1936).

Several commentators have pointed to the problem in one form or another. For Maurice Friedman, Jung's philosophy is a sort of Berkeleian idealism bordering on solipsism (1966-67, pp. 600, 602-3). Kaune adds the perceptive comment that this same contradiction between realism and idealism applied to Jung's very description of the psyche, which at one moment appears as a transempirical subject, and at the next as an objective "given" (1967, p. 84).

42. 132, 1938/1954, p. 76.

43. 51, 1920/1960, p. 304; 136, 1939, p. 243; letter to F. Lerch, 10 September 1956. Jung took obvious delight in his personal affinities with Kant, and even went so far as to suggest that the *Kritik* was decisively influenced by Kant's (also) introverted personality type (132, 1938/1954, p. 77), which he defined alternatively as "normal" and as "extremely pure" (51, 1920/1960, pp. 313, 383).

44. In one seminar talk Jung remarked that the Kantian categories "are only an intellectual application of the archetypes" (73, 1929, Part I, p. 98). Similar comments occur in 38, 1948, p. 274 n. 17; 44, 1928, p. 169 n. 7; 49, 1919, p. 136;

51, 1920/1960, p. 438; 193, 1952/1955, p. 436.

45. "The archetype would thus be, to borrow from Kant, the noumenon of the image which intuition perceives and, in perceiving, creates" (51, 1920/1960, pp. 400-401; cf. 120, 1936/1954, p.59). It is in this sense that he refers to the archetypes and the collective unconscious as "negative borderline concepts" that point to an unknowable *Ding-an-sich* (32, 1912, p. 140; 140, 1939/1955, p. 505; 75, 1929/1938, p. 54). Another contradiction appears in Jung's references to the archetype of the Self: he both asserts and denies that it is to be considered a *Grenzbegriff* like the archetypes (150, 1941/1954, p. 262 n. 18; 156, 1943, p. 182; 221, 1958, p. 410.

46. 128, 1937/1940, pp. 5-6; cf. 37, 1914, pp. 192-93.

47. The three sets of terms are used interchangeably. Note also that on occasion Jung substituted *teleological* and *final,* although he explicitly rejected the former in several places because he held it to carry the unwarranted connotation of a specific and consciously entertained goal, in addition to the general meaning of orientation to a goal (cf. 38, 1914/1948, p. 241; 44, 1916, pp. 294-95 n. 19; 59, 1925, p. 119; 69, 1928, p. 4 n. 4).

48. 45, 1917, pp. 296-97. Jung's use of Kantian language gets him in a tangle here again. By identifying the "causal" with the "mechanistic," he implies, incorrectly, that causality was a regulative, and not a constitutive, principle for Kant.

49. Jung first hazarded this opinion in a lecture delivered in 1913 (34, pp. 508-9), and later developed it at greater length (30, 1916, pp. 391 ff.; 51, 1920/1960, pp. 60-63; cf. also 36, 1913, p. 275).

50. Jung's longest treatment of these two models is found in his essay "On Pyschic Energy" (69, 1928). In his later work, as less and less stress was put on the libido theory, the term *energic* was gradually replaced by *final.* Possibly criticism of his outmoded use of the concept and laws of energy had something to do with the change. At any rate, Jung would hardly have agreed with Bennett's claim that developments in microphysics had deprived him of the main pillar of his methodology (1961, p. 272).

51. 56, 1946, p. 105. Jung's defense occasionally slips into unfairness toward those espousing opposing points of view, as in the following remark included in his obituary tribute (!) to Freud: "Freud's psychology moves within the narrow confines of nineteenth-century scientific materialism. Its philosophical premises were never examined, thanks obviously to the Master's insufficient philosophical equipment. So it was inevitable that it should come under the influence of local and temporal prejudices . . . " (138, 1939, p. 47).

52. An exhaustive treatment can be found in 193, 1952/1955. A very fine analysis of Jung's arguments has been done by M. Fordham (1957, pp. 35-50), whose efforts Jung himself praised highly (218, 1957, p. ix).

53. In referring to synchronicity as an "acausal" connecting principle, Jung does not mean to dispense with causality altogether, as H. H. Price understands him to

have done (1953, pp. 34-35). In fact, he states explicitly that "wherever a cause is even remotely thinkable, synchronicity becomes an exceedingly doubtful proposition" (193, 1952/1955, p. 461). In practice, however, the horizons of the "thinkable" are rather narrower for Jung than for most of his critics, as I shall note later more specifically.

54. "Everything human is relative, because everything rests on an inner polarity; for everything is a phenomenon of energy. Energy necessarily depends on a pre-existing polarity, without which there could be no energy" (30, 1925/1942, p. 75; cf. 124, 1936, 1: 17; 167, 1946/1954, p. 212).

55. Referring to the tendency of the unconscious to compensate the state of consciousness, Jung chose another term, from Heraclitus: *enantiodromia.* He says of it: "This characteristic phenomenon practically always occurs when an extreme, one-sided tendency dominates conscious life; in time an equally powerful counterposition is built up, which first inhibits the conscious performance and subsequently breaks through the conscious control" (51, 1920/1960, p. 426; cf. 30, 1916/1942, p. 72). The change in terminology here does not signify anything more than an application of the general principle of opposition. We should note, to be precise, that whereas the general concept of enantiodromia ("a running-counter-to") is clearly Heraclitean, the term itself is not. Jung took it from Stobaeus's collection of the fragments, many of which are now known to be inauthentic. The fragment in question (cited in 51, 1920/1960, p. 425 n. 37) shows Stoic and Platonic elements, and hence is not attributable to Heraclitus.

56. Walder's view that the male-female polarity is basic and normative for Jung, inasmuch as his polarities are fundamentally symbolical and not ideational, overlooks the origins of the energic viewpoint in Jung's early work, and cannot find sufficient support in the later writings (1951, pp. 11–12).

57. 100, 1934, Part I, p. 95. Cf. 84, 1931, 2:228.

58. 73, 1928, Part I, pp. 94-95; 109, 1937, 8: 27.

59. From a letter to E. Neumann written in 1952 (237, p. 375).

60. Note the following statement by one of Jung's disciples: "Dr. Jung has carefully worked out his theory of knowledge and explicitly stated it in many places. He is an excellent philosopher . . . and has subjected his methods to careful intellectual scrutiny" (Sanford, 1971, p. 92). And again: "His findings were presented within a careful and critical philosophical framework, which is seldom found among empirical scientists today. In addition he had the knowledge and the interest to do an adequate job" (Kelsey, 1971, p. 188).

61. His own defense of the separation of fact and theory is not convincing theoretically, but it does admittedly succeed often in communicating Jung's lack of interest in such philosophical niceties. For example, he wrote: "If criticism confines itself to the method, it may easily come one day to deny the existence of facts merely because the method of finding them betrays certain theoretical defects—a standpoint that would happily carry us back to the depths of the Middle Ages" (22, 1910, p. 75; cf. 32, 1912, pp. 102-3).

62. "When the projection corresponds to a quality actually present in the object, the projected content is nevertheless present in the subject too, where it forms a part of the object-imago. The object-imago itself is a psychological entity that is distinct from the actual perception of the object. . . . The autonomy of the image is therefore not recognized by the conscious mind and is unconsciously projected on the object. . . . This naturally endows the object with a compelling reality in relation to the subject and gives it an exaggerated value" (38, 1928/1948, p. 274). Jung is speaking here of the interpretation of dream material, *not* of his own empirical data.

63. We find Jung slipping into occasional revelations of this position, as when he writes: "Personal and theoretical prejudices are the most serious obstacles in the way of psychological judgment. They can, however, be eliminated with a little good will and insight" (188, 1951, p. 115; cf. 89, 1931, p. 147).

64. Jung's favoritism toward the final viewpoint as against the causal is symptomatic of this same confusion. His study of the Miller case (1911-12) represents both the first and the last attempt to combine both points of view. The longest recorded case history in the Jungian corpus, the eleven-volume seminar series entitled *The Interpretation of Visions* (84, 1930-34), almost totally neglects mention of the causal viewpoint. Moreover, when Jung spoke of points of view as subjective projections, he gave causality as an example, but not finality (ibid., 1933, 10: 169; 1934, 11: 173).

65. 87, 1931, p. 54.

66. 185, 1950, p. 590.

67. Price, 1953, pp. 33-34.

68. This is Flew's view of the synchronicity principle. He has also pointed out that the phrase "*meaningful coincidence*" is misleading, since coincidences are *always* meaningful, else their occurrence would go unnoticed (1953, pp. 198-201).

69. Jung's interpretation of the UFOs as synchronistic phenomena is a clear instance of this usage (see Chap. 3§3 above).

70. This is the origin of Jung's further claim that the synchronicity principle may help to clear up the mind-body problem (193, 1952/1955, p. 506) by positing a "psychoid" substratum that is common to both and the ultimate seat of the archetypes.

71. Jahoda (1967) rejects the principle of synchronicity on logical grounds, favoring the view that the coincidences of which Jung speaks are wholly subjective phenomena. Koestler argues similarly, accusing Jung of using the archetypes as "pseudo-causes" (1972, pp. 94-101).

72. "No matter what you say . . . all your philosophy is nothing more than a psychological fantasy . . . . A philosophy is merely the reflection of one's individual psychology" (84, 1931, 2: 228-29).

73. See above, chap. 4, n. 118.

74. In the English translation, *Glaube* is rendered both as "faith" and as "belief," with no connotative difference. This corresponds to Jung's own use of the terms when he wrote or spoke in English.

75. "Psychology as the science of the soul has to confine itself to its subject and guard against overstepping its proper boundaries by metaphysical assertions or other professions of faith. . . . The religious-minded man is free to accept whatever metaphysical explanations he pleases. . . ; not so the intellect (*sic*), which must keep strictly to the principles of scientific interpretation and avoid trespassing beyond the bounds of what can be known" (156, 1943, p. 14). Numerous such passages have been cited in Part I of this essay.

76. The origin of this usage can probably be traced to Kant's attack on "speculative" and "transcendent" metaphysics, both in its philosophical and in its theological forms. (Jung would surely have rejoiced at Kant's description of the latter as *"eine Zauberlaterne von Hirngespinsten."*) No exception is made, however, for Kant's "transcendental metaphysics," even though Jung himself tried to adopt many of its principles in his methodology.

77. One can hardly overlook the importance that the title of scientist held for Jung personally. In one particularly *ad hominem* gesture of self-defense, he wrote to a local critic of his method: "Supposing that my attitude really does exhibit such easily recognizable faults, how do you square this with the fact that I unite at least seven honorary doctorates upon my unscientific and/or benighted head? I am, by your leave, an honorary member of the Academy of German Scientists and Physicians, a Fellow of the Royal Society, Doctor Scientiae of Oxford and Harvard University, and was one of the four guests of honor and representatives of Swiss Science at the Tercentenary of the latter University. Do these august bodies really consist of nothing but simpletons incapable of judgment, and is the Philosophical Faculty of Zurich University the brain of the world? (letter to A. Künzli, 4 February 1943; cf. also 22, 1910, p. 75).

One passage in the seminar notes deserves mention as an odd reversal of Jung's usual stance. Speaking of the commitment of science to the principle of causality, Jung is reported to have remarked: "What I am doing is not science. There is a fundamental difference between science and psychology" (84, 1931, 2: 234). On the other hand, his statements against rationalism are not to be considered as a renunciation of the scientific posture. Rather, Jung saw that the truly scientific attitude was one that acknowledged the mysterious reality of the psyche, which theories can only partially contain. His anti-rationalism was therefore, at least in his methodology, a recognition of the limits of scientific knowledge.

78. ". . . The fact that metaphysical ideas exist and are believed in does nothing to prove the actual existence of their content or of the object they refer to . . . . Once metaphysical ideas have lost their capacity to recall and evoke the original experience they have not only become useless but prove to be actual impediments on the road to wider development" (174, 1948/1950, p. 34). "True faith seems

nonsense to me; the experience exists or it does not exist" (100, 1939, Part II, pp. 142-43 (This passage was somehow misplaced in the edited version of 1959; it appears in vol. 4, lecture 9 (1940) of the original notes.)). Cf. also 95, 1932, pp. 173-74; 156, 1943, p. 13,

The resultant identification of the "true" and the "factual" is another instance of Jung's undisciplined philosophical language, for which he has often been attacked. White epitomizes the criticisms in the succinct remark: "To call any idea 'psychologically true' simply on the ground that it exists is at least open to misunderstanding, and we are left guessing what could possible be 'psychologically false' " (1960, p. 50). Eric Fromm goes too far in his attack on Jung's notion of truth (cf. 135, 1939, p. 544) when he writes: "Contrary to him, I believe that a lie is never a 'spiritual fact' (Fromm thus translates Jung's "*seelische Tatsache*"), nor any other fact for that matter, escept that of being a lie" (1960, p. 116). Surely the defense of the canons of objective truth does not require us to deny that even false statements can be deeply significant for those who believe them. The point is so fundamental to psychoanalysis that we can scarcely take Fromm seriously here, though Jung's phrasing is hardly clear (e.g., 32, 1912, p. 132).

Of the many, many attempts to effect a rapprochement between Jung's psychological theory and philosophical metaphysics, the most promising I know of appears in a recent work by the theologian David Burrell (1974, pp. 182-237). Burrell suggests how uncovering the metaphysic implicit in Jung's own theories and highlighting Jung's many positive insights into the psychology implicit in' much of traditional metaphysics could overcome Jung's accustomed, intemperate attacks on metaphysics, and so also provide creative links to theological reflection that Jung himself did not perceive.

Chapter 5 *Imago Dei:* Fact and Interpretation

1. In his introduction to a book on palmistry, Jung refers favorably to the author's method as one that is highly intuitive, i.e., where only special talent, duly trained, can yield the relevant data (160, 1944, p. xii). This is the precise point I wish to argue here in reference to Jung's own method. A draft of the ideas presented here appeared in an earlier publication (1976).

2. Jung himself claimed that this refusal to reduce his method to a "technique" was an argument in favor of its status as a science (77, 1929; 83, 1931, 2: 45; 161, 1945, p. 88). Progoff's reference to "the details of the method by which Jung attempted to achieve individuation through psychotherapeutic techniques" goes wholly against the spirit of Jung's thinking (1953, p. 144). Likewise Hostie's claim that "throughout his life Jung had followed a very definite method" (1957, p. 7), clearly exceeds Jung's own appraisal of his life's work (cf. 197, 1952, p. 11).

3. Rather complete descriptive summaries of Jung's analytical techniques can be found in Adler, 1966, pp. 22-91; Fordham, 1958, pp. 168-79.

4. Frequent references to active imagination and painting occur in Jung's works (cf. von Franz, 1959; Humbert, 1971; Hull, 1971). The use of dancing, sculpture, and automatic writing is rare and not too clear (cf. 42, 1916/1958, p. 84; 167, 1946/1954, p. 202; Fierz, 1968).

5. I use this phrase to refer to the "directed association" that Jung contrasts with Freud's "free association." In Jung's method, the patient "associates" under the direction of the therapist, who focuses attention on an image or complex of images acquired in practice of one of the techniques mentioned above. Amplification on the *objective* level is more concerned with interpretation than with the gathering of raw data, and will be treated later. This distinction, vague in Jung's writings, has been clearly developed in Hobson's valuable article (1971).

6. Jung himself recognized that even in the dream state there was a modicum of consciousness at work. But its only function was to observe; it *could not* affect the workings of the unconscious (55, 1923, p. 59). Moreover, to him any distinction between the dream as lived through and the dream as narrated by the patient is irrelevant (cf., e.g., 161, 1945, p. 85), an opinion that I wish to question here.

7. Note that Jung distinguishes memory-images from those images proceeding directly from the unconscious mind (73, 1929, Part II, p. 49).

8. Precisely what is meant by this term is unclear. In some contexts *absolute* seems to indicate the undeniable, prereflective immediacy of the experience. Yet surely it can be claimed that in all experience of the world around us, including the most intellectually disciplined and sophisticated, there is an element of immediacy and thus room for this special sense of *absolute.* In other places the word seems to suggest an acceptance of unconscious events by a cautious refusal to suppress them as frivolous or dangerous.

   If the word is puzzling and not always helpful, we must still ask whether Jung "relativizes" God over against the *imago Dei* of personal experience, as many critics have claimed. Von Franz's assertion that Jung's stress on the absolute nature of experience frees him from all such criticism (1971, p. 31) fails to reckon with this obscurity.

9. For example, he cites at length the case of a woman whose dreams revealed that her "God" was her bank account (84, 1931, 2: 136 ff.). He used the same principle in speaking of *conscious* attitudes as well. Thus he called sex Freud's "God" (237, 1961, p. 151), respectability the "God of the West" (59, 1925, p. 73; 73, 1930, Part II, pp. 140, 164; 84, 1933, 10: 101-2), yellow gold the "God" of Rockefeller (84, 1933, 8: 133-34), etc.

10. I shall here restrict myself to visual imagery, although *sensu stricto* "God-image" includes the hearing of voices, the entertaining of abstract ideas, the evocation of a numinous presence, etc., all of which may occur in the absence of any visual image.

11. Jung clearly acknowledges this point (99, 1933, 1: 103-4).

12. *Coincidentia, conjunctio, complexio, unio,* and their German equivalents are all used synonymously by Jung in this connection, irrespective of the philosophical,

astrological, alchemical, or mathematical overtones peculiar to one or the other of them.

13. This same distinction holds for fantasies, visions, and products of active imagination. A further factor, unique to the dream, is that it is the rare person who is able to recall even a small fraction of his dreams. This would appear to increase the dissatisfaction of equating nocturnal experience with the waking narration.

14. Stekel, 1960, 1: 13. An example of such a phenomenon is given by one of Jung's own patients who recalls how, after beginning therapy with Jung, her dreams at once began to reveal "Jungian" material (Bügler, 1963, p. 24). Sargant gives the example of a patient undergoing three months of analysis by a Freudian and three months by a Jungian, resulting in different dreams (1957, p. 58). G. Adler comments on this case: "All one can say is that with different schools, different aspects or levels of the unconscious are either activated or observed" (1961, p. 45). Shortly thereafter, in apparent contradiction to this view, he comments that we must simply "assume" that there is no influence of consciousness on the processes of the unconscious (p. 47).

15. On one occasion, during a seminar lecture, Jung referred to his "picture-method" —by which he encouraged patients to depict their fantasies or feelings in paintings —as a "hypothesis" (84, 1930, 1: 2, 6, 7). This qualification then promptly disappears from his further elaboration of the data.

16. As de la Croix has correctly pointed out, Jung's descriptive models tend to shift from the indicative to the imperative mood, taking on a normative task and thus sacrificing the very scientific status Jung intended for them (1960, pp. 207-8).

17. 124. 1936, 1: 8; 156, 1943, p. 42.

18. Westmann, 1958, p. 180.

19. Jung's sole reference to this is cryptic, vaguely suggesting that "interpretation" is in fact necessary in the gathering of primary material: "No interpretations worth mentioning were then attempted because the dreamer, owing to his excellent scientific training and ability, did not require any assistance. Hence conditions were really ideal for unprejudiced observation and recording" (156, 1943, p. 42).

20. Several of Jung's critics have accused him of denying conscious and rational reflection on the reality of God its rightful place as a psychological datum (cf. White, 1960, pp. 53-54; Hostie, 1957, p. 222; Haendler, 1953, p. 214). This failure can be seen in part to follow from this general obscurity in his notion of "unconscious facts."

21. The only occasion on which Jung attempted to give a definition of image was in 1920 (51, 1920/1960, pp. 442-47).

22. Following Wundt, Jung defines *apperception* as "a psychic process by which a new content is articulated with similar, already existing contents in such a way that it becomes understood, apprehended, or "clear" (ibid., p. 412).

23. These two qualities appear to be correlatives, as are those of the personal and the pathological (see Jacobi, 1959, p. 25); but the point is not clear in Jung.

24. 213, 1956, p. x.

25. A general account of Jung's theory of projection can be found in an essay by C. A. Meier (1959a).

26. Many critics like Medard Boss (1957, p. 53) and Igor Caruso (1964, pp. 10-12) have rightly criticized Jung for dismissing Freud's causal models while at the same time slipping into his theory of the archetypes his own causal explanations, which differ from Freud's only in being tacit and disguised.

27. Jung defines projection as the expulsion of a subjective content into an object. It is "passive" when it occurs unintentionally, autonomously; "active" when it concerns the attaching of a subjective judgment to an object. All projection is an unconscious process (to draw the logical conclusion from his classification of projection under what he calls "identity") (51, 1920/1960, pp. 457-58, 441). Had Jung made much use of the notion of active projection, he would likely have seen the necessity of examining the inconsistencies and obscurities this gives rise to. In practice, the distinction was irrelevant to Jung's method.

28. Raising similar criticisms against Jung's use of spatial metaphors, White has tried to offer an alternative basis to this theory of projection in Aristotelean-Thomistic categories (1952, pp. 102-25).

29. A systematic and complete treatment of the complex with accompanying textural references from Jung's work, but without critical appraisal, has been done by Jacobi (1959, pp. 6-30).

30. I am here paraphrasing Christou's conclusions (1963, p. 34).

31. Presumably this is the reason for Jung's apparently contradictory claims that the collective unconscious itself is capable of being "scientifically established" (187, 1951, p. v), while asserting elsewhere that "there is no hope that the validity of any statement about unconscious states or processes will ever be verified scientifically" (167, 1946/1954, p. 214).

32. Jung translates the religious dictum, "We are in the hands of God," to mean that we have acknowledged "a certain psychological principle which is supposed to be more comprehensive than consciousness. . . . The totality is expressed by the Self," which one can become unaware of but cannot lose, any more than one can lose touch with God (84, 1934, 11: 106-7). Elsewhere he remarks, speaking of the Self as goal "We never grow into the divine stature; we are never with our God" (73, 1929, Part I, p. 185).

33. Kaune has argued well that the "symbols of totality" or "uniting symbols" do not of themselves justify the conclusion that only such symbols are able to represent the essence of the psyche (1967, pp. 97-98).

34. Dry shows other shades of meaning in addition to these (1961, p. 91).

35. 158, 1944/1948, pp. 291-93.

36. Hence Jung writes, without proof: "The most careful inquiry has never revealed any possibility of the patients being acquainted with the relevant literature or having other information about such ideas" (128, 1937/1940, p. 103).

37. To my knowledge the only occasion on which Jung acknowledged the possibility of thought transference, only to dismiss it immediately and with good cause, was in relation to the well-known case in 1906 of the "sun-phallus" vision of a schizophrenic patient. Four years later Jung discovered an exact parallel to the vision in an ancient Mithraic document that had been published after the patient had been committed to the hospital (64, 1927/1931, pp. 150-51). Ellenberger remarks that in fact a similar image is to be found in Creuzer's *Symbolic* (1841), opening up the remote possibility that Jung, who was acquainted with the work, had already met it previously (1970, p. 743 n. 140). A further complication arises from the fact—disguised in later accounts of the case and even in the revision of the original passage—that it was not Jung himself but a pupil of his, J. Honeger, who had first discovered the patient's vision (cf. 24, 1911-12, pp. 108-9 and 186, 1950, p. 101).

It is also interesting to note that in a seminar lecture Jung makes reference to the notion of "mental contagion," giving the case of a man whom he analyzed through his son's dreams (73, 1928, Part I, p. 18; cf. 73, 1930, Part II, p. 195)! He did not, however, consider the possible consequences for his hypothesis of the collective unconscious that such a case suggests.

38. 82, 1930/1950, p. 105. Elsewhere Jung remarks: "Even though we do not understand the dream, it is working and causing changes. If we understand, however, we have the privilege of working with the timeless spirit in ourselves" (73, 1928, Part I, p. 164). Meier calls this "the principle of omniscience," adding that it is a good example of how, *nolens volens,* Jung involves himself in metaphysics (1959b, p. 76). Jung himself is sometimes more cautious, observing that such an idea is not capable of empirical verificaton: "If I even discovered a case in which such a higher intelligence was absolutely certain, it would make a great impression on me. It has looked suspiciously like it sometimes, but I have never met an absolutely certain case" (100, 1939, Part II, p. 213; cf. 38, 1928/1948, p. 256; 165, 1945/1947, p. 240 n. 1; letter to H. Goodrich, 20 May 1940).

39. Although modern biology had exploded this cliché, Jung quite simply accepted it as a demonstrable principle (cf., e.g., 141, 1939, p. 287; Fordham, 1957, pp. 28-33). Among Jung's disciples, Eric Neumann is best known for having developed this idea at greater length. For a short summary of his approach, see Neumann, 1961.

40. The phrase is taken from Lévy-Bruhl, whom Jung cites. When Lévy-Bruhl recanted the notion in his *Carnets,* Jung lamented the fact, since he claimed it had a "sound psychological basis" (203, 1954, p. 250 n. 662). Jung's critics have proved less sympathetic to the notion. Even Paul Radin, perhaps the most important anthropologist to express his profound debt to Jung's psychology, dismisses this aspect of his thought (cf., e.g., 1956, pp. 39, 69).

41. Here again we have an instance of creeping generalization, for Jung totally denied the relevance of cultural factors on psychological phenomena once he had fixed on the notion of a collective psyche. Among his critics, some have completely dismissed his explanation in favor of a purely cultural explanation for

the origin of myth (e.g., Malinowski, 1960, p. 157), while others have tried to tread a middle path that makes use of both models (e.g., Kerényi, 1967, p. xxvi).

42. An affinity with the notion of the "pleroma" in the *Septem sermones* has already been noted (chap. 1 above, §3). The idea appears most often in the seminar notes (cf. 71, 1928, p. 54; 73, 1928, Part I, p. 40; 84, 1930, 1: 213; 84, 1933, 9: 109; see also 239, n.d., p. 63), but also slips into his published work (203, 1954, p. 300; 87, 1931, p. 69). These passages lend support to Gebser's comment that the step "which Jung could not take as a *scientist* he had probably already taken as a *man*," namely, the positing of the collective unconscious as a "cosmic ground of being" (1943, pp. 190-92).

43. Jung himself was aware of the danger of falling into this trap (78, 1929, p. 109), but succumbed nonetheless.

44. Balmer has given a lengthy but unsystematic synopsis of the whole tangle of senses that Jung attributed to the archetype (1972, pp. 74-101). Although his criticisms derive in part from an inadequate presentation of Jung's thought, his montage of quotations amply demonstrates the lack of care with which Jung expressed himself at times. Rümke differentiates five possible definitions of the archetype, concluding that the theory is scientifically unreliable (1950, p. 457).

45. Thus Jung compared the archetypes to Kant's categories as *transcendental* conditions for the possibility of knowledge. But he also hints at their having a *physical* basis in the brain, so that they might then be transmitted genetically. It would be misleading to say that he argued his case; rather, he merely speculated on its possibility. Critics are divided in their judgment. Some think that with the further development of genetics it will be seen how the archetypes can be successfully reduced, without remainder, to physiological processes. Others hold that Jung erred in attempting to align his doctrine of the archetypes to genetic theory, since they refer only to the fundamental realities and experiences of life, constant and universal because they belong to human nature or because they merely broaden the age-old conception of "natural law." By far the majority of commentators, however, stress the importance of sociocultural patterns. These Jung himself all but totally ignores in his explanation. One of Jung's ablest and severest critics, Medard Boss, presents a rather odd, almost Leibnizian, alternative by asserting that one must attribute the repetition of archaic motifs in unconscious fantasies to the direct intervention of God in an act of self-revelation whereby a coordinated unity, akin to the preestablished harmony of the monads, is established (1963, pp. 54-55; 1957, pp. 53-54).

46. Hübscher's description of the archetypes as (in Goethe's phrase) a sort of "alphabet of the World Spirit" (1957, p. 183) is well chosen, because it indicates the way in which Jung posits intelligible content in the archetypes and establishes a quasi-syntactical similarity among the variety of archetypal images. It is interesting to recall here the criticism of Lévi-Strauss, who points to what he sees as Jung's basic but tacit assumption of a necessary and self-evident connection between a given mythic pattern and a certain meaning as "comparable to the long-supported error that a sound may possess a certain

affinity with a meaning" (1963, p. 208). A rather hasty attempt by Cooley (1968-69) to reconcile the views of the two thinkers correctly points out that Jung understood the meaning of an archetype as broader than that of any specific archetypal symbol that expressed it; but he fails to criticize the principles on which Jung established the meaning-content of the archetypes, thus missing the main point of the debate.

47. I find no support in Jung's writings, lectures, or correspondence for the assertion that he had tried to provide a scientifically based theodicy, as some of his commentators claim (cf., e.g., Thornton, 1965, p. 138; Froboese-Thiele, 1950, p. 346).

48. I find myself wholly out of sympathy with those who claim that Jung has simply *identified* God and the psyche as metaphysical equivalents (e.g., Granjel, 1948, p. 294; Affemann, 1957, pp. 17-18; Frischknecht, 1945, pp.25-27).

49. Von Franz's testimony here is clear: "He was personally convinced that God was an objective reality transcendent to the psyche" (1971, p. 34).

50. It is helpful in this regard to read through Jung's exchange of letters with E. A. Bennet in 1960 (1961, pp. 95-103).

51. I have hitherto neglected to mention Glover's uncompromising attack on Jung's work (1950). Although the book contains a number of valid criticisms, there is hardly a page that does not show up the gross distortions to which Glover's unsympathetic approach to Jung and his avid loyalty to Freud have led. In later years Glover himself softened his attitude toward Jung's work, but his book continued to exercise considerable influence among non-Jungian psychologists. For example, Fortis's 1968 comparison of Freud and Jung repeats most all of Glover's exaggerations without question.

52. Jung considered this a strength of his approach, in contrast to that of Freud which was, in Jung's words, "originally gleaned from morbid minds" (85, 1931, p. xviii).

53. I cite two passages (which, incidentally, contradict one another) by way of illustration: "One of the unbreakable rules in scientific research is to take an object as known only so far as the inquirer is in a position to make scientifically valid statements about it. 'Valid' in this sense simply means what can be verified by facts" (165, 1945/1947, p. 207). "We find that the validity of psychic facts cannot be subjected either to epistemological criticism or to scientific verification" (62, 1926, p. 328).

54. Cf. 30, 1942, pp. 111-112; 77, 1929, pp. 42-43; 89, 1931, pp. 145-47; 101, 1934, p. 66; 109, 1937, 8:78.

55. Mairet, a student of Adlerian psychology, summarizes these criticisms succinctly: "Of the increasing number of people who have adopted the Master of Zurich as their chief spiritual guide and interpreter, the majority is probably alienated from any church, and had adopted Jungianism as a way of life *extra ecclesiam*. It is true that Júng is always warning people that he is an empirical thinker; that psychology is essentially different from religion. . . . All this does not save

him from his being regarded by not a few of the professing Christians who know his work as a gnostic and heresiarch whose teaching is a danger to the faith" (1956, p. 69). On the other side, one may refer to the interesting attempt by Ivan Alm (1935) to go into the question somewhat more critically, studying Jung's views in the light of Otto's notion of mysticism and pointing up both the similarities and the differences between the two.

56. 51, 1920/1960, p. 253.

57. Jung did not settle on any single name for this method, referring to it as "comparative," "synthetic," "historical," and the like (cf. 30, 1943, pp. 80-89; 32, 1912, pp. 145-47; 37, 1914, p. 187; 51, 1920/1960, p. 423; 156, 1943, p. 289: 186, 1950, pp. xxv-vi, 367-68; 221, 1958, pp. 340, 389, 406).

58. A recent work by James Hillman (1975) is perhaps the most revolutionary attempt made to date to question the biases that psychological models impose on God-images appearing as psychic phenomena. Working out of a basically Jungian position, he goes beyond Jung in the notion of a single imperial ego to the interpretation of God-images in a fundamentally monotheistic frame of reference. Fairness to psychic data, Hillman insists, requires a polytheistic psychology, and a decentralization of subjectivity, which views the ego as but one member of a commune of possible imaginal centers. Freud's suspicion about Jung (stated in a letter of 12 November 1911) that "his horizon has been too narrowed by Christianity," is taken seriously in this exceedingly important book and raises the sort of critical questions about Jung's notion of the *imago Dei* that I have had, rightly or wrongly, to neglect in focusing on methodological issues.

59. I am using *mythology* here as a shorthand to cover the entire range of related disciplines to which Jung refers.

60. Paul Ricoeur argues that Freud's psychology can be seen essentially to operate from the opposite hermeneutic pole, working as a demystification of language in terms of repressed desires (1970, p. 26). Although he has nothing to say of Jung's work, finding it too confused (p. 76), there is good reason to suppose that his approach to psychoanalysis would be equally valid for analytical psychology.

61. "Just as psychological knowledge furthers our understanding of the historical material, so, conversely, the historical material can throw light on individual psychological problems" (186, 1950, p. 5).

62. The distinction between *Geisteswissenschaften* and *Naturwissenschaften* does not figure in Jung's writings. Toni Wolff had made use of a similar distinction in her 1935 essay on Jung's methodology, which Jung referred to casually in a revision of an earlier lecture with these words: "In respect of its natural subject-matter and its method of procedure, modern empirical psychology belongs to the natural sciences, but in respect of its method of explanation it belongs to the human sciences" (56, 1946, p. 90). Jung's usual preference for the unqualified term *Wissenschaft* is indicative of his hesitation in locating his

work exclusively with either the natural or the human sciences, and indeed in attempting a clarification on this level.

63. Writing of dream interpretation, Jung comments. "I must content myself wholly with the fact that the result means something to the patient and sets his life in motion again. I may allow myself only one criterion for the result of my labors: Does it work? As for my scientific hobby—my desire to know *why* it works—this I must reserve for my spare time" (77, 1929, pp. 42-43). The view argued here is that Jung's "scientific" ventures were purely and simply a consequence of his "interpretative" therapeutics, a reflection on his procedure and not a separate project with a different strategy and set of principles.

64. This implies that in Jung's methodology, as set out above, only his general remarks on the "energic point of view" accurately reflect the nature of his method.

To my knowledge, the only commentator seriously to suggest such a project has been Peter Homans (1969). Yet he overlooks all those problems related to Jung's methodological reflections which I have made the focus of my attention.

Bibliography

Works by C. G. Jung

The following list includes only those of Jung's works, and only those revisions and editions, which have been specifically referred to in the text and notes of the foregoing study. A complete bibliography of the Corpus Jungianum is being prepared for vol. 19 of the *Collected Works,* to be published in the near future.

In their English translation, the *Collected Works* (C.W.) are being published in the United States by the Bollingen Foundation in conjunction with Princeton University Press, and in England by Routledge and Kegan Paul of London. The latest editions have been used here.

Certain titles have been marked with an asterisk (*) to indicate the original German edition of a specific edition otherwise cited in the English translation. They are similarly indicated in the text and notes, an asterisk following the respective page number.

As explained above (chap. 1, n. 1), the dates of individual works, given here before the titles, do not always correspond to the actual dates of publication.

1 1896. Die Grenzen der exacten Wissenschaften. Lecture to Zofingia on 28 November 1896.

2 1897. Einige Gedanke über Psychologie. Lecture to the Zofingia on 15 May 1897.

3 1898. Gedanken über Wesen and Wert spekulativer Forschung. Lecture to the Zofingia on 21 May 1898.

4 1899. Gedanken über die Auffassung des Christentums mit Bezug auf die Lehre Albrecht Ritschls. Lecture to the Zofingia on 7 January 1899.

5 1901. Sigmund Freud: On Dreams. A report given to the staff of the Burghölzli Hospital in Zurich on 25 January 1901, and printed in *Spring* (1973), pp. 171-79.

6 1902. On the Psychology and Pathology of So-called Occult Phenomena. C. W., 1: 3-88.

7 1903. On Manic Mood Disorder. C. W., 1: 109-34.

8 1903. On Simulated Insanity. C. W., 1: 159-87.

9 1905. Cryptomnesia. C. W., 1: 95-106.

10 1905. An Analysis of the Associations of an Epileptic. In *Studies in Word-Association*, pp. 206-26. London: Routledge and Kegan Paul, 1969.

11 1906. The Psychological Significance of the Association Experiment. *Archiv für Kriminalanthropologie und Kriminalistik* 22 (1906): 145-62.

12 1906. The Psychology of Dementia Praecox. C. W., 3: 1-151.

13 1906-61. *C. G. Jung Letters, 1906-1961*. Published in three volumes by Walter Verlag, Olten Freiburg, 1972-73. Vol. 1 (of two vols.) of the English translation was published by Routledge and Kegan Paul, 1973. *The Freud-Jung Letters*. Princeton, N.J.: Princeton University Press, 1974.

14 1907. Associations d'idées familiales. *Archives de psychologie* 7; no. 26 (1907): 160-68.

1909. The Familial Constellation. In *Collected Papers on Analytical Psychology*, pp. 119-32. London: Baillière, Tindall and Cox, 1920.

15 1908. The Freudian Theory of Hysteria. C. W., 4: 10-24.

16 1908. The Content of the Psychoses. C.W., 3: 158-78.

17 1909. The Significance of the Father in the Destiny of the Individual. C.W., 4: 301-23.

1948. Ibid. The revision is indicated in the text and notes by use of brackets.

18 1909. The Analysis of Dreams. C.W., 4: 25-34.

19 1910. Randbemerkungen zu dem Buch von Fr. Wittels: *Die sexuelle Not. Jahrbuch für psychoanalytische und psychopathologische Forschungen* 2 (1910): 312-15.

20 1910. Referate über psychologische Arbeiten schweizerischer Autoren (bis Ende 1909). *Jahrbuch für psychoanalytische und psychopathologische Forschungen* 2 (1910): 356-88.

21 1910. A Contribution to the Psychology of Rumor. C.W., 4:35-47.

22 1910. On the Criticism of Psychoanalysis. C.W., 4:74-77.

23 1911. On the Significance of Number Dreams. C.W., 4:48-55.

24 1911-12. Psychology of the Unconscious. London: Kegan Paul, 1917; New York; Moffat Yard, 1916.

25 1911. A critical review of Morton Prince's *The Mechanism and Interpretation of Dreams*. C.W., 4:56-73.

26 1911. A Criticism of Bleuler's Theory of Schizophrenia. C.W., 3: 197-202.

27 1911. A Case of Neurosis in a Child. C. W., 4: 204-26.

28 1912. Über die psychoanalytische Behandlung nervöser Leiden. *Correspondenzblatt für Schweizer Ärzte* 42 (1912): 1079-80, 1083-84.

29 1912. Concerning Psychoanalysis. C.W., 4: 78-81.

30 1912. New Paths in Psychology. C.W., 7:245-68.

1916. Ibid. The revision is indicated in the text and notes by use of brackets.

1925. The Unconscious in the Normal and Pathological Mind. In *Two Essays on Analytical Psychology*, London: Ballière, Tindall and Cox, 1928.

1942. On the Psychology of the Unconscious. C.W., 7: 7-119.

31 1912. America Facing its Most Tragic Moment. An interview printed in the *New York Times*, 29 September 1912.

32 1912. The Theory of Psychoanalysis. Lectures given at Fordham University, New York, September 1912. C.W., 4: 85-203.

33 1913. Letter from Dr. Jung. *Psychoanalytic Review* 1 (1913): 117-18.

34 1913. Contribution to the Study of Psychological Types. C.W., 6: 499-509.

35 1913. General Aspects of Psychoanalysis. C.W., 4: 229-42.

36 1913. Some Crucial Points in Psychoanalysis: A Correspondence between Dr. Jung and Dr. Löy. C.W., 4: 252-89.

37 1914. On Psychological Understanding. C.W., 3:179-93.

38 1914. The Psychology of Dreams, In *Collected Papers on Analytical Psychology*, pp. 299-311. London: Baillière, Tindall and Cox, 1920.

1928. Allgemeine Gesichtspunkte zur Psychologie des Traumes. In *Über die Energetik der Seele*, pp. 112-84. Zurich: Rascher, 1928.

1948. General Aspects of Dream Psychology. C.W., 8:237-80.

39 1916. Preface to the first edition of *Collected Papers on Analytical Psychology*. C.W., 4: 290-93.

40 1916. Septem sermones ad mortuus, written by Basilides in Alexandria, the City where the East toucheth the West. Reprinted in *Memories, Dreams, Reflections*, recorded and ed. Aniela Jaffé, pp. 378-90. New York: Vintage Books, 1961.

41 1916. Adaptation. A posthumous paper, written in 1916 and reprinted in *Spring* (1970), pp. 170-73.

42 1916. The Transcendent Function. Original manuscript published in English by the Students Association of the C.G. Jung Institute, 1957 (privately printed).

1958. Ibid., revised. C.W., 8: 67-91.

43 1916. Individuation and Collectivity. A posthumous paper, written in 1916 and reprinted in *Spring* (1970) pp. 174-76.

44 1916. The Structure of the Unconscious. C.W., 7: 269-304.

1928. The Relations between the Ego and the Unconscious. C.W., 7: 127-241.

45 1917. Preface to the second edition of *Collected Papers on Analytical Psychology*. C.W., 4: 293-97.

46 1918. The Role of the Unconscious. C.W., 10: 3-28.

47 1919. Introduction to Elida Evans, *The Problem of the Nervous Child*. London: Kegan Paul, 1921, pp. v-viii.

48 1919. On the Problem of Psychogenesis in Mental Diseases. C.W., 3: 211-25.

49 1919. Instinct and the Unconscious. C.W., 8: 129-38.

50 1919. The Psychological Foundations of Belief in Spirits. In *Contributions to Analytical Psychology*, pp. 250-69. London: Kegan Paul, 1928.

1948. Ibid. C.W., 8:301-18.

51 1920. Psychological Types. London: Kegan Paul, 1923.

1949. Psychologische Typen. Zurich: Rascher, 1950.

1960. Psychological Types. C.W., 6:1-495.

52 1922. On the Relation of Analytical Psychology to Poetry. C.W., 15: 65-83.

53 1922. The Love Problem of a Student. C.W., 10: 97-112.

54 1923. Human Relationships in Relation to the Process of Individuation. Notes of a seminar at Polzeath, Cornwall, England. Summer 1923.

55 1923. Child Development and Education. C.W., 17: 49-62.

56 1923-24. Analytical Psychology and Education. In *Contributions to Analytical Psychology*, pp. 313-82. London: Kegan Paul, 1928.

1946. Ibid., C.W., 17: 63-132.

57 1924. Foreword to the second Swiss edition of *Wandlungen und Symbole der Libido*. C.W., 5: xxviii-ix.

58 1925. Marriage as a Psychological Relationship. C.W., 17: 189-201.

59 1925. Notes on the Seminar on Analytical Psychology. Zurich, 23 March to 6 July 1925 (privately printed, 1926). 16 lectures.

60 1925. Dreams and Symbolism. Notes of a seminar at Swange, England. Summer 1925, 12 lectures.

61 1925. The Significance of the Unconscious in Individual Education. C.W., 17: 149-64.

62 1926. Spirit and Life. C.W., 8:319-37.

63 1926. Foreword to the second edition of "The Significance of the Father in the Destiny of the Individual." C.W., 4:301-2.

64 1927. Mind and Earth. In *Contributions to Analytical Psychology*, pp. 118-40. London: Kegan Paul, 1928.

1931. In the revision, the original article was broken up into two articles: The Structure of the Psyche. C.W., 8:139-58. Mind and Earth. C.W., 10:29-49.

65 1927. Analytical Psychology and Weltanschauung. In *Contributions to Analytical Psychology*, pp. 141-63. London: Kegan Paul, 1928.

1931. Ibid., C.W., 8:358-81.

66 1927. Woman in Europe. C.W., 10: 113-33.

67 1927. Memorial to J.S. *Spring* (1955), p. 63.

68 1928. Psychoanalysis and the Cure of Souls. C.W., 11:348-54.

69 1928. On Psychic Energy. C.W., 8:3-66. (This paper was originally framed in 1912.)

70 1928. Das Seelenproblem des modernen Menschen. *Europäische Revue* 4, nos. 2/9 (1928): 700-15.

1931. The Spiritual Problem of Modern Man. C.W., 10: 74-94.

71 1928. Lectures on Dream Analysis. Notes on lectures given at a seminar in Zurich, 7 November to 12 December 1928. (privately printed, 1928). 6 lectures.

72 1928. A Psychological Theory of Types. C.W., 6:524-41.

73 1928-30. Dream Analysis. Notes of seminars given at Zurich. The original mimeographed edition contained five volumes plus an index volume. It was later reedited into two volumes by Carol Baumann (1958) and privately printed:

Part I: Vols. 1 and 2 of the original notes.

Part II: Vols. 3, 4, and 5 of the original notes. The lectures for 1929 begin on p. 67; those for 1930 on p. 108.

74 1929. Freud and Jung: Contrasts. C.W., 4: 333-40.

75 1929. Commentary on *The Secret of the Golden Flower*. In *The Secret of the Golden Flower*. London: Kegan Paul, 1930.

1938. Ibid., C.W., 13: 1-56.

76 1929. Problems of Modern Psychotherapy. C.W., 16:53-75.

77 1929. The Aims of Psychotherapy. C.W., 16: 36-52.

78 1929. The Significance of Constitution and Heredity in Psychology. C.W., 8:107-13.

79 1930. Die seelischen Probleme der menschlichen Altersstufen. *Neue Züricher Zeitung*, 14 and 16 March 1930.

1931. The Stages of Life. C.W., 8: 387-403.

80 1930. Richard Wilhelm: *In Memoriam*. C.W., 15:53-62.

81 1930. Introduction to Kranefeldt's *Secret Ways of the Mind*. C.W., 4: 324-32.

82 1930. Psychology and Literature. In *Modern Man in Search of a Soul*, pp. 175-99. London: Kegan Paul, 1933.

1950. Ibid., C.W., 15:84-105.

83 1930–31. Berichte über die deutschen Seminare. Lectures given in Küsnacht-Zürich. Privately printed in Stuttgart, 1931-32.

Vol. 1: lectures from 6 to 11 October 1930.
Vol. 2: lectures from 5 to 10 October 1931.

84 1930–34. Interpretation of Visions. Notes of seminars given at Zurich. Privately printed in Zurich, 1930-34.

Vol. 1: lectures from 15 October to 9 December 1930.
Vol. 2: lectures from 21 January to 25 March 1931.
Vol. 3: lectures from 6 May to 15 June 1931.
Vol. 4: lectures from 11 November to 16 December 1931, with index.
Vol. 5: lectures from 20 January to 16 March 1932.
Vol. 6: lectures from 4 May to 29 June 1932.
Vol. 7: lectures from 2 November to 7 December 1932.
Vol. 8: lectures from 18 January to 8 March 1933.
Vol. 9: lectures from 3 May to 21 June 1933.
Vol 10: lectures from 4 October to 13 December 1933.
Vol. 11: lectures from 24 January to 21 March 1934.

85 1931. Foreword to Charles Roberts Aldrich, *The Primitive Mind and Modern Civilization*, pp. xv-xvii. New York: Harcourt, Brace and Co., 1931. Pp. xv-xvii.

86 1931. Introduction to Frances Wickes, *Analyse der Kinderseele*. C.W., 17:37-46.

87 1931. Archaic Man. C.W., 10:50-73.

88 1931. The Basic Postulates of Analytical Psychology. In *Modern Man in Search of a Soul*. London: Kegan Paul, 1933.

1934. Ibid., C.W., 8:338-57.

89 1931. The Practical Use of Dream Analysis. C.W., 16:139-61.

90 1932. Die Hypothese des Kollektiven Unbewussten. Autoreferat. In *Vierteljahrschrift der Naturforschenden Gesellschaft in Zürich* 77, no. 2 (1932): iv-v.

91 1932. Sigmund Freud in His Historical Setting. C.W., 15:33-40.

92 1932. Psychotherapists or the Clergy. C.W., 11:327-47.

93 1932. The Real and the Surreal. C.W., 8:382-84.

94 1932. The Kundalini Yoga. Notes on the seminar by Hauer with commentary by C.G. Jung. Zurich, 1932.

*Psychologischer Kommentar zu Hauers Seminar über den Tantra-Yoga. Zurich, 1932.

95 1932. The Development of Personality. C.W., 17:165-86.

96 1933. Review of G.R. Heyer, *Der Organismus der Seele. Europäische Revue* 9, no. 10 (1933): p. 639.

97 1933. Über Psychologie. In *Neue Schweizer Rundschau* 1 (1933): 21-28, 98-106.

1934. The Meaning of Psychology for Modern Man. C.W., 10:134-56.

98 1933. Brother Klaus. C.W., 11: 316-23.

99 1933. Bericht über das Berliner Seminar. Berlin, 1933. Privately printed. Lectures from 26 June to 1 July 1933.

100 1933-40. Modern Psychology. Notes on lectures given at the Eidgenössische Technische Hochschule in Zurich, originally delivered in German. The original notes, in six volumes, are here brought together in three volumes, privately printed in Zurich, 1959-60. Parts II and III bear the subtitle: The Process of Individuation.

Part I: Vol. 1 (lectures from 20 October 1933 to 23 February 1934; 1934 material begins on p. 43); Vol. 2 (lectures from 20 April 1934 to 12 July 1935; 1935 material begins on p. 170).

Part II: Vol. 3, Eastern Texts (lectures from 28 October 1938 to 23 June 1939; 1939 material begins on p. 52); Vol. 4, *Exercitia Spiritualia* of St. Ignatius of Loyola (lectures from 16 June 1939 to 8 March 1940; 1940 material begins on p. 212).

Part III: Vols. 5 and 6, Alchemy, with index. Vol. 5 (lectures from 8 November 1940 to 28 February 1941; 1941 material begins on p. 64); Vol. 6 (lectures from 5 May 1941 to 11 July 1941).

101 1934. Bericht über das Basler Seminar. Lectures from 1 to 6 October, 1934. Privately printed, Basel, 1935. Reprinted in *L'Homme à la découverte de son âme*, pp. 97-197, 273-332. Geneva: Editions du Mont-Blanc. 1970. This latter edition is cited in the text.

102 1934. The State of Psychotherapy Today. C.W., 10:157-73.

103 1934. A Rejoinder to Dr. Bally. C.W., 10:535-44.

104 1934. The Soul and Death. C.W., 8:404-15.

105 1934. A Study in the Process of Individuation. In *The Integration of the Personality*, pp. 30-51. London: Kegan Paul, Trench, Trubner and Co., 1940.

1950. Ibid., C.W., 9, no. 1: 290-354.

106 1934. La Révolution Mondiale. C.W., 10:496-502.

107 1934. Does the World Stand on the Verge of Spiritual Rebirth? *Hearst's International-Cosmopolitan*, April 1934, pp. 24-25, 179-82.

108 1934. Archetypes of the Collective Unconscious. In *The Integration of the Personality*, pp. 52-95. London: Kegan Paul, Trench, Trubner and Co., 1940.

1954. Ibid., C.W., 9, no. 1: 3-41.

109 1934-39. Psychological Analysis of Nietzsche's *Zarathustra*. Seminars given in Zurich, privately printed, 1934-42, with index:

Vol. 1: 8 lectures from 2 May to 27 June 1934.
Vol. 2: 10 lectures from 10 October to 12 December 1934.
Vol. 3: 8 lectures from 23 January to 13 March 1935.
Vol. 4: 8 lectures from 8 May to 26 June 1935.
Vol. 5: 9 lectures from 16 October to 11 December 1935.
Vol. 6: 7 lectures from 22 January to 4 March 1936.
Vol. 7: 8 lectures from 6 May to 24 June 1936.
Vol. 8: 9 lectures from 5 May to 30 June 1937.
Vol. 9: 7 lectures from 4 May to 22 June 1938.
Vol. 10: 12 lectures from 19 October to 15 February 1939.

110 1935. Presidential address to the 8th General Congress for Psychotheraphy, Bad Nauheim, 1935. C.W., 10:554-56.

111 1935. Foreword to Rose Mehlich, *J.H. Fichtes Seelenlehre und ihre Beziehung zur Gegenwart*, pp. 7-11. Zurich: Rascher, 1935.

112 1935. Foreword to Olga Freün von Koenig-Fachsenfeld, *Wandlungen des Traumproblems von der Romantik bis zur Gegenwart*, pp. iii-vi. Stuttgart: Ferdinand Enke, 1935.

113 1935. Editorial. C.W., 10:547-51.

114 1935. Psychologischer Kommentar zum *Bardo Thödol.* In *Das Tibetanische Totenbuch*, ed. W. Y. Evans-Wentz, pp. 15-35. Zurich: Rascher, 1936.

1953. Psychological Commentary on "The Tibetan Book of the Dead." C.W., 11: 509-52.

115 1935. Principles of Practical Psychotheraphy. C.W., 16:3-20.

116 1935. Analytical Psychology: Its Theory and Practice. Five lectures delivered under the auspices of the Institute of Medical Psychology, London, 30 September to 4 October 1935. London: Routledge and Kegan Paul, 1968.

117 1935. Dream Symbols of the Process of Individuation. In *The Integration of the Personality*, pp. 96-204. London: Kegan Paul, Trench, Trubner and Co., 1940.

118 1936. Wotan. C.W., 10:179-93.

119 1936. Yoga and the West. C.W., 11:529-37.

120 1936. Über den Archetypus, mit besonderer Berücksichtigung des Animabegriffes. *Zentralblatt für Psychotherapie und ihre Grenzgebiete* 9, no. 5 (1936): 259-74.

1954. Concerning the Archetype with Special Reference to the Anima Concept. C.W., 9, no. 1: 54-172.

121 1936. Psychology of Dictatorship. An interview printed in the *Observer* (London), 18 October 1936, p. 15.

122 1936. The Concept of the Collective Unconscious. C.W., 9, no. 1: 42-53.

123 1936. The Idea of Redemption in Alchemy. In *The Integration of the Personality*, pp. 205-80. London: Kegan Paul, Trench, Trubner and Co., 1940.

*Die Erlösungsvorstellungen in der Alchemie. *Eranos Jahrbuch*, 1936, pp. 13-111. Zurich: Rhein, 1937.

124 1936-37. Dream Symbols of the Individuation Process. Notes of a seminar at Bailey Island, Maine (vol. 1) and New York City

(vol. 2). Privately printed, Zurich, 1937-38:

Vol 1: 6 lectures from 20 to 25 November 1936.
Vol. 2: 5 lectures from 16 to 26 October 1937.

125 1936-37. Seminar über Kinderträume und ältere Literatur uber Traum-Interpretation. Given at the E.T.H., Zurich. Privately printed, Zurich, 1937.

126 1937. Bericht über die Berliner Vorträge von C. G. Jung. Seminar report. Privately printed, Berlin, 1937.

127 1937. The Realities of Practical Psychotherapy. A posthumous paper. C.W., 16: 327-38.

128 1937. Psychology and Religion. New Haven, Conn.: Yale University Press, 1938.
1940. Ibid., C.W., 11: 3-105.

129 1937. Notes on a talk of 1937, marking the end of a seminar. *Spring* (1972), pp. 144-48.

130 1937. Einige Bemerkungen zu den Visionen des Zozimos. In *Eranos Jahrbuch*, 1937, pp. 15-54. Zurich: Rhein, 1938.

1954. The Visions of Zozimos. C.W., 13:58-108.

131 1938. Foreword to the third edition of *Psychic Conflicts in a Child*. C.W., 17:6-7.

132 1938. Psychological Aspects of the Mother Archetype. *Spring* (1943), pp. 1-31.

1954. Ibid., C.W., 9, no. 1: 73-110.

133 1938-39. Psychologische Interpretation von Kinderträumen. Seminar at the E.T.H. in Zurich. 16 lectures from 25 October 1938 to 7 March 1939 (1939 material begins p. 70). Privately printed, Zurich, 1939.

134 1939. What India Can Teach Us. C.W., 10:525-30.

135 1939. Foreword to Daisetz Teitaro Suzuki, *Introduction to Zen Buddhism*. C.W., 11: 538-57.

136 1939. On the Psychogenesis of Schizophrenia. C.W., 3: 233-49.

137 1939. The Dreamlike World of India. C.W., 10:515-24.

138 1939. In Memory of Sigmund Freud. C.W., 15: 41-49.

139 1939. The Symbolic Life. Seminar talk given 5 April 1939 to the Guild of Pastoral Psychology, London (Lecture no. 80).

140 1939. Psychological Commentary on *The Tibetan Book of the Great Liberaton*, In *The Tibetan Book of the Great Liberation*, ed. W.Y. Evans-Wentz, pp. xxix-lxiv. London: Oxford University Press, 1954.

1955. Ibid. C.W., 11: 475-508.

141 1939. Conscious, Unconscious and Individuation. C.W., 9, no. 1: 275-89.

142 1939. Preface to Jolande Jacobi, *The Psychology of C.G. Jung*, p. ix. London: Routledge and Kegan Paul, 1969.

143 1939-40. Psychologische Interpretation von Kinderträumen. Seminar held at the E.T.H. in Zurich. 10 lectures. Privately printed, Zurich, 1939-40.

144 1940. Die verschiedenen Aspekte der Widergeburt. *Eranos Jahrbuch*, 1939, pp. 399-447. Zurich: Rhein, 1940.

1950. Concerning Rebirth. C.W., 9, no. 1: 111-47.

145 1940. The Psychology of the Child Archetype. In *Essays on a Science of Mythology*, pp. 97-138. New York: Panteheon Books, 1949.

1951. Ibid. C.W., 9, no. 1: 151-81.

146 1940. Zur Psychologie der Trinitätsidee. *Eranos Jahrbuch*, 1940/1941, pp. 31-64. Zurich: Rhein, 1942.

1948. A Psychological Approach to the Dogma of the Trinity. C.W., 11: 108-200.

147 1941. Psychological Aspects of the Kore. In *Essays on a Science of Mythology*, pp. 217-45. New York: Pantheon Books, 1949.

1951. Ibid. C.W., 9, no. 1: 182-203.

148 1941. Paracelsus as a Spiritual Phenomenon. C.W., 13: 111-89.

149 1941. Foreword to *Paracelsica: Zwei Vorlesungen über den Arzt und Philosophen Theophrastus*. C.W., 13: 110.

150 1941. Das Wandlungssymbol in der Messe. *Eranos Jahrbuch*, 1940/1941, pp. 67-155. Zurich: Rhein, 1942.

1954. Transformation Symbolism in the Mass. C.W., 11:201-96.

151 1941. Psychotherapy Today. C.W., 16:94-110.

152 1942. Der Geist Mercurius. *Eranos Jahrbuch*, 1942, pp. 179-236. Zurich: Rhein, 1943.

1947. The Spirit Mercurius. C.W., 13: 191-250.

153 1942. Psychotherapy and a Philosophy of Life. C.W., 16:76-83.

154 1943. The Psychology of Eastern Meditation. C.W., 11:558-75.

155 1943. Depth-Psychology and Self-Knowledge, *Spring* (1969) pp. 129-39.

156 1943. Psychology and Alchemy. C.W., 12: x, 1-483.

157 1944. The Holy Men of India. C.W., 11: 576-86.

158 1944. Vom Wesen des Traums. *Ciba Zeitschrift* 9, no. 99 (1944): 3546-57.

1948. On the Naure of Dreams. C.W., 8: 81-97.

159 1944. Epilogue to *L'Homme à la découverte de son âme*, pp. 333-34. Geneva: Éditions du Mont-Blanc, 1970.

160 1944. Foreword to Julius Spier, *The Hands of Children*, pp. xi-xii. London: Kegan Paul, Trench, Trubner and Co., 1944.

161 1945. Medicine and Psychotherapy. C.W., 16:84-93.

162 1945. After the Catastrophe. C.W., 10:194-217.

163 1945. The Enigma of Bologna. C.W., 14:56-88.

164 1945. Werden die Seelen Frieden finden? Ein Interview mit Dr. C.G. Jung. *Weltwoche* 13, no. 600 (1945): 3.

165 1945. Zur Psychologie des Geistes. *Eranos Jahrbuch*, 1945, pp. 385-448. Zurich: Rhein, 1946.

1947. The Phenomenology of the Spirit in Fairy Tales. C.W., 9, no. 1: 207-54.

166 1945. The Psychology of the Transference. C.W., 16: 163-323.

167 1946. The Spirit of Psychology. In *Spirit and Nature: papers from the Eranos Yearbooks*, pp. 371-444. London: Routledge and Kegan Paul, 1955.

1954. On the Nature of the Psyche. C.W., 8:159-234.

168 1947. Foreword to *Symbolik des Geistes*. Zurich: Rascher, 1948.

169 1947. Foreword to Mary Esther Harding, *Psychic Energy: Its Source and Goal*, pp. xi-xii. New York: Pantheon Books, 1947.

170 1948. Rede gehalten von Prof. Dr. C G. Jung anlässlich der Gründungsitzung des C. G. Jung-Institutes Zürich am 24. April 1948. Privately circulated.

171 1948. The Shadow, Anima and Animus. C.W., 9, no. 2: 8-22.

172 1948. Foreword to Edward White, *Uneingeschränktes Weltall*, pp. 7-14. Zurich: Origo, 1948.

173 1948. De Sulphure, *Nova acta paracelsica* 5 (1948): 27-40.

1954. Sulphur. C.W., 14:110-28.

174 1948. Über das Selbst, *Eranos Jahrbuch*, 1948, pp. 285-315. Zurich: Rhein, 1949.

1950. The Self. C.W., 9, no. 2: 23-35.

175 1948. Foreword to Lily Abegg, *Ostasien Denkt Anders*, pp. 3-4. Zurich: Atlantic, 1949.

176 1949. Foreword to Mary Esther Harding, *Woman's Mysteries*, pp. ix-xii. New York: Pantheon Books, 1955.

177 1949. Foreword to C. A. Meier, *Antike Inkubation und moderne Psychotherapie*. Zurich: Rascher, 1949.

178 1949. Foreword to Eric Neumann, *Depth-Psychology and a New Ethic*, pp. 11-18. London: Hodder and Stoughton, 1969.

179 1949. Foreword to Gerhard Adler, *Studies in Analytical Psychology*, pp. 3-5. London: Hodder and Stoughton, 1966.

180 1949. Dr. Carl Jung on the Occult. An interview by Norman Colgan. *Prediction* 15, no. 2 (1949): 7-10.

181 1950. Concerning Mandala Symbolism. C.W., 9, no. 1: 355-84.

182 1950. Foreword to Fanny Moser, *Spuk: Irrglaube oder Wahrglaube?* Baden-Zurich: GYR Verlag, 1950. 1: 9-12.

183 1950. Fall von Professor Jung. In *Spuk: Irrglaube oder Wahrglaubé?* Baden-Zurich: GYR Verlag, 1950. 1:253-60.

184 1950. *Aion: Researches into the Phenomenology of the Self.* C.W., 9, no. 2.

185 1950. Foreword to the *I Ching*. C.W., 11: 589-608.

186 1950. *Symbols of Transformation*. C.W., 5.

187 1951. Prefatory note to the English edition of *Psychology and Alchemy*. C.W., 13: v.

188 1951. Fundamental Questions of Psychotherapy. C.W., 16: 111-25.

189 1951. On Synchronicity. C.W., 8: 520-31.

190 1951. *Answer to Job*. C.W., 11: 359-470.

191 1951. Foreword to Zwi Werblowsky, *Lucifer and Prometheus*. C.W., 11: 311-15.

192 1952. Foreword to John Custance, *Wisdom, Madness, Folly*. New York: Pellegrini and Cudahy, 1952.

193 1952. Synchronizität als ein Prinzip akausaler Zusammenhänge. In *Naturerklärung und Psyche*, pp. 1-107. Zurich: Rascher, 1952.

1955. Synchronicity: An Acausal Connecting Principle. C.W., 8: 418-519.

194 1952. "Religion und Psychologie." *Merkur* 4, no. 5 (1952): 467-73.

195 1952. Foreword to Victor White, *God and the Unconscious*. C.W., 11:299-310.

196 1952. The Challenge of the Christian Enigma. *New Republic*, 27 April 1953, pp. 18-9.

197 1952. Foreword to Frieda Fordham, *An Introduction to the Psychology of C. G. Jung*, p. 11. Harmondsworth: Penguin Books, 1968.

198 1953. Foreword to John Weir Perry, *The Self in Psychotic Process*, pp. v-viii. London: Cambridge University Press, 1953.

199 1953. The Philosophical Tree. C.W., 13:251-349.

200 1954. On the Psychology of the Trickster Figure. C.W., 9, no. 1: 255-72.

201 1954. Mach immer alles ganz und richtig. . . *Weltwoche* 22, no. 1100 (1954): 31.

202 1954. C.G. Jung zu den fliegenden Untertassen. *Weltwoche* 22, no. 1078 (1954): 7.

203 1954. Mysterium Conjunctionis. C.W., 14.

204 1955. Mandalas. C.W., 9, No. 1: 387-90.

205 1955. The Meaning of the Christian Myth. *New Republic*, 21 February 1955, pp. 30-31.

206 1955. Men, Women and God. *Daily Mail.* An interview with Frederick Sands, in five parts. Part 5: "I Believe in God," 29 April, p. 6.

207 1955. Human Nature Does Not Easily Yield to Idealistic Advice. *New Republic*, 16 May 1955, pp. 18-19.

208 1955. Seelenarzt und Gottesglaube: Eine Stunde mit Prof. Dr. med. C. G. Jung. An interview with Georg Gerster in *Weltwoche* 23, no. 1116 (1955): 7.

209 1955. Carl Gustav Jung. An 80th birthday interview with Stephen Black in *News-Chronicle* (London), 26 July 1955, p. 4. The complete transcript of the interview is printed in E.A. Bennet, *C.G. Jung*. London: Barrie and Rockliff, 1961. pp. 146-53.

210 1955. How I Wrote My Answer to Job. C.W., 11:357-58.

211 1955. Statement in a publisher's brochure announcing K. Neumann's translation of *Die Reden Gotama Buddhas*. In *Gesammelte Werke*, 11:690-93. Zurich: Rascher, 1963.

212 1956. Wotan und der Rattenfänger. *Der Monat* 9, no. 97 (October 1956): 75-76.

213 1956. Foreword to Jolande Jacobi, *Complex, Archetype, Symbol in the Psychology of C. G. Jung*, New York: Pantheon Books, 1959, pp. 9-11.

214 1956. The Undiscovered Self: Present and Future. C.W., 10: 245-305.

215 1956-58. Answers to questions raised by Howard L. Philp in correspondence, in Philp, *Jung and the Problem of Evil*, pp. 5-7, 8-21, 209-25, 226-54. London: Salisburg Square, 1958.

216 1957. Foreword to Felicia Froboese-Thiele, *Träume—Eine Quelle religiöser Erfahrung?*, pp. 18-19. Göttingen: Vanderhoeck und Ruprecht, 1957.

217 1957. Foreword to Aniela Jaffé, *Apparitions and Precognition*, pp. v-viii. New Hyde Park, N.Y.: University Books, 1963.

218 1957. Foreword to Michael Fordham, *New Developments in Analytical Psychology*, pp. xi-xiv. London: Routledge and Kegan Paul, 1957.

219 1957. *Conversations with Carl Jung, and Reactions from Ernest Jones*, ed. Richard I. Evans. Princeton, N.J.: Van Nostrand Insight Books, 1964.

220 1958. Letter to E. Thornton, 7 July 1958. In James Aylward et al., *Spectrum psychologiae*, pp. 141-42.

221 1958. Flying Saucers: A Modern Myth of Things Seen in the Skies. C.W., 10: 308-433.

222 1958. A Psychological View of Conscience. C.W., 10: 437-55.

223 1958. Contribution to a symposium on the question: "If Christ Walked the Earth Today. . . ." *Cosmopolitan* 145, no. 6. (December 1958): 30.

224 1958. Definition of the "Self," C.W., 6: 460-61.

225 1959. Foreword to Toni Wolff, *Studies in Jungian Psychology*. C.W., 10: 469-76.

226 1959. Good and Evil in Analytical Psychology. C.W., 10: 456-68.

227 1959. Uber Psychotherapie und Wunderheiligen. In Wilhelm Bitter, ed, *Magie und Wunder in der Heilkunde*, pp. 7-9. Munich: Kinder, 1959.

228 1959. On the Frontiers of Knowledge. *Spring* (1960), pp. 7-20.

229 1959. Dr. Jung on Life and Death. A report by F. Fordham of John Freeman's interview with Jung. *Listener* 62 (1959): 722-25.

230 1959-60. Interviews with and letters from Jung, in Miguel Serrano, *C. G. Jung and Hermann Hesse: A Record of Two Friendships*, pp. 47-61, 68, 69-70, 74-75, 83-93, 96-102. New York: Schocken Books, 1970.

231 1960. Dr. Jung Looks Back and On. An interview with Hugo Charteris, in *The Daily Telegraph* (London), 21 January 1960, p. 8.

232 1960. The Art of Living. An interview with Gordon Young, in the *Sunday Times* (London), 17 July 1960, pp. 21, 36.

233 1960. Foreword to Miguel Serrano, *The Visits of the Queen of Sheba*, pp. v-vi. London: Asia Publishing House, 1960.

234 1960. Letter to the editor, *Listener* 63 (21 January 1960): 133.

235 1960. Yoga, Zen and Koestler. *Encounter* 16, no. 2 (1961): 56-58.

236 1961. Why I Believe in God. An interview with Frederick Sands, in *Good Housekeeping* 153 (December 1961): 64, 139-41.

237 1961. Memories, Dreams, Reflections. Recorded and ed. Aniela Jaffé. New York: Vintage Books, 1961.

*Erinnerungen, Träume, Gedanken. Zurich: Buchclub Ex Libris, 1961.

238 1961. Approaching the Unconscious. In *Man and His Symbols*, pp. 18-103. London: Aldus Books, 1964.

239 n.d. *From Conversations with C. G. Jung*, ed. Margaret Ostrowski-Sachs. (Remarks transcribed during analytical sessions and discussions after Eranos meetings, all undated.) Privately printed, Zurich, 1971.

Since the preparation of this bibliography for publication, Princeton University Press has issued two additional volumes of Jung's work that conveniently gather together many of the titles listed above: *The Symbolic Life, Collected Works*, Vol. 18 (1976) and *C. G. Jung Speaking*, ed. William McGuire and R.F.C. Hull (1977).

Works by Other Authors

Abenheimer, Karl M.

1968. The Ego as Subject. In Joseph B. Wheelright, ed., *The Reality of the Psyche: Proceedings of the 3rd Annual Congress for Analytical Psychology*, pp. 61-73. New York: C. G. Jung Foundation for Analytical Psychology.

Abraham, Karl.

1914. Review of Jung, *Versuch einer Darstellung der psychoanalytischen Theorie. Internationale Zeitschrift für ärztliche Psychoanalyse* 2:72-82.

1955. *Critical Papers and Essays on Psychoanalysis.* London: Hogarth.

1965. *A Psychoanalytic Dialogue: The Letters of Sigmund Freud and Karl Abraham, 1907-1926.* Ed. H. C. Abraham and E. L. Freud. London: Hogarth Press and Institute of Psychoanalysis.

Adler, Gerhard.

1961. *The Living Symbol: A Case Study in the Process of Individuation.* London: Routledge and Kegan Paul.

1966. *Studies in Analytical Psychology.* London: Hodder and Stoughton.

Affemann, Rudolf.
1957. *Psychologie und Bibel: eine Auseinandersetzung mit C. G. Jung*. Stuttgart: Klett.

Alm, Ivar.
1935. Die Analytische Psychologie als Weg zum Verständnis des Mystik. In *Die kulturelle Bedeutung der Komplexen Psychologie. Festschrift zum 60. Geburtstag von C. G. Jung,* ed. the Psychological Club, Zurich, pp. 298-313. Berlin: Springer.
1936. *Den Religiösa Funktionen I Människosjälen Studien Till Frågan om Religionens Inneböerd och Människans Väsen I Modern Psychologi Särskilt Hos Freud och Jung.* Stockholm: Svenska Kyrkans Diakonistyrelses Bokförlag.
1963. C. G. Jungs Erfahrungen in theologischer Sicht. *Theologische Zeitschrift* 19: 352-59.

Altizer, Thomas J. J.
1966. *The Gospel of Christian Atheism.* Philadelphia: Westminster.

Balmer, Heinrich.
1972. *Die Archetypentheorie von C. G. Jung: Eine Kritik.* Berlin: Springer.

Baudouin, Charles.
1963. *L' Ouvre de Jung et la psychologie complexe.* Paris: Payot.

Baumann, Hans H.
1935. Jungs Psychologie im Ausland. *Neue Schweizer Rundschau* 3: 254-56.

Baynes, Helton Godwin.
1923. Translator's preface to Jung, *Psychological Types.* London: Kegan Paul.

Bennet, E. A.
1961. *C. G. Jung.* London: Barrie and Rockliff.
1966. *What Jung Really Said.* London: Macdonald.

Bennett, A. A. G.
1961. The Work of Jung. *Maha-Bodhi* 69, no. 9: 264-73.

Bernet, Walter.
1955. *Inhalt und Grenze der religiösen Erfahrung. Eine Untersuchung der Probleme der religiösen Erfahrung in Auseinandersetzung mit der Psychologie C. G. Jungs.* Bern: Paul Haupt.

Bertine, Eleanor.
1960. The Perennial Problem of Good and Evil. *Spring,* pp. 21-33.

Bertrand, R.
1955. C. G. Jung et les nombres. *Le Disque vert,* pp. 330-38.

Bleuler, Paul Eugen.
1925. Review of Jung, *Wandlungen und Symbole der Libido.* 2d ed. *Münchner medizinische Wochenschrift* 72: 1746.

Bloch, Iwan.
1914. Review of Jung, *Wandlungen und Symbole der Libido. Klinisch-therapeutische Wochenschrift* 21: 749.

Boss, Medard.
1957. *The Analysis of Dreams.* London: Rider.
1963. *Psychoanalysis and Daseinanalysis.* London: Basic Books.

Bradway, Katherine.
1964. Jung's Psychological Types. *Journal of Analytical Psychology* 9, no. 2: 129-35.

Broad, C. D.
1953. *Religion, Philosophy and Psychical Research.* London: Routledge and Kegan Paul.

Brunneton, J. L.
1933. C. G. Jung, l'homme, sa vie, son caractère. *Revue d'Allemagne* 7: 673-89.

Buber, Martin.
1953a. Religion and Modern Thinking. In *The Eclipse of God: Studies in the Relation Between Religion and Philosophy,* pp. 87-122, 179-84. London: Victor Gollancz.
1953b. Reply to C. G. Jung. In *The Eclipse of God: Studies in The Relation Between Religion and Philosophy,* pp. 171-76. London: Victor Gollancz.

Bügler, Käthe.
1963. Die Entwicklung der analytischen Psychologie in Deutschland. In Michael Fordham, *Contact with Jung.* London: Tavistock.

Buonaiuti, Ernesto.
1964. *Pellegrino di Roma.* Bari: Laterza.

Buri, Fritz.
1952. C. G. Jungs *Antwort auf Hiob. National-Zeitung,* 27 April.

Burrell, David.
1974. *Exercises in Religious Understanding.* Notre Dame, Ind.: University of Notre Dame Press.

Carstens, Erik.
1964. *Freud, Jung og Freeman: Et problemdrama om psykoanalyse og kultur i fire akten.* Copenhagen: Borgens.

Caruso, Igor.
1964. *Existential Psychology: From Analysis to Synthesis.* London: Dartin, Longman and Todd.

Christou, Evangelos.
1963. *The Logos of the Soul.* Zurich: Donquin.

Clark, James M.
1959. C. G. Jung and Meister Eckhart. *Modern Language Review* 54: 239-44.

Clark, Robert A.
1961. Recent Developments in Psychiatry and Allied Fields: Analytic Psychology Today. *American Journal of Psychotherapy* 15: 193-204.

Cooley, Rob.
1968-1969. Jung, Lévi-Strauss and the Interpretation of Myth. *Criterion* 8 (Autumn-Winter): 12-16.

Corbin, Henry.
1953. La Sophia éternelle. *Revue de culture européenne* 3:11-44.

Corrie, Joan.
1929. *A-B-C of Jung's Psychology.* London: Kegan Paul, Trench, Trubner and Co.

Corti, Walter Robert.
1955. Vingt ans d'Eranos. *Le Disque vert,* pp. 288-97.

Cox, David.
1959. *Jung and St. Paul: A Study of the Doctrine of Justification by Faith and Its Relation to the Concept of Individuation.* London: Longmans, Green and Co.

Dahrendorf, Malte.
1959. Herman Hesses Demian und C. G. Jung. *Germanischromanische Monatsschrift* 8: 81-97.

De La Croix, Michel-Marie.
1960. Contribution to Débat sur psychologie et religion. *Recherches et débats, no. 30: L'Armée et la nation,* pp. 206-14. Paris: Fayard.

Dillistone, Frederick William.
1959. The Christian Doctrine of Man and Modern Psychological Theories. *Hibbert Journal* 54: 154-60.

Dry, Avis Mary.
1961. *The Psychology of Jung: A Critical Interpretation.* London: Methuen.

Edinger, Edward F.
1964. Trinity and Quaternity. In *Der Archetyp. The Archetype. Proceedings of the 2d International Congress for Analytical Psychology,* ed. Adolf Guggenbühl-Craig, pp. 81-87. Basel and New York.
1966. Christ as Paradigm of the Individuating Ego. *Spring,* pp. 5-23.

Eitingon, Max.
1914. Über das Unbewusste bei Jung und seine Wendung ins Ethische. *Internationale Zeitschrift für ärztliche Psychotherapie* 2: 99-104.

Eliade, Mircea.
1955. Note sur Jung et l'alchimie. *Le Disque vert,* pp. 97-109.
1962. *The Forge and the Crucible.* London: Rider.

Ellenberger, Henri.
1970. *The Discovery of the Unconscious: The History and Evolution of Dynamic Psychiatry*. London: Allen Lane, the Penguin Press.

Eschenbach, Helmut W.
1967. Studie zur Psychologie C. G. Jungs: eine Erfassungsmodell. *Der Landarzt* 43: no. 28: 1353-61.

Evans, Erastus.
1956. The Phases of Psychic Life. In Philip Mairet, ed., *Christian Essays in Psychiatry*, pp. 109-26. London: SCM Press.

Ferenczi, Sandor.
1913. Review of Jung, *Wandlungen und Symbole der Libido. Internationale Zeitschrift für ärztliche Psychoanalyse* 1: 391-403.

Fierz, Heinrich Karl.
1968. Plastic Works of Art in the Therapy of Psychosis. In *The Reality of the Psyche*, pp. 35—41.

Fite, Warner.
1916. Review of Jung, *Psychology of the Unconscious. Nation* 103 (10 August): 127.

Flew, Anthony.
1953. Coincidence and Synchronicity. *Journal of the Society for Psychical Research* 37: 198-201.

Fodor, Nándor.
1964. Jung's Sermons to the Dead. *Psychoanalytic Review* 51: 74-78.

Fordham, Frieda.
1968. *An Introduction to Jung's Psychology*. Harmondsworth: Penguin Books.

Fordham, Michael.
1945. Professor C. G. Jung. *British Journal of Medical Psychology* 20, no. 3: 221-35.
1955. An Appreciation of *Answer to Job*. *British Journal of Medical Psychology* 28, no. 4: 271-73.
1956. The Evolution of Jung's Researches. *British Journal of Medical Psychology* 29: 3-8.
1957 *New Developments in Analytical Psychology*. London: Routledge and Kegan Paul.
1958 *The Objective Psyche*. London: Routledge and Kegan Paul.
1962a *The Self in Jung's Writings*. Guild of Pastoral Psychology, Lecture no. 117. London.
1962b *An Evaluation of Jung's Work*. Guild of Pastoral Psychology, Lecture no. 119. London.
1963. The Empirical Foundation and Theories of the Self in Jung's Work. *Journal of Analytical Psychology* 8, no. 1: 1-23.

1971. Religious Experience in Childhood. In Hilda Kirsch, ed, *The Well-Tended Tree: Essays into the Spirit of Our Times*, pp. 79-89. New York: G. P. Putnam's Sons.

Forti, Filippo.
1968. *Il contrasto Freud/Jung e le nuove direzioni della psicoanalisi.* Rome: Silva.

Freud, Sigmund.
1957. *On the History of the Psychoanalytic Movement.* Collected Works, Standard Edition, pp. 7-71. London: Hogarth.
1963. *Psychoanalysis and Faith: The Letters of Sigmund Freud and Oskar Pfister.* Ed. Heinrich Meng and Ernst Freud. London: Hogarth.
1966. (with Lou Andreas-Salomé). *Briefwechsel.* Ed. Ernst Pfeiffer. Frankfurt am Main: Fischer.

Friedman, Maurice.
1966-1967. Jung's Image of Psychological Man. *Psychoanalytic Review* 53, no. 4: 595-608.

Friedman, Paul, and Goldstein, Jacob.
1964. Some Comments on the Psychology of C. G. Jung. *Psychoanalytic Quarterly* 22, no. 2: 194-225.

Froboese-Thiele, Felicia.
1950. Die religiöse Funktion des Unbewussten. *Der Psychologe* 2: 343-51.

Fromm, Erich.
1960. Psychoanalysis and Zen Buddhism. In *Zen Buddhism and Psychoanalysis.* New York: Harper and Brothers.

Gaffney, James.
1963. Symbolism of the Mass in Jung's Psychology. *Revue de l'Université d'Ottawa* 33: 214*-31*.

Gebser, J.
1943. *Abendländische Wandlung. Abriss der Ergebnisse moderner Forschung in Physik, Biologie und Psychologie: Ihre Bedeutung für Gegenwart und Zukunft.* Zurich: Oprecht.

Glover, Edward.
1950. *Freud or Jung?* London: Allen and Unwin.

Goldbrunner, Josef.
1940. *Die Tiefenpsychologie von Carl Gustav Jung und christliche Lebensgestaltung.* Freiburg im Breisgau.
1964. *Individuation.* University of Notre Dame Press.

Granjel, Luís S.
1949. La psicología de C. G. Jung en la historia de las relaciones entre medicina y religión. *Archivos ibero-americanos de historia de la medicina* 1: 189-297.

Gregory, Marcus.
1939. *Psychotherapy, Scientific and Religious.* London: Macmillan & Co.

Grinstein, Alexander.
1957. *The Index of Psychoanalytic Writings.* 5 vols. New York: New York International Universities Press.

Haendler, Otto.
1953. Komplexe Psychologie und theologische Realismus. *Theologische Literaturzeitung* 78: 199-215.

Harding, Mary Esther.
1959. Jung's Contribution to Religious Symbolism. *Spring,* pp. 1-16.
1965. *The "I" and the "Not I." A Study in the Development of Consciousness.* New York: Pantheon.

Haynes, Renee.
1956. Wrestling Jacob. *Tablet* 207 (11 February): 134.

Hegel, G. W. F.
1967. *The Phenomenology of Mind.* New York: Harper Torchbooks.

Heisig, James W.
1970. Man and God Evolving: Altizer and Teilhard. In John B. Cobb, Jr., ed., *The Theology of Altizer: Critique and Response,* pp. 93-111. Philadelphia: Westminster.
1971. La nozione di Dio secondo Carl Gustav Jung. *Humanitas* (Brescia), n.s. 36, no. 10: 777-802.
1972. The *VII Sermones:* Play and Theory. *Spring,* pp. 206-18.
1973a. Depth-Psychology and the *Homo Religiosus. Irish Theological Quarterly* 40: 148-61.
1973b. Jung and Theology: A Bibliographical Essay. *Spring,* pp. 204-55.
1976. Jung and the *Imago Dei:* The Future of an Idea. *Journal of Religion* 56, no. 1: 88-104.

Hellens, Franz.
1955. C. G. Jung écrivain. *Synthèses* 10: 433-37.

Hesse, Herman.
1934. Über einige Bücher. *Neue Rundschau* 45, no. 2: 321-28.

Heyer-Grote, Lucy.
1956. Freud und Jung. *Die Heilkunst* 69: 173-76.

Hillman, James.
1970. Why "Archetypal" Psychology? *Spring,* pp. 212-17.
1975. *Re-Visioning Psychology.* London and New York: Harper and Row.

Hinkle, Beatrice Moses.
1919. Jung's Libido-Theory and the Bergsonian Philosophy. *New York Medical Journal* 99: 1080-86.

Hobson, Robert F.
1971. Imagination and Amplification in Psychotherapy. *Journal of Analytical Psychology* 16, no. 1: 79-105.

Hoch, Dorothee.
1963. Zum Credo von C. G. Jung. *Kirchenblatt für die reformierte Schweiz* 119: 66-68.

Homans, Peter.
1969. Psychology and Hermeneutics: Jung's Contribution. *Zygon* 4: 333-55.

Hostie, Raymond.
1957. *Religion and the Psychology of Jung.* London: Sheed and Ward.

Howes, Elizabeth Boyden.
1961. Contribution to *In Memoriam Carl Gustav Jung (1875-1961).* Privately printed by the Analytical Psychology Club of San Francisco.

Hübscher, Arthur.
1957. *Denker unserer Zeit.* vol. 2. Munich: R. Piper.

Hull, R. F. C.
1971. Bibliographical Notes on Active Imagination in the Works of C. G. Jung. *Spring,* pp. 115-20.

Humbert, Elie G.
1971. Active Imagination: Theory and Practice. *Spring,* pp. 101-14.

Huxley, Aldous.
1956. *Adonis and the Alphabet.* London: Chatto and Windus.

Isham, M. K.
1923. Dr. Jung Expounds the Psychology of Individuation. *New York Times Book Review,* 10 June, pp. 9, 16.

Jacobi, Jolande.
1949. Aspects psychologiques de l'homme religieux. *Études carmélitaines,* pp. 115-35.
1956. Freud and Jung: Meeting and Parting. *Swiss Review of World Affairs* 6, no. 5: 18-23.
1959. *Complex, Archetype, Symbol in the Psychology of C. G. Jung.* New York: Pantheon Books.
1967. *The Way of Individuation.* London: Hodder and Stoughton.
1969. *The Psychology of C. G. Jung.* London: Routledge and Kegan Paul.

Jacobs, Hans.
1961. *Western Psychotherapy and Hindu-Sâdhanâ. A Contribution to Comparative Studies in Psychology and Metaphysics.* London: Allen and Unwin.

Jaffé, Aniela.
1970. *The Myth of Meaning in the Work of C. G. Jung*. London: Hodder and Stoughton.
1971. *From the Life and Work of C. G. Jung*. London: Hodder and Stoughton.
1972. The Creative Phases in Jung's Life. *Spring,* pp. 162-90.

Jahoda, Gustav.
1967. Jung's "Meaningful Coincidences." *The Philosophical Journal* 4: 35-42.

Jantz, Harold.
1962. Goethe, Faust, Alchemy and Jung. *German Quarterly* 35: 129-41.

Jones, Alfred Ernest.
1948. *Papers on Psycho-analysis.* London: Ballière, Tindall and Cox.

Josey, Charles C.
1938. Review of Jung, *Psychology and Religion. Journal of Religion* 18: 458.

Kantor, J. R.
1923. Review of Jung, *Psychological Types. Journal of Philosophy* 20: 636-40.

Kaune, Fritz Jürgen.
1967. *Selbstverwirklichung. Eine Konfrontation der Psychologie C. G. Jungs mit der Ethik.* Munich: Ernst Reinhardt.

Kelsey, Morton.
1971. Jung as Philosopher and Theologian. In Hilda Kirsch, ed., *The Well-Tended Tree: Essays into the Spirit of Our Times,* pp. 184-96. New York: G. P. Putnam's Sons.

Kerényi, Karl.
1967. *Eleusis: Archtypal Image of Mother and Daughter.* New York: Pantheon Books.

Kiesow, Ernst-Rüdiger.
1962. *Katholizismus und Protestantismus bei Carl Gustav Jung.* Ph.D. dissertation for the theological faculty of the University of Berlin (Humboldt).

Koestler, Arthur.
1972. *The Roots of Coincidence.* London: Hutchinson.

Künzli, Arnold.
1955. Carl Gustav Jung. *Deutsche Rundschau* 81: 942-44.

Lambert, Kenneth.
1962. Jung's Later Work: Historical Studies. *British Journal of Medical Psychology* 35, no. 3: 191-97.

Lawrence, D. H.
1971. *Fantasia of the Unconscious* and *Psychoanalysis and the Unconscious.* Harmondsworth: Penguin Books.

Lévi-Strauss, Claude.
1963. *Structural Anthropology.* New York and London: Basic Books.

Lewis, Aubrey.
1957. Jung's Early Work. *Journal of Analytical Psychology* 2, no. 2: 119-35.

Lippmann, Walter.
1916. An Epic of Desire. *New Republic* 7, pp. 21-22.

Looser, Günther.
1966. Jung's Childhood Prayer. *Spring,* pp. 76-80.

Macintosh, Douglas Clyde.
1940. *The Problem of Religious Knowledge.* London: Harper and Bros.

McClintock, James I.
1970. Jack London's Use of Carl Jung's *Psychology of the Unconscious. American Literature* 42: 336-47.

McLeish, John.
1961. Carl Jung, Psychology and Catholicism. *Wiseman Review* 489 (Fall): 264-76; 490 (Winter 1961-62): 313-18.

Mairet, Philip.
1956. Presuppositions of Psychological Analysis. In *Christian Essays in Psychiatry,* pp. 40-72. London: SCM Press.

Malinowski, Bronislaw.
1960. *Sex and Repression in Savage Society.* London: Routledge and Kegan Paul.

Mann, Ulrich.
1965. Tiefenpsychologie und Theologie. *Lutheranische Monatshefte* 4: 188-92.
1971. Die Gotteserfahrung des Menschen bei C. G. Jung. In Wolfgang Böhme, ed., *C. G. Jung und die Theologen. Selbsterfahrung und Gotteserfahrung bei C. G. Jung,* pp. 7-24. Stuttgart: Radius.

Meier, Carl Alfred.
1959a. Projection, Transference and the Subject-Object Relation in Psychology. *Journal of Analytical Psychology* 4, no. 1: 21-34.
1959b. *Jung and Analytical Psychology.* Newton, Mass.: Andover-Newton Theological School, Department of Psychology.

Meyer, Werner.
1961. In Memoriam Carl Gustav Jung. *Reformatio* 10: 331-36.

Michaëlis, Edgar.
1953. Le Livre de Job interprété par C. G. Jung. *Revue de théologie et de philosophie* 3: 183-95.
1954. Satan—die vierte Person der Gottheit? Zu C. G. Jungs Deutung des Buches Hiob. *Zeitwende* 25: 368-77.

Mrokwa, Klaus.
1968. *"Archetypus" und "kollektive Unbewusstes" im psychologischen System von Carl Gustav Jung. Eine kritische Studie zum Mystizismus und Irrationalismus in der Psychologie der Gegenwart.* Ph.D. dissertation, Martin-Luther Universität, Halle/Wittenberg.

Mueller, Fernand-Lucien.
1970. *L'Irrationalisme contemporaine.* Paris: Payot.

Munz, Peter.
1961. C. G. Jung. In *Symposium on the Life and Work of Carl Gustav Jung.* Victoria University, Wellington, New Zealand, 13 July (privately printed). 17 pp.

Murphy, Gardner.
1966. *Personality: A Biosocial Approach to Origins and Structure.* New York and London: Basic Books.

Neumann, Eric.
1961. The Significance of the Genetic Aspect for Analytical Psychology. In Gerhard Adler, ed., *Current Trends in Analytical Psychology. Proceedings of the 1st International Congress for Analytical Psychology,* pp. 37-53. London: Tavistock.

Perrot, Etienne.
1970. *La voie de la transformation d'après C. G. Jung et l'alchimie.* Paris: Libraire de Médicis.

Philp, Howard L.
1958. *Jung and the Problem of Evil.* London: Salisbury Square.

Piaget, Jean.
1945. Hommage à C. G. Jung. *Schweizerische Zeitschrift für Psychologie und ihre Anwendungen* 4: 169-71.

Price, H. H.
1953. Review of Jung and Pauli: *Naturerklärung und Psyche. Journal of the Society for Psychical Research* 37: 26-35.

Prinzhorn, Hans.
1932. *Psychotherapy: Its Nature, Its Assumptions, Its Limitations.* London: Jonathan Cape.

Progoff, Ira.
1953. *Jung's Psychology and Its Social Meaning.* New York: Julian Press.

Quispel, Gilles.
1970. C. G. Jung und die Gnosis: Die *Septem sermones ad mortuos* und Basilides. *Eranos Jahrbush,* pp. 277-98. Zurich: Rhein.

Radin, Paul
1956. *Primitive Man as Philosopher.* New York: Dover.

Reik, T.
1921. The Science of Religion. *International Journal of Psychoanalysis* 2: 80-93.

Ricoeur, Paul.
1970. *Freud and Philosophy: An Essay on Interpretation.* New Haven and London: Yale University Press.

Rudin, Josef.
1964. C. G. Jung und die Religion. *Orientierung* 28: 238-42.

Rümke, H. C.
1950. Aantekeningen over det instinct, den archetypus, den existentiaal, over de Werelden, die zij oproepen, over reductie en misvorming van het mensbeeld. In *Pro regno, pro sanctuario. Een bundel studies en bijdragen van vrienden en vereerders bij de zestigste verjaardag van Prof. Dr. C. Van der Leeuw,* ed. W. J. Kooiman and J. M. Van Veen, pp. 451-67. Nijkerk: Callenbach.

Andreas-Salomé, Lou.
1965. *The Freud Journal of Lou Andreas-Salomé.* London: Hogarth.

Sanday, W.
1910. *Christologies Ancient and Modern.* Oxford: At the Clarendon Press.

Sanford, John A.
1971. Analytical Psychology: Science or Religion? An Exploration of the Epistemology of Analytical Psychology. In Hilda Kirsch, *The Well-Tended Tree: Essays into the Spirit of Our Times,* pp. 90-105. New York: G. P. Putman's Sons.

Sargant, William.
1957. *Battle for the Mind: A Physiology of Conversion and Brainwashing.* London: Heinemann.

Sborowitz, Arië.
1951. Das religiöse Moment in der Tiefenpsychologie. *Psyche* 5: 278-89.

Schär, Hans.
1951. *Religion and the Cure of Souls in Jung's Psychology.* London: Routledge and Kegan Paul.

Schmidt, Ernst.
1954. Hiob, Jung and Bultmann. *Neue Deutsche Hefte* 1: 699-705.

Sinclair, May.
1923. Psychological Types. *English Review* 36: 436-39.

Smith, Huston.
1966. Foreword to Philip Kapleau, ed., *The Three Pillars of Zen: Teaching, Practice and Enlightenment.* New York: Harper and Row.

Speiser, Andreas.
1942. Die Platonische Lehre vom unbekannten Gott und die christliche Trinität. *Eranos Jahrbuch, 1940/1941,* pp. 11-29. Zurich: Rhein.

Spiegelberg, Herbert.
1972. *Phenomenology and Psychiatry.* Evanston, Ill.: Northwestern University Press.

Staub, Josef.
1948. Die Auffassung von Gott und Religion bei C. G. Jung. *Annalen der Philosophischen Gesellschaft Innerschweiz und Ostschweiz* 4, no. 1: 1-37.

Stein, L.
1958. Analytical Psychology: A "Modern" Science. *Journal of Analytical Psychology* 3: no. 1: 43-50.

Steiner, Gustav.
1965. Erinnerungen an Carl Gustav Jung. Zum Entstehung der Autobiographie. *Basler Stadtbuch,* pp. 117-63.

Stekel, Wilhelm.
1960. *The Interpretation of Dreams.* 2 vols. London: Vision.

Stern, Karl.
1953. Jung and the Christians. *Commonweal* 58: 229-31.

Sykes, Gerald.
1962. *The Hidden Remnant.* London: Routledge and Kegan Paul.

Tansley, A. G.
1920. *The New Psychology and Its Relation to Life.* London: Allen and Unwin.

Thiry, A.
1957. Jung et la religion. *Nouvelle revue théologique* 79: 248-76.

Thorburn, J.M.
1924. Analytical Psychology and Religious Symbolism. *Monist* 34: 96-111.

Thornton, Edward.
1965. Jungian Psychology and the Vedanta. In *Spectrum psychologiae* (various authors), pp. 131-42. Zurich: Rascher.

Thurneysen, Eduard.
1963. C. G. Jungs *Erinnerungen, Träume, Gedanken. Kirchenblatt für die reformierte Schweiz* 119: 162-65, 178-81.

Ulanov, Ann Belford.
1971. *The Feminine in Jungian Psychology and in Christian Theology.* Evanston, Ill.: Northwestern University Press.

Urban, Wilbur Marshall.
1949. *Beyond Realism and Idealism.* London: Allen and Unwin.

Van Den Bergh Van Eysinga, Gustav Adolf.
1953. *Godsdienstwetenschappelijke Studiën XIV.* Haarlem: H. D. Tjeenk Willink and Zoon N. V.

Van Der Hoop, J. H.
1923. *Character and the Unconscious: A Critical Exposition of the Psychology of Freud and Jung.* London: International Library of Psychology, Philosophy and Scientific Method.

Vestdijck, S.
1955. La Pensée de C. G. Jung. *Le Disque vert,* pp. 231-35.

Vetter, August.
1936. Die Deutung der unbewussten Seele bei C. G. Jung. *Zeitwende* 12: 213-24.

Von Franz, Marie-Louise.
1959. Die aktive Imagination in der Psychologie C. G. Jungs. In Wilhelm Bitter, ed., *Meditation in Religion und Psychotherapie. Ein Tagungsbericht,* pp. 136-48. Stuttgart: Klett.
1963. Die Bibliotek C. G. Jungs in Küsnacht. *Librarium* 6: 95-104.
1971. Die Selbsterfahrung bei C. G. Jung. In Böhme, *C. G. Jung und die Theologen. Selbsterfahrung und Gotteserfahrung bei C. G. Jung,* pp. 25-45. Stuttgart: Radius.

Von Weizaecker, Viktor.
1958. Reminiscences of Freud and Jung. In Benjamin Nelson, ed., *Freud and the Twentieth Century,* pp. 59-74. London: Allen and Unwin.

Walder, Peter.
1951. *Mensch und Welt bei C. G. Jung.* Zurich: Origo.

Watkin, E.
1955. Religion? *Dublin Review* 229: 337-40.

Westmann, Heinz.
1958. Erna Rosenbaum, 1897-1957. *Journal of Analytical Psychology*
3, no. 2: 180.

White, Victor.
1942. *Frontiers of Theology and Psychology.* Guild of Pastoral Psychology, Lecture no. 19. London.
1952a *God and the Unconscious.* London: Harvill Press.
1952b. Review of Vol. 9, no. 2 of Jung's Collected Works. *Dominican Studies* 5: 240-43.

1956. Jung et son livre sur Job. *La Vie spirituelle, Supplément* 9: 199-209.

1960. *Soul and Psyche.* London: Collins.

Wildberger, Hans.
1954. Das Hiobproblem uns seine neuste Deutung. *Reformatio* 3 (1954): 355-63, 439, 448.

Winnicott, D.
1964. Review of Jung, *Memories, Dreams, Reflections. International Journal of Psychoanalysis* 45: 450-55.

Wittels, Fritz.
1924. *Sigmund Freud: His Personality, His Teaching and His School.* London: Allen and Unwin.

Wolff. Toni.
1935. Einführung in die Grundlagen der Komplexen Psychologie. In *Die kulturelle Bedeutung der Komplexen Psychologie. Festschrift Zum 60. Geburtstag von C. G. Jung, ed. the Psychological Club, Zurich,* pp. 1—168. Berlin: Springer.

Zacharias, Gerhard Paulus.
1954. *Psyche und Mysterium.* Zurich: Rascher.

Anon.
1923. Review of Jung, *Psychological Types. Saturday Review* 135 (9 June): 773.

Anon.
1952. Antwort auf C. G. Jungs Antwort Auf Hiob. *Für ein jüdisches Lehrhaus Zürich* 2 (September): 22-24.

Anon.
1955. The Old Wise Man. *Time,* 14 February, pp. 62-70.

Anon.
1918. Review of Jung, *Die Psychologie der unbewussten Prozesse. Schweizerische Theologische Zeitschrift* 35: 35.

Index